THE RIGHT HONOURABLE
WILLIAM EWART GLADSTONE

GEORGE W. E. RUSSELL

First published 1891
This edition published 2007

Copyright © in this edition Nonsuch Publishing Limited, 2007

Nonsuch Publishing
Cirencester Road, Chalford, Stroud, Gloucestershire, GL6 8PE, UK
www.nonsuch-publishing.com

Nonsuch Publishing is an imprint of NPI Media Group

All rights reserved. No part of this book may be reprinted or reproduced or utilised in any form or by any electronic, mechanical or other means, now known or hereafter invented, including photocopying and recording, or in any information storage or retrieval system, without the permission in writing from the Publishers.

British Library Cataloguing in Publication Data
A catalogue record for this book is available from the British Library

ISBN 978-1-84588-376-8

Typesetting and origination by NPI Media Group
Printed in Great Britain

Contents

	Introduction to the Modern Edition	7
	Prefatory Note	11
I	Birth, parentage, and education	13
II	Enters Parliament—Early speeches—Office—Opposition	28
III	Religious opinions—Book on Church and State—Marriage—Becomes Vice-President of the Board of Trade—Admitted to the Cabinet—Resigns	44
IV	Free Trade—The Repeal of the Corn Laws—Retires from the representation of Newark—Returned for the University of Oxford—Growth and transition—Loss of a child—The Gorham judgment—Secession of friends	61
V	Don Pacifico—Civis Romanus—The Neapolitan prisons—The Papal aggression—Triumph over Mr Disraeli—The Coalition Government—Chancellor of the Exchequer—First Budget	77
VI	The Crimean War—Resignation—Ecclesiastical troubles—A free lance—The 'Arrow'—The Divorce Bill—Opposition to Lord Palmerston—Declines to join Tory Government—Lord High Commissioner to the Ionian Islands—Chancellor of the Exchequer in Whig Government—The French Treaty and the Paper Duties—Conflict with the House of Lords—Opinion on the American War	91

| VII | Growth in Liberal principles—The General Election of 1865—Defeated at Oxford—Returned for South Lancashire—The Death of Lord Palmerston—Leader of the House of Commons—The Reform Bill—The Cave of Adullam—Defeat and resignation | 112 |

| VIII | The Tory Reform Bill—Liberal mutiny—Triumphant Opposition—Proposes to disestablish the Irish Church—The General Election of 1868—Defeated in South-West Lancashire—Returned for Greenwich—Liberal majority—Prime Minister—The Disestablishment of the Irish Church | 134 |

| IX | The Irish Land Act—The abolition of Purchase—The 'Alabama' claims—Disaffection at Greenwich—Waning popularity—Dissolution—Defeat—Resignation—Retirement from leadership—Theological controversy | 149 |

| X | The Eastern Question—The Midlothian campaign—The General Election of 1880—Liberal triumph—Prime Minister a second time—Ireland and Egypt—Defeat and resignation—The General Election of 1885—Home Rule—Prime Minister a third time—The Home Rule Bill defeated—The General Election of 1886—Resignation—Leadership of Opposition—Golden wedding—Life at Hawarden | 168 |

| XI | Analysis of Character—Religiousness—Attitude towards Nonconformity—Love of power—Political courage—Conservative instincts—Love of beauty—Literary tastes—Love of finance—Business-like aptitude—Temper—Courtesy—Attractiveness in private life | 181 |

Introduction to the Modern Edition

The Liberal Party was the most successful electoral force of the second half of the nineteenth century, and Liberal governments were in power almost continuously throughout this period. William Ewart Gladstone alone led four Liberal ministries, of sixteen years' duration in total, and he came to personify the transformation of Britain from a country governed largely by a land-owning aristocracy into one of mass representative democracy and secret-ballot voting. His influence upon the rise and fall of the party's fortunes cannot be exaggerated; his own transformation from a Tory into a Liberal shaped much of its early success, and later peaks of Liberal popularity coincided with his return to power. That is not to deny that a multitude of other factors also had their part to play in the Liberal domination of politics in this period, and also in its decline by the early years of the twentieth century. What is clear, nevertheless, is that Gladstone was *the* political giant of his lifetime—almost as much of an epitome of the Victorian age as the great queen herself—and that many of the principles and aspirations he brought to public life hold fast to this day.

The history of Liberalism as a formal political party stretches back 150 years to the establishment of the Liberal Party in 1859. However, Liberal political thought in general can be traced back much further than this: 200 years previously the reaction that set in after the restoration of the monarchy following the Civil War was characterised by ideas that would later become central to Liberalism. The late seventeenth century saw the writings of John Locke distil these principles for the first time into a discernable philosophy that could potentially be capable of forming the framework of a government. His ideas concerning political liberty, the primacy of the individual, private property and free enterprise were expounded in his *Treatises on Government* in 1690, and he became the first in a long line of British Liberal thinkers. A formal political party that took on these principles was still, however, far from existing.

It was not until the eighteenth century that the establishment of formal parliamentary groupings in general began to occur. This at first took the form of the Whigs and the Tories. The Tories were viewed, broadly speaking, as the defenders of the Crown and the established Anglican Church, whereas, on the other hand, the Whigs asserted the primacy of Parliament over monarch. The terms 'Whigs' and 'Tories' echoed the divisions between Parliamentarians and Royalists from the Civil War era, and would continue to carry these associations into the eighteenth century, despite the redefinition of the two factions. By this time the Tories were often identified with the 'old' landowning gentry class and the Whigs with the 'new' wealth of financiers and merchants. The two groups were, nevertheless, in many ways similar in their ideologies, although the differences they did have spawned a great deal of bitter rivalry.

Towards the end of the eighteenth century events in the wider world, such as the French Revolution, opened up and helped popularise new debate over the ideological basis of government, and were to lead to the development of political groups with more conflicting principles. The Whigs resisted the Tory government's attempts to stifle such debate, which reached a peak during the wars with France in the 1790s, and their lengthy period of opposition encouraged them to embrace popular opinion about many different issues, such as electoral reform and religious toleration. The Whigs began to call for parliamentary reform as a means to reflect the changes in society that had been initiated by the Industrial Revolution, and they seized their chance when Tory divisions allowed a Whig government under Lord Grey to pass the Reform Act of 1832. This was the first step on the road to extending the franchise, which would lead to the necessity of greater political interaction with a wider section of society, both ordinary voters and more radical groups. It was at this time that the Conservative Party came into existence, and at the same time the demand for something that would represent liberal elements began to be felt, although a cohesive party would take two more decades to form. Support for a liberal political ideology was fostered by the Peelites, a small but influential group of former Conservatives (Gladstone numbered amongst them) who had broken with their previous party over the repeal of the Corn Laws. This move, which was underpinned by support for the principles of free trade, was strongly opposed by traditional land-owning interests and could only mean an irrevocable split with the Conservatives. It was also what took Gladstone towards his adherence to what would come to be known as the Liberal Party.

This finally took shape on 6 June 1859, when a combination of Peelites, Whigs and Radicals overthrew a minority Conservative government, and the new Liberal Party that was established went on to govern Britain for the greater part of the next thirty years. The underlying philosophy of the party was summed up in the slogan 'peace, retrenchment and reform'. It instituted moves further to extend the franchise in 1867 and again in 1885, and above all free trade was championed as a means of generating prosperity for all. Gladstone's specific impact upon the history of the Liberal Party and its nineteenth-century domination was comprehensive. He made lasting financial innovations, such as replacing taxes upon goods and customs duties with a progressive income tax, and establishing parliamentary accountability for government spending. Ireland was a continuing issue for him: he disestablished the Church of Ireland in 1869 and passed an Irish Land Act to tackle unfair landlords. His devotion to defending the rights of oppressed minorities was a continuing passion, and was partly responsible for his return to power in 1880 after a Conservative win in 1874; he attacked the government at this time over their weak response to Turkish brutality in the Balkans.

The Liberal government now focused on the increasing problems in Ireland, where sectarian differences and economic issues were coming to a head. The growing electoral support for a home rule party became a major issue in Britain, and was increasingly problematic for both the Liberal Party and the Conservatives. Gladstone took up the home rule cause himself and tried to introduce a devolution bill, but this was rejected twice and led to splits within the Liberal Party. This, coupled with other dissensions within the party as to who would succeed Gladstone, weakened the Liberals, and they lost their clear sense of direction. The chosen successor, Lord Rosebery, failed to end the party's deepening conflicts over social policy, and the traditional liberals who wanted government to stay out of economic affairs stood at odds with those who saw state involvement as paramount to alleviating issues such as poverty and ill health. The popularity of the more interventionist approach was what drove the brief Liberal revival in the twentieth century—when progressive social reform became the order of the day—but until then the Liberal Party largely lost favour in Britain, with only a short minority administration in the twenty years that followed the resignation of Gladstone.

Nevertheless, the Liberal Party did achieve a lasting legacy during the twentieth century: it was one of the greatest reforming administrations of that century, laying the foundations for the modern welfare state as we know it today. It failed, however, to survive the strains of the First World War, proved unable to resist the rise of the Labour Party and never returned to the general election success it had enjoyed under Gladstone.

Prefatory Note

The task of writing this Biography is one for which I should certainly not have volunteered. When Mr Stuart Reid proposed it to me, I undertook it with reluctance. I pointed out that this was one of the cases where personal acquaintance with the subject of the book was a positive disqualification for the work. I could not consent to embellish my pages with traits and incidents which I had observed in the sacred intercourse of social life; and the official relation in which I had stood to Mr Gladstone made it difficult for me to sit in judgment on his public acts. These objections were overruled; but it is right to state that Mr Gladstone is in no way or degree responsible for what I have written. When, before undertaking the work, I applied to him for his sanction, he said that he would put no obstacles in the way; and there his connexion with the matter ends.

This book aims at little more than a clear statement of facts chronologically arranged. The successive events of a great man's life, and his own recorded words, have been allowed to speak for themselves; and, where comment was required, it has been sought in the writings of contemporary observers. Original criticism has been used as sparingly as possible.

The space at disposal being strictly limited, I have touched lightly on those later events of Mr Gladstone's career which are within general recollection, and I have bestowed more detailed attention on the early stages, which are now, to most people, either unknown or forgotten.

The books which I have consulted are too numerous to be specified but I am under peculiar obligation to Mr Barnett Smith's painstaking and accurate 'Life of the Right Hon. William Ewart Gladstone'; to Mr Justin McCarthy's 'History of Our Own Times'; to 'The Life of Bishop Wilberforce'; and to the 'Memoirs of James Robert Hope-Scott.'

My special thanks are due to his Eminence Cardinal Manning; the Lord Bishop of Bath and Wells; the Lord Bishop of St Andrews; Lord Napier and

Ettrick; the Very Rev. the Dean of Christ Church; the Venerable Archdeacon Denison; the Right Hon. Sir Thomas Acland, Bart; Mr Arthur Godley, CB; Mr Milnes-Gaskell, MP; Mr E. Hamilton, of Charters; Mr F. Cornish, of Eton; and Mr W. Cory, who have helped me with invaluable recollections, or have given me access to interesting records.

To this list must be added, with regretful respect, the name of the late Dean of St Paul's.

For the admirable portrait which forms the frontispiece I am indebted to the kindness of Mr Rupert Potter, whose skill in photography requires no praise from me.

Here and there I have borrowed from previous writings of my own; and I have done so on the ground that, when a writer has carefully chosen certain words to express his meaning, he can seldom alter them with advantage.

G.W.E.R.
June 1, 1891.

I

Birth, parentage, and education

WILLIAM EWART GLADSTONE WAS BORN on December 29, 1809. His birthplace was No 62. Rodney Street, Liverpool; but for his ancestry we must look further north than Lancashire.

The parish of Libberton lies near the town of Biggar, in the upper ward of Lanarkshire, and here, from very early times, a family of Gledstanes owned a property from which they took their name. They were Gledstanes of Gledstanes, or, in Scottish phrase, Gledstanes of that ilk. The derivation of the name is obvious enough to anyone who has seen the spot. *Gled* is a hawk, and that fierce and beautiful bird would have found its natural home among the *stanes*, or rocks, of the craggy moorlands which surround the fortalice of Gledstanes. As far back as 1296, Herbert de Gledestane figures in the Ragman Roll as one of the lairds who swore fealty to Edward I. His descendants for generations held knightly rank, and bore their part in the adventurous life of the Border. As years went on their estates dwindled, and their social standing underwent a change. By the beginning of the seventeenth century the estate of Gledstanes was sold. The adjacent property of Arthurshiel remained in the hands of the family for nearly a hundred years longer. Then the son of the last Gledstanes of Arthurshiel removed to the neighbouring town of Biggar, and opened the business of a maltster there.

His grandson, Thomas Gladstones (for so the name was modified), became a corn-merchant at Leith. It chanced that, in pursuit of his business, this Mr Thomas Gladstones had occasion to sell a cargo of grain which had arrived at Liverpool, and he sent his eldest son, John, to transact the sale at the port. John Gladstone's energy and aptitude attracted the favourable notice of a leading corn-merchant of Liverpool, on whose recommendation the young man settled in that city. He began his commercial career as a clerk in his patron's house. He lived to become one of the merchant-princes of Liverpool, a baronet, and a member of Parliament. He died in 1851, at the age of eighty-seven. He seems to have been a man of unbending will, of inexhaustible energy, of absolute self-reliance; a stern, strong, imperious nature, pre-eminent in all those qualities which overcome obstacles, conquer fortune, and command the respect of the world.

Sir John Gladstone was a pure Scotchman, a Lowlander by birth and descent. He married Anne, daughter of Andrew Robertson, of Stornoway, sometime Provost of Dingwall. Provost Robertson belonged to the Clan Donachie, and by this marriage the robust and business-like qualities of the Lowlander were blended with the poetic imagination, the sensibility and fire of the Gael. John and Anne Gladstone had six children. The third son—WILLIAM EWART—was named after a merchant of Liverpool, who was his father's friend.

He was born at a critical moment in the fortunes of England and of Europe. Abroad, the greatest genius that the world has ever seen was wading through slaughter to a universal throne, and no effectual resistance had as yet been offered to a progress which menaced the liberty of Europe and the existence of its States. At home, a crazy king and a profligate heir-apparent presided over a social system in which all civil evils were harmoniously combined. A despotic Administration was supported by a parliamentary representation as corrupt as illusory; a Church, in which spiritual religion was all but extinct, had sold herself as a bondslave to the governing classes. Rank and wealth and territorial ascendency were divorced from public duty, and even learning had become the handmaid of tyranny. The sacred name of justice was prostituted to sanction a system of legal murder. Commercial enterprise was paralyzed by prohibitive legislation; public credit was shaken to its base; the prime necessaries of life were ruinously dear. The pangs of poverty were aggravated by the concurrent evils of war and famine, and the common people, fast bound in misery and iron, were powerless to make their sufferings known or to seek redress, except by the desperate methods of conspiracy and insurrection. None of the elements of revolution were wanting, and the fates seemed to be hurrying England to the brink of a civil catastrophe. The general sense of insecurity and apprehension, inseparable from such a condition of affairs, produced its effect upon even the robustest minds.

Sir John Gladstone was not a likely victim of panic, but he was a man with a large stake in the country, the more precious because acquired by his own exertion: he believed that the safeguards of property and order were imperilled by foreign arms and domestic sedition; and he had seen with indignation and disgust the excesses of a factious Whiggery which was not ashamed to exult in the triumph of the French over the English Government. Under the pressure of these influences, Sir John Gladstone gradually separated himself from the Whigs, with whom in earlier life he had acted, and became a close ally of Mr Canning, whose return for Liverpool he actively promoted. A deep and lasting friendship grew up between the statesman-adventurer and his merchant-ally. The fascination of genius exercised its inevitable spell, and the enlightened and gracious Toryism which Mr Canning taught became his friend's political gospel.

Sir John Gladstone was a man whose opinions could hardly fail to produce their effect upon those with whom he lived, and over whom he exercised a patriarchal authority. In the penetrating gaze, the strongly-marked features, the compressed and resolute mouth, which the skilful brush of the ill-fated William Bradley has perpetuated, it is easy to read the signs of a temper which brooked no resistance. In the town of Liverpool his political influence, backed by his wealth and station, was widely felt, and in his own home it probably was irresistible. His son has thus described him:

'His eye was not dim, nor his natural force abated; he was full of bodily and mental vigour; "whatsoever his hand found to do, he did it with his might;" he could not understand or tolerate those who, perceiving an object to be good, did not at once and actively pursue it; and with all this energy he joined a corresponding warmth and, so to speak, eagerness of affection, a keen appreciation of humour, in which he found a rest, and an indescribable frankness and simplicity of character, which, crowning his other qualities, made him, I think (and I strive to think impartially), nearly or quite the most interesting old man I have ever known.'

It was his habit to discuss all manner of questions with his children, and an eye-witness has observed that 'nothing was ever taken for granted between him and his sons. A succession of arguments on great topics and small topics alike—arguments conducted with perfect good humour, but also with the most implacable logic—formed the staple of the family conversation. The children and their parents argued upon everything ... They would debate as to whether the trout should be boiled or broiled, whether a window should be opened, and whether it was likely to be fine or wet next day. It was all perfectly good-humoured, but curious to a stranger because of the evident care which all the disputants took to advance no proposition, even as to the prospect of rain, rashly.'

Sir John Gladstone's house was, by all accounts, a home pre-eminently calculated to mould the thoughts and direct the course of an intelligent and receptive nature. There was the father's masterful will and keen perception, the sweetness and piety of the mother, wealth with all its substantial advantages and few of its mischiefs, a strong sense of the value of money, a rigid avoidance of extravagance and excess; everywhere a strenuous purpose in life, constant employment, and concentrated ambition.

After some tuition at the Vicarage of Seaforth, where Arthur Penrhyn Stanley was among his fellow-pupils, William Gladstone left home for Eton. From a provincial town, from mercantile surroundings, from an atmosphere of money-making, from a strictly-regulated life, the impressionable boy was transplanted, at the age of eleven, to the shadow of Windsor and the banks of the Thames, to an institution which belongs to history, to scenes haunted by the memory of the most illustrious Englishmen, to a free and independent existence among companions who were the very flower of English boyhood. A transition so violent and yet so delightful was bound to produce an impression which lapse of time was powerless to efface, and no one who knows the man and the school can wonder that for seventy years Mr Gladstone has been the most enthusiastic of Etonians.

He entered Eton after the summer holidays of 1821, under the Head-Mastership of the terrific Dr Keate. To quote the emphatic testimony of Sir Roderick Murchison, he was then 'the prettiest little boy that ever went to Eton.' He boarded at Mrs Shurey's, a house at the south end of the broad walk in front of the schools and facing the chapel, and rather nearer the famous 'Christopher Inn' than would nowadays be thought desirable. On the wall opposite the house (which now belongs to Mr Carter) the name of 'Gladstone,' carved, it is believed, by the statesman's own hand, may still be traced. His tutor was the Rev. Henry Hartopp Knapp. His brothers, Thomas and Robertson Gladstone, were already at Eton, and boarded in Mrs Shurey's house. Thomas was in the Fifth Form, and William, who was placed in the middle remove of the Fourth Form, became his eldest brother's fag.

A famous line in Lord Lytton's 'New Timon' has recorded the fact that Mr Gladstone was what Etonians, with classical elegance, designate a 'sap.' In other words, he was not ashamed to fulfil the purpose for which boys are, at any rate in theory, sent to school. He worked hard at his classical lessons, and supplemented the ordinary business of the school by studying mathematics in the holidays. His interest in work was first aroused by Mr Hawtrey, afterwards Head Master, who commended a copy of his Latin verses, and 'sent him up for good.' This experience first led the young student to associate intellectual work with the ideas of ambition and success. He was not a fine scholar, in that restricted sense of the term which implies a special aptitude for turning English into Greek and Latin or for original versification in the classical languages. 'His composition,' we read, 'was stiff,' but he was imbued with the substance of his authors; and a contemporary who was in the Sixth Form with him remarks that 'when there were thrilling passages of Virgil or Homer, or difficult passages in the *Scriptores Graeci* to translate, he or Lord Arthur Hervey was generally called up to edify the class with quotation or translation.'

By common consent, he was pre-eminently God-fearing, orderly, and conscientious. 'At Eton,' said the late Bishop Hamilton, of Salisbury, 'I was a thoroughly idle boy; but I was saved from some worse things by getting to know Gladstone.' To have exercised, while still a schoolboy, an influence for good on one of the greatest of contemporary saints is surely such a distinction as few Prime Ministers ever attained. A schoolfellow still living remembers seeing William Gladstone turn his glass upside down and decline to drink a coarse toast proposed, according to annual custom, at an election-dinner at the 'Christopher.' He was not only pure-minded and courageous, but humane. He stood forth as the champion of some wretched pigs, which it was the custom to torture at Eton Fair on Ash Wednesday, and, when bantered by his schoolfellows for his humanity, offered to write his reply 'in good round hand upon their faces.'

His most intimate friend was Arthur Hallam, by universal acknowledgment the most remarkable Etonian of his day; in mind and character not unworthy of the magnificent eulogy of 'In Memoriam.' Although they boarded in different houses, Gladstone and Hallam always breakfasted together, and, when separated by the holidays, corresponded diligently with one another. On August 23 1826, Hallam wrote to a common friend: 'I heard from Gladstone shortly after your letter reached me—a long and very orderly epistle, as you may suppose, full of lamentations about Liverpool, the country and the Ministry, and of high-flying eulogiums on Walter Scott's "Woodstock."'

Among their schoolfellows were John Hanmer, afterwards Lord Hanmer; Sir James Colvile, Chief Justice at Calcutta; Frederic Rogers, Lord Blachford; Spencer Walpole, Home Secretary in the days of the Reform League; Gerald Wellesley, Dean of Windsor; Frederick Tennyson, Sir George Cornewall Lewis, William Selwyn, William Cavendish, now Duke of Devonshire; Lord Arthur Hervey, now Bishop of Bath and Wells; George Selwyn, successively Bishop of New Zealand and of Lichfield; Alexander Kinglake, Sir Francis Doyle, Henry Denison, James Milnes-Gaskell, MP for Wenlock; James Bruce, afterwards Earl of Elgin; James Hope, afterwards Hope-Scott; Charles Canning, afterwards Earl Canning and Governor-General of India; Walter Hamilton, afterwards Bishop of Salisbury; and his brother, Edward Hamilton, now of Charters:

Young Gladstone took no delight in games. One of his contemporaries has often declared, 'without challenge or contradiction, that he was never seen to run'; but he was fond of sculling, and kept a 'lock-up,' or private boat, for his own use. He walked fast and far; and his chief amusement, when he was not debating or reading or writing, was to roam about the delightful neighbourhood of Windsor in the congenial company of a few like-minded friends. One of these, James Milnes-Gaskell, writing to his mother on June 30, 1826, says: 'I was out all yesterday evening with Gladstone, who is one of the cleverest and most sensible people I ever met with'—odd praise in a schoolboy's mouth. At the end of 1827, Charles Canning writes: 'Handley, Gladstone, Mr Bruce, Lord Bruce, Hodgson, and myself, set up a Salt Hill

Club at the end of the half. We met every whole holiday or half, as was convenient, after twelve, and went up to Salt Hill to bully the fat waiter, eat toasted cheese, and drink egg-wine.' It is startling to learn, on the same unimpeachable authority, that 'in all our meetings, as well as at almost every time, Gladstone went by the name of Mr Tipple.'

But beyond this intimate circle Gladstone was not generally popular or even widely known. He was seen to the greatest advantage, and was most thoroughly at home, in the debates of the Eton Society, learnedly called 'The Literati' and vulgarly 'Pop,' and in the editorship of the *Eton Miscellany*. The Eton Society in Gladstone's day was a remarkable group of brilliant boys. Its meetings were held over Miss Hatton's 'sock-shop.' Its tone was intensely Tory. Current politics were forbidden subjects, but political opinion disclosed itself through the thin disguise of historical or academical questions. The execution of Strafford and Charles I, the characters of Oliver Cromwell and Milton, the 'Contrat Social' of Rousseau, and the events of the French Revolution, laid bare the speakers political tendencies as effectually as if the conduct of Queen Caroline, the foreign policy of Lord Castlereagh, or the repeal of the Test and Corporation Act, had been the subject of debate. Mr Gladstone was elected a member of the Society on October 15, 1825. On the 29th of the same month he made his maiden speech on the question, 'Is the education of the poor on the whole beneficial?' The contemporary scribe records that 'Mr Gladstone rose and eloquently addressed the House' in favour of education; and one who heard him says that his opening words were, 'Sir, in this age of increased and increasing civilization.' It almost oppresses the imagination to picture the shoreless sea of eloquence which rolls between that exordium and the oratory to which we still are listening, and hope to listen for years to come.

During the remainder of his time at Eton, Mr Gladstone took a leading part both in the debates and in the private business of the Society. We find him introducing promising members, among them Mr Kinglake, agitating for more readable and instructive newspapers, proposing rules calculated to ensure orderly and decorous conduct, moving fines on those guilty of disorder or breaches of rule, and himself the subject of a fine for putting down an illegal question. In debate he champions the claims of metaphysics against those of mathematics, and defends aristocracy against democracy. He confesses 'innate feelings of dislike to the French.' He protests against the disarmament of the Highlanders as 'in the name of policy inexpedient, in the name of God unjust.' In a debate on the fate of Strafford he deplores the action of the House of Commons, which we ought to be able to 'revere as our glory and confide in as our protection.' The peroration of his speech on the question whether Queen Anne's Ministers, in the last four years of her reign, deserved well of their country, is so characteristic, both in substance and in form, that it deserves reproduction here:

Thus much, Sir, I have said, as conceiving myself bound in fairness not to regard the names under which men have hidden their designs so much as the designs themselves. I am well aware that my prejudices and my predilections have long been enlisted on the side of Toryism—(cheers)—and that in a cause like this I am not likely to be influenced unfairly against men bearing that name and professing to act on the principles which I have always been accustomed to revere. But the good of my country must stand on a higher ground than distinctions like these. In common fairness and in common candour, I feel myself compelled to give my decisive verdict against the conduct of men whose measures I firmly believe to have been hostile to British interests, destructive of British glory, and subversive of the splendid and, I trust, lasting fabric of the British Constitution.

The following extracts are from the diary of the Hon. William Cowper, afterwards Lord Mount-Temple. On Saturday, October 27, 1827, the subject for debate was:

'Whether the deposition of Richard II was justifiable or not.' Jelf opened: not a good speech. Doyle spoke *extempore*, made several mistakes, which were corrected by Jelf. Gladstone spoke well. The Whigs were regularly floored; only four Whigs to eleven Tories, but they very nearly kept up with them in coughing and 'Hear, hears.' Adjourned to Monday, after 4.

Monday, 29.—Gladstone finished his speech, and ended with a great deal of flattery of Doyle, saying that he was sure he would have courage enough to own that he was wrong. It succeeded. Doyle rose amidst reiterated cheers to own that he was convinced by the arguments of the other side. He had determined before to answer them and cut up Gladstone!

December 1.—Debate, 'Whether the Peerage Bill of 1719 was calculated to be beneficial or not.' Thanks voted to Doyle and Gladstone; the latter spoke very well: will be a great loss to the Society.

The foregoing extracts indicate pretty clearly the political colour of the young orator's opinions. It is further illustrated by the following anecdote of Sir Francis Doyle's: 'One day I was steadily computing the odds for the Derby, as they stood in a morning newspaper. He (Mr Gladstone) leant over my shoulder to look at the lot of horses named. Now it happened that the Duke of Grafton owned a colt called Hampden, who figured in the aforesaid lot. "Well," cried Mr Gladstone, reading off the odds, "Hampden, at any rate, I see, is in his proper place, between *Zeal* and *Lunacy*," for such, in truth, was the position occupied by the four-footed namesake of that illustrious rebel.'

In 1827 Mr Gladstone took part in launching the *Eton Miscellany*. Under the pseudonym of 'Bartholomew Bouverie,' he was at once the editor and the most copious contributor. The first number appeared on June 4, 1827, and the magazine lived till the following December, which, as school journalism goes, must be considered an instance of longevity. Among the principal contributors were Sir James Colvile, Sir Francis Doyle, Mr Milnes-Gaskell, Arthur Hallam, Lord Hanmer, and Bishop Selwyn. Mr Gladstone turned his hand to every kind of authorship. He wrote prologues, epilogues, leading articles, historical essays, satirical sketches, classical translations, and humorous poetry: His tribute to the memory of Mr Canning, in a paper on 'Ancient and Modern Genius Compared,' is full of feeling and rhetorical force.

> It is for those who revered him in the plenitude of his meridian glory to mourn over him in the darkness of his premature extinction: to mourn over the hopes that are buried in his grave, and the evils that arise from his withdrawing from the scene of life. Surely if eloquence never excelled and seldom equalled—if an expanded mind and judgment whose vigour was paralleled only by its soundness—if brilliant wit—if a glowing imagination—if a warm heart, and an unbending firmness—could have strengthened the frail tenure, and prolonged the momentary duration of human existence, that man had been immortal! But nature could endure no longer. Thus has Providence ordained that inasmuch as the intellect is more brilliant, it shall be more short-lived; as its sphere is more expanded, more swiftly is it summoned away. Lest we should give to man the honour due to God—lest we should exalt the object of our admiration into a divinity for our worship—He who calls the weary and the mourner to eternal rest hath been pleased to remove him from our eyes.

As a sample of his humorous style we take these lines from his mock-heroic 'Ode to the Shade of Wat Tyler':

> Shade of him whose valiant tongue
> On high the song of freedom sung;
> Shade of him, whose mighty soul
> Would pay no taxes on his poll;
> Though, swift as lightning, civic sword
> Descended on thy fated head,
> The blood of England's boldest poured,
> And numbered Tyler with the dead!
>
> Still may thy spirit flap its wings
> At midnight o'er the couch of kings;
> And peer and prelate tremble, too,
> In dread of nightly interview!

> With patriot gesture of command,
> With eyes that like thy forges gleam,
> Lest Tyler's voice and Tyler's hand
> Be heard and seen in nightly dream.
>
> I hymn the gallant and the good
> From Tyler down to Thistlewood,
> My muse the trophies grateful sings,
> The deeds of Miller and of Ings;
> She sings of all who, soon or late,
> Have burst Subjection's iron chain,
> Have seal'd the bloody despot's fate
> Or cleft a peer or priest in twain.
>
> Shades, that soft Sedition woo,
> Around the haunts of Peterloo!
> That hover o'er the meeting-halls,
> Where many a voice stentorian bawls!
> Still flit the sacred choir around,
> With 'Freedom' let the garrets ring,
> And vengeance soon in thunder sound
> On Church, and constable, and king.

Will it be credited that a Tory critic, anxious to prove that the Liberal leader was a revolutionist from his cradle, has gravely cited this ode as a serious effusion of youthful Radicalism?

Sir Francis Doyle writes: 'Hallam, Selwyn, and the other contributors left Eton at Midsummer (or Election, as we used to call it), 1827. Mr Gladstone and I remained behind as its chief supporters, or rather it would be more like the truth if I said that Mr Gladstone supported the whole burden upon his own shoulders. I was unpunctual and unmethodical, so also were his other vassals; and the *Miscellany* would have fallen to the ground but for Mr Gladstone's untiring energy, pertinacity, and tact. I may as well remark that my father, a man of great ability as well as of great experience of life, predicted Gladstone's future eminence from the manner in which he handled this somewhat tiresome business. "It is not," he remarked, "that I think his papers better than yours or Hallam's—that is not my meaning at all; but the force of character he has shown in managing his subordinates, and the combination of ability and power that he has made evident, convince me that such a young man cannot fail to distinguish himself hereafter."

The impression which he made upon those of his schoolfellows who were brought into contact with him may be gathered from one or two quotations from contemporaries, themselves of no common promise. James Milnes-Gaskell, urging his wish to go to Oxford instead of Cambridge, which his mother had preferred, gives as one of the reasons for his choice that it would allow of his continued intimacy with Gladstone: 'Gladstone is no ordinary individual; and, perhaps, if I were called on to select the individual I am intimate with to whom I should first turn in an emergency, and whom I thought in every way pre-eminently distinguished for high excellence, I think I should turn to Gladstone … If you finally decide in favour of Cambridge, my separation from Gladstone will be a source of great sorrow to me.'

And Arthur Hallam says: 'Whatever may be our lot, I am confident that *he* is a bud that will bloom with a richer fragrance than almost any whose early promise I have witnessed.'

Gladstone left Eton at Christmas, 1827. He read for six months, with private tutors, one of whom was Dr Turner, afterwards Bishop of Calcutta.

With reference to this part of his life, he wrote: 'I resided with Dr Turner, at Wilmslow (in Cheshire) from January till a few months later. My residence with him was cut off by his appointment to the Bishopric of Calcutta … My companions were the present (1877) Bishop of Sodor and Man, and Sir C. A. Wood, Deputy-Chairman of the G. W. Railway. We employed our spare time in gymnastics, in turning, and in rambles. I remember paying a visit to Macclesfield. In a silk factory the owner showed us his silk handkerchiefs, and complained much of Mr Huskisson for having removed the prohibition of the foreign article. The thought passed through my mind at the time: why make laws to enable people to produce articles of such hideous pattern and indifferent quality as this? Alderley Edge was a favourite place of resort. We dined with Sir John Stanley (at Alderley) on the day when the King's Speech was received and I recollect that he ridiculed (I think very justly) the epithet *untoward,* which was applied in it to the Battle of Navarino.'

In October 1828, Gladstone went up to Christ Church, where, in the following year, he was nominated to a Studentship. The House was then in its days of glory. The Dean was Dr Samuel Smith, shortly after succeeded by Dr Gaisford; the Rev. T. Vowler Short, afterwards Bishop of St Asaph, and the Rev. Daniel Veysie were the Censors. Among the undergraduates were Lord Canning, Lord Lincoln, afterwards Duke of Newcastle; Sir Robert Phillimore, Walter Hamilton, Charles Wordsworth, now Bishop of St Andrews; Lord Abercorn, Lord Douglas, afterwards Duke of Hamilton; H. G. Liddell, now Dean of Christ Church; Sir Francis Doyle, Sir Thomas Acland and his brother Arthur Acland-Troyte, Henry Ker Seymer, MP for Dorset; Joseph Anstice, Professor of Greek and Latin at King's College, and Henry Denison, whose career of promise was cut short by an accident in Australia. Among the conspicuous undergraduates at other colleges were Henry Edward Marining now Cardinal-Archbishop; Archibald

Campbell Tait, Archbishop of Canterbury; Lord Elgin, Sidney Herbert, James Hope, Robert Lowe, now Lord Sherbrooke; Robert Scott, Dean of Rochester, and Sir George Cornewall Lewis.

In December 1829, a deputation from the Union at Cambridge paid a visit to Oxford, and took part in a great debate on the respective merits of Byron and Shelley. One of the orators from Cambridge was Richard Monckton Milnes, afterwards Lord Houghton, and in a letter of December 5, 1829, describing his visit to Oxford, he says: 'The man that *took* me most was the youngest Gladstone of Liverpool—I am sure, a very superior person.'

Mr Gladstone's first rooms were in the 'old library,' near the hall; but for the greater part of his time he occupied the right-hand rooms on the first floor of the first staircase on the right as the visitor enters Canterbury Gate. He was, alike in study and in conduct, a model undergraduate, and the great influence of his character and talents was used with manly resolution against the riotous conduct of the 'Tufts,' whose brutality caused the death of one of their number in 1831. We read this note in the correspondence of a friend: 'I heard from Gladstone yesterday; he says that the number of Gentlemen Commoners has increased, is increasing, and ought to be diminished.' Everyone who has experienced the hubristic qualities of the Tufted race, and its satellites, will cordially sympathize with this sentiment of an orderly and industrious undergraduate. He was conspicuously moderate in the use of wine. His good example in this respect affected not only his contemporaries but also his successors at the University; men who followed him to Oxford ten years later found it still operative, and declare that undergraduates drank less in the forties, because Gladstone had been courageously abstemious in the thirties.

The course of study necessary at this time for classical honours was comprehensive, and the method of examination searching. A man who aimed at a first-class would 'take in' a list comprising from twelve to twenty books, which he was supposed to have mastered very completely, so as to be prepared to bear a pretty close examination in their subjects and language. These might be Homer, Æschylus, Sophocles, part of Aristophanes, Herodotus, Thucydides, perhaps Polybius, Virgil, Horace, perhaps Lucretius, portions of Livy and Tacitus, Aristotle's Ethics, Politics, and Rhetoric, perhaps the Republic of Plato or two of the shorter dialogues, and Butler's Analogy or Sermons. The actual examination on paper would be something of this kind. First day, Logic; and translation from English into Latin. Second, English Essay; translation from Greek into English. Third, Latin Essay; translation from English into Greek. Fourth, questions on Aristotle and Plato; Greek History, text, substance, critical questions. Fifth, questions on Butler and Ethics; Latin History. Then came the *vivâ voce* by one after another of the four examiners, who 'heckled' the candidate as much as they thought fit in all his books and subjects. This, with good examiners and good candidates, was a very interesting process, as minute knowledge, as well as intelligence and general views, came into play. The Divinity came in at the *vivâ voce*. The candidate was supposed to be at home in the Four Gospels; he ought to know something of St Paul, and he was expected to have a close knowledge of the language and general meaning of the Thirty-nine Articles. If he 'took in' Butler, questions might arise out of that. Metaphysic was not formally recognized; but he might in his Logic expect questions from Aristotle's Organon, and other philosophical treatises; and his study of Logic was supposed to have given him some acquaintance with such subjects. The examination was designed to try, not a man's general cleverness or even knowledge, but his power of mastering books intelligently and usefully; to test the way in which he had employed himself in reading during his three years at Oxford. Many brilliant men failed in it for want of knowledge; but it was also a trial of a man's intellectual power generally, as well as of his observation and memory. It was meant to enforce thoroughness of work, not to give honour to cleverness.

Not content with the intellectual exertion which this examination involved, Mr Gladstone also read for mathematical honours. It is said that he read steadily, but, till he neared his final schools, not laboriously. Nothing was ever allowed to interfere with his morning's work. He read for four hours, then he took a constitutional walk, and though not averse to hospitality in the way of suppers and wine-parties, he always read for two or three hours before bed-time. His tutor was the Rev. Robert Briscoe, whose lectures on Aristotle attracted some of the best men in the University; and he also attended the lectures of Dr Burton on Divinity and of Dr Pusey on Hebrew. He read classics privately with the present Bishop of St Andrews. The Long Vacation of 1830 he spent with a small reading-party at Cuddesdon Vicarage. 'It is curious,' writes a contemporary, 'to remember reading Plato with Bruce (Lord Elgin), seeing Manning hard at work getting up the text of the Bible so as to command great facility in applying it, Gladstone working at Hooker, whilst Hamilton (Bishop of Salisbury) was more inclined, I think, to indulge in Aristophanes.'

Mr Gladstone's chosen friends and associates were all industrious and steady men; not a few of them more distinctly religious than is, or was, common in undergraduate life. A more secularly-minded friend, writing in 1829, notes his regret that 'Gladstone has mixed himself up as much as he has done with the St Mary Hall and Oriel set, who are really, for the most part, only fit to live with maiden aunts and keep tame rabbits.'

He founded and presided over an essay society, called after him the WEG. The following were the original members: T. D. Acland, J. Anstice, J. B. Coll, F. Coll, F. H. Doyle, J. M. Gaskell, W. E. Gladstone, B. Harrison, J. T. Leader, H. Moncrieff, F. Rogers, and H. Ker Seymer.

The following members joined later: The Hon. J. Bruce, the Hon. F. Bruce, T. Egerton, H. G. Liddell, the Earl of Lincoln, F. D. Maurice, N. Oxnam, C. Thornton, H. H. Vaughan, and C. Marriott.

One of the surviving members of this society remembers Mr Gladstone reading an elaborate essay on Socrates' belief in immortality.

During the latter part of his undergraduate career, he took a brief but brilliant share in the proceedings of the Union, of which he was successively Secretary and President. He made his maiden speech on February 11, 1830. Brought up in the nurture and admonition of Mr Canning, whose fascinating eloquence he had heard at Liverpool and in the House of Commons, and whose society he had enjoyed at Eton, he was true to his great master's teaching. He defended Catholic emancipation, and thought the Duke of Wellington's Government unworthy of national confidence. He opposed the removal of Jewish disabilities, arguing, we are told by a contemporary, 'on the part of the Evangelicals,' and pleaded for the gradual extinction, in preference to the immediate abolition, of slavery. But his great achievement was his speech against the Whig Reform Bill. In April, 1831, Arthur Hallam writes: 'I have had a long letter from Gladstone; he is very bitter against the Reform Bill'; and when he came to deliver his sentiments in debate, his genuine indignation raised him to an unusual pitch of eloquence. He denounced the Bill as destined to change our form of government, and to break up the foundations of social order. One who heard this famous discourse says that it 'converted Alston, the son of the member for Hertford, who immediately on the conclusion of Gladstone's speech walked across from the Whig to the Tory side of the House, amidst loud acclamations.'

Another who heard it says: 'Most of the speakers rose, more or less, above their usual level, but when Mr Gladstone sat down we all of us felt that an epoch in our lives had occurred. It certainly was the finest speech of his that I ever heard.' Bishop Charles Wordsworth says that his experience of Mr Gladstone at this time 'made me (and, I doubt not, others also) feel no less sure than of my own existence that Gladstone, our then Christ Church undergraduate, would one day rise to be Prime Minister of England.'

In December 1831 Mr Gladstone crowned his career by taking a double first-class. The late Lord Halifax used to say, with reference to the increase in the amount of reading requisite for the highest honours: 'My double-first must have been a better thing than Peel's; Gladstone's must have been better than mine,'

Among the purely intellectual effects produced on Mr Gladstone by the discipline of Oxford, it is obvious to reckon an almost excessive exactness in the statement of propositions, a habit of rigorous definition, a microscopic care in the choice of words, and a tendency to analyze every sentiment and every phrase, and to distinguish with intense precaution between statements almost exactly similar. From Aristotle and Bishop Butler and Edmund Burke he learned the value of authority, the sacredness of law, the danger of laying rash and inconsiderate hands upon the ark of State. In the political atmosphere of Oxford he was taught to apply these principles to the civil events of his time, to dread innovation, to respect existing institutions, and to regard the Throne and the Church as inseparably associated by Divine ordinance.

The Toryism of the place was of a romantic and old-fashioned type, as far as possible removed from the utilitarian Conservatism of a later day. Charles I was a saint and martyr, and loyalty to the Stuarts was a sentiment which, though no longer practical, still lingered in the dreams of men. The claims of rank and birth were admitted with a childlike cheerfulness. The high function of government was the birthright of the few. The people had nothing to do with the laws, except to obey them. Mr Gladstone has told us that in academical circles liberty was regarded with jealousy and fear, as something which could not be dispensed with, 'but which was continually to be watched for fear of excess.'

The distinctly religious effect of Oxford on Mr Gladstone's mind was perhaps less direct than has been generally supposed. His was what Tertullian calls '*anima naturaliter Christiana.*' He had been carefully brought up. His father was a God-fearing man according to his light and opportunity, his mother a devout Evangelical. At Eton he had been honourably distinguished by simple devotion and stainless living. When he entered Oxford the Catholic revival had not yet begun. Cardinal Newman taught us to date it from the 14th of July, 1833. But the High Church party held the field. With the exception of a handful of Evangelicals at one obscure college, the religious clergy and laity of Oxford were High Churchmen of the traditional type. Dr Routh still survived to 'report,' as Cardinal Newman said, 'to a forgetful generation what had been the theology of their fathers'; though his influence was not felt beyond the walls of Magdalen College. The Caroline divinity still lingered. Men believed in the Church as a Divine society, as well as a chief institution of the realm; they set store upon her Orders and Sacraments, and at least professed great respect for, if they did not cultivate intimate acquaintance with, the writings of her standard divines. At the same time, they had a holy horror of Popish usurpation, and Sir Robert Peel's concession of the Catholic claims had just cost him his seat for the University. But these influences produced no immediate or conscious effect on Mr Gladstone's mind. The ecclesiastical atmosphere of the place was High and Dry, and therefore as little as possible attractive to an ardent and spiritual nature. Had his undergraduate career been a few years later, when the fascinating genius and austere sanctity of Cardinal Newman had begun to leaven the University, he would probably have been numbered with that band of devoted disciples who followed the great Oratorian whithersoever he went. But between 1829 and 1832 there was no leader of paramount authority in the religious world of Oxford, and the young student of Christ Church was left to develop his own opinions and frame his own course. The blameless schoolboy became a blameless undergraduate; diligent, sober, regular alike in study and devotion, giving his whole energies to the duties of the place, and quietly abiding in the religious faith in which he had been trained. Bishop Charles Wordsworth says that no man of his standing in the University habitually read his Bible more or knew it better. Cardinal Manning remembers him walking to church with his 'Bible and Prayer-book tucked under his arm.' He paid surreptitious visits to Dissenting chapels; denounced Bishop Butler's doctrine that human nature is not wholly corrupt; was enraged by a University sermon in which Calvin had been placed on the same level of orthodoxy as Socinus; and quitted Oxford with a religious belief still untinctured by Catholic theology. But the great change was not far distant, and he had already formed some of the friendships which, in their development, were destined to affect so profoundly the course of his religious thought.

Leaving the University in this devout though not ecclesiastical frame of mind, Mr Gladstone pondered carefully the choice of a profession. Conscious of great powers, keenly anxious to use them for God's glory and the service of men, and relieved by his father's wealth from the necessity of making his own fortune, he turned his thoughts to Holy Orders. There still exists a deeply interesting letter in which he urges, with characteristic earnestness, the reasons which impelled him to a clerical career. But his father had resolved otherwise, and the paternal will prevailed. Quitting Oxford in the spring of 1832 Mr Gladstone spent six months in Italy, learning the language, studying the art, and revelling in the natural beauties of that glorious land. In the following September, he was suddenly recalled to England, to undertake his first parliamentary campaign.

II

Enters Parliament—Early speeches—Office—Opposition

The English nation had now reached one of the main turning-points in its history. That which the Duke of Wellington so aptly described as a revolution by due course of law had taken place, and the most extravagant expectation of its results filled the air. The enthusiastic friends of freedom looked with sanguine hope to the consequences of an act which had admitted large classes, hitherto unrepresented, to the rights of citizenship. Prudent patriots believed that, by a timely concession of reform, they had weakened the forces of revolution and averted the necessity for larger change. Philanthropists cherished the amiable illusion that a purely political process would go far towards abolishing ignorance and poverty and disease, and would precipitate a social millennium. On the other hand, the rich and the privileged classes, timid men, and lovers of the ancient ways, were terrified by the scenes of bloodshed and violence which had prepared the way for the great reform. A revolution had just occurred in France, and might at any moment be reproduced in England. Ireland was in a state of scarcely-veiled insurrection. Great political forces, hostile to the established order, and encouraged by a momentous victory, were no longer restrained by the strong hand of executive authority. Credit was disturbed, property was insecure, commercial enterprise at a standstill. Everywhere the signs of change were visible. The horizon was overcast with the dark clouds of coming danger. Natural disasters were added to political alarms. A mysterious and in tractable pestilence ravaged the great cities. Men's hearts were failing them for fear and for looking after those things that were coming on the earth. Religious people, assembling themselves together for the study of sacred prophecy, discerned all around them the signs of the end, and persuaded themselves that the world had already entered upon that Great Tribulation which is appointed to precede the Second Coming of Christ. The terrors of the time begat a hundred forms of strange fanaticism; and among men who were not fanatics there was a deep and wide conviction that national judgments were overtaking national sins, and that the only hope of safety for England lay in a return to that practical recognition of religion in the political sphere which had been the characteristic glory of Englishmen at the proudest moments of English history. 'The beginning and the end of what is the matter with us in these days,' wrote Mr Carlyle, 'is that we have forgotten God.'

It was a moment well calculated to awake the enthusiasm of an ardent and gifted youth, educated in an Evangelical home, trained to dread revolution and to abhor infidelity, and conscious of exceptional qualifications for the service of the State; and we who know the man, have seen his career, and have watched the workings of his fiery spirit, can imagine the solemn eagerness with which, in the autumn of 1832, the young politician turned his steps from Italy to England.

The fifth Duke of Newcastle was one of the chief potentates of the High Tory party. His frank claim to 'do what he liked with his own' in the representation of Newark has given him a place in political history. But that claim had been rudely disputed by the return of a Radical lawyer at the election of 1831. The Duke was anxious to obtain a capable candidate to aid him in regaining his ascendancy over the rebellious borough. His son, Lord Lincoln, who was to contest Nottinghamshire, had been a friend, at Eton and Oxford, of Mr William Gladstone, had heard his memorable speech against the Reform Bill delivered in the Oxford Union, and had written home that 'a man had uprisen in Israel.' At his suggestion, the Duke invited the young student of Christ Church to stand for Newark in the Tory interest, against Mr Serjeant Wilde, afterwards Lord Chancellor Truro. He could scarcely have found a more suitable instrument for the accomplishment of his design.

William Ewart Gladstone was now twenty-two years old, with a physical constitution of unequalled vigour, the prospect of ample fortune, great and varied knowledge, a natural tendency to political theorization, and an inexhaustible copiousness and readiness of speech. In person he was striking and attractive, with strongly-marked features, a pale complexion, abundance of dark hair, and eyes of piercing lustre. People who judged only by his external aspect considered that he was delicate.

His address to the electors was all that such a document should be. He was bound by the opinions of no man and no party, but felt it a duty to watch and resist that growing desire for change which threatened to produce, 'along with partial good, a melancholy preponderance of mischief.' The first principle to which he looked for national salvation was that the 'duties of Governors are strictly and peculiarly religious, and that Legislatures, like individuals, are bound to carry throughout their acts the spirit of the high truths they have acknowledged.' The condition of the poor demanded special attention; labour should receive adequate remuneration, and he thought favourably of the 'allotment of cottage grounds.' He regarded slavery as sanctioned by Holy Scripture, but the slaves were to be educated, and gradually emancipated.

The nomination took place on December 11. Mr Gladstone spoke amid continuous interruption, and was subjected to a severe cross as to the circumstances of his candidature, his father's connexion with slavery, and his own view of capital punishment. Here his dialectical ingenuity stood him in good stead, and one can almost sympathize with the perplexity of the Radical elector who, on asking the Tory candidate if he was the Duke of Newcastle's nominee, was met by the intimation that, before answering that question, Mr Gladstone must have the questioner's definition of the term 'nominee.' 'Mr Gillson said he meant a person sent by the Duke of Newcastle to be pushed down the electors' throats whether they would or not.' Really, as times go, this seems not a bad definition; but Mr Gladstone replied that, according to that definition, 'he was not a nominee. He came to Newark by the invitation of the Red Club, than whom none were more respectable and intelligent.'

The contest was fought out with great spirit and determination, and when it closed Mr Gladstone was returned at the head of the poll. The borough returned two members: another Tory was second, and Serjeant Wilde was defeated. A few weeks before the election Mr Arthur Hallam, writing of his friend, 'the old WEG,' says: 'I shall be very glad if he gets in … We want such a man as that. In some things he is likely to be obstinate and prejudiced; but he has a fine fund of high, chivalrous, Tory sentiment, and a tongue, moreover, to let it loose with.' And on December 15 he exclaims, 'And Gladstone has turned out the Serjeant … What a triumph for him! He has made his reputation by it; all that remains is to keep up to it.'

The following descriptive prophecy is taken from a poem by one of Mr Gladstone's Liberal opponents in the Union at Oxford, and it is worthy of quotation as showing the impression which his talents and character had made even upon those of his contemporaries whose political opinions were the most remote from his own:

> Yet on one form, whose ear can ne'er refuse
> The Muses' tribute, for he lov'd the Muse,
> (And when the soul the gen'rous virtues raise,
> A friendly Whig may chant a Tory's praise),
> Full many a fond expectant eye is bent
> Where Newark's towers are mirror'd in the Trent.
> Perchance ere long to shine in senates first,
> If manhood echo what his youth rehears'd,
> Soon Gladstone's brows will bloom with greener bays

Than twine the chaplet of a minstrel's lays;
Nor heed, while poring o'er each graver line,
The far, faint music of a lute like mine.
His was no head contentedly which press'd
The downy pillow in obedient rest,
Where lazy pilots, with their canvas furl'd,
Set up the Gades of their mental world;
His was no tongue which meanly stoop'd to wear
The guise of virtue, while his heart was bare;
But all he thought through ev'ry action ran;
God's noblest work—I've known one honest man.*

The first Reformed Parliament met on January 29, 1833, and the young member for Newark took his seat for the first time in an assembly which he was destined to adorn, delight, and astonish for more than half a century, and over which, for a great portion of that period, he was to wield an unequalled and a paramount authority. The House of Commons contained more than three hundred new members. The Whigs, led by Lord Althorp, had a large majority; but there was a compact minority of Tories, ranged under the skilful leadership of Sir Robert Peel, and a body of Irish members who followed O'Connell, and who might be reckoned as hostile to the Ministry.

The subjects which loomed largest in the public mind were the social condition of Ireland and the position of the Established Church in that island, the discontent and misery of the poor in England, and slavery in the British Colonies. No reference to the last-named subject was made in the Speech from the Throne, but, under salutary pressure from some of their supporters, the Government resolved to deal with it. The Colonial Secretary, Mr Stanley (afterwards fourteenth Earl of Derby and Prime Minister), brought forward a series of Resolutions in favour of the extinction of slavery in the British colonies. All children of slaves, born after the passing of the Act, and all children of six years old and under, were declared free. But the rest of the slaves were to serve a sort of apprenticeship; three-fourths of their time was for a certain number of years to remain at the disposal of the masters; the other fourth was their own, to be paid for at a fixed rate of wages. The planters were to be fairly compensated out of the exchequer. The discussion of these resolutions was signalized by Mr Gladstone's maiden speech in Parliament. It was delivered in reply to what was almost a personal challenge. On the first night of the debate Lord Howick (now Lord Grey), who had been Under-Secretary for the Colonies, and who opposed the resolu-

---

* *Black Gowns and Red Coats*: a satirical poem. By George Cox, MA, Fellow of New College, Oxford. 1834.

tions as proceeding too gradually towards abolition, cited certain occurrences on Sir John Gladstone's plantation in Demerara to illustrate his contention that the system of slave-labour in the West Indies was attended by great mortality among the slaves. On May 17 Mr Gladstone delivered his reply to Lord Howick. Among those who knew the young member for Newark his speech was anticipated with lively expectation.

He was riding that morning in Hyde Park, a noticeable figure on his grey Arabian mare, with 'his hat, narrow brimmed, high up on the centre of his head, sustained by a crop of thick, curly hair.' A passer-by pointed him out to another new member—Lord Charles Russell—and said, 'That is Gladstone. He is to make his maiden speech to-night. It will be worth hearing.' The speech began with all due modesty. Lord Howick, he said, had attacked the management of his father's estates. He met some of the noble Lord's statements with denials, and some with explanations. There was no great mortality and no excessive hardship on the plantation. The particular form of cultivation practised in Demerara was no doubt more severe than some others; but house-painting and working in lead-mines were also known to be more dangerous to life than other occupations. His father's manager was the kindest of men, and the slaves under his charge were the happiest, healthiest, and most contented of their race.

Fortunate indeed, perhaps unduly so, was the venerable slave-owner who could command the services of such parliamentary advocate as this. On June 3 Mr Gladstone spoke more fully in the same sense, deprecated slavery, condemned cruelty, was favourable to emancipation, but thought that it should be effected gradually, and after due preparation. The slaves must be educated, and 'stimulated to spontaneous industry,' as the owners must be fully compensated. During the same Session Mr Gladstone spoke on the question of bribery and corruption at Liverpool, and on July 8 he made an elaborate speech on the Church Temporalities (Ireland) Bill.

The condition of Ireland was then, as now, the most urgent of all the problems which awaited the Ministry. Mr Macaulay 'solemnly declared that he would rather live in the midst of many civil wars that he had read of than in some parts of Ireland at this moment.' Sydney Smith did not over-colour the picture when he described 'those Irish Protestants whose shutters are bullet-proof; whose dinner-table is regularly spread out with knife, fork, and cocked pistol; salt-cellar, and powder-flask; who sleep in sheet iron nightcaps; who have fought so often and so nobly before their scullery-door, and defended the parlour passage as bravely as Leonidas defended the pass of Thermopylæ.'

In the province of Leinster alone, in the previous July, August, and September, there had been 1,279 crimes, and in the following three months the number had risen to 1,641. During the year, the catalogue of outrages contained 172 homicides, 465 robberies, 568 burglaries, 454 acts of cruelty to cattle, 2,095 illegal notices, 425 illegal meetings, 796 malicious injuries to property, 753 attacks on houses, 280 arsons, and 3,156 serious assaults—in all, more than 9,000 crimes connected with the disaffected state of the people. To remedy this condition, the Government, on February 15, introduced a stringent Coercion Bill. Power was placed in the hands of the Lord Lieutenant to suppress every meeting or association which he regarded as dangerous to the preservation of peace and to declare any district to be in a disturbed state. In a district so proclaimed, the inhabitants were to be confined to their houses from an hour after sunset to sunrise; the right of meeting and petitioning was withdrawn; and they were placed under martial law. The Bill further gave power to enter houses in search of arms, forbade the distribution of seditious papers, and suspended the Habeas Corpus Act in the disturbed districts. Mr Gladstone gave silent votes for the Bill, which duly passed into law. Meanwhile, in order to render this drastic Act more palatable, the Ministry, on February 12, introduced a Bill for the regulation of the Irish Church. Even the warmest defenders of that institution could scarcely deny that it stood in need of some reform. In a country with some eight millions of inhabitants, the Established Church boasted some eight hundred thousand members. It had four Archbishops and eighteen bishops, with an aggregate income of £150,000 a year, and a body of parochial clergy supported by tithes which were exacted, not only from the Protestant minority, but from the six millions of Catholics. Besides the payment of tithes, a special tax, or 'Church cess,' for the maintenance of the ecclesiastical fathers and their services, was levied indiscriminately on members of all religions, but administered exclusively by Protestant vestries. It was estimated that from first to last the income of the Church was more than £800,000 a year. To remedy these anomalies, without too violently disturbing Protestant sentiment or endangering the security of property, was the object of the Ministerial Bill. It was proposed to destroy ten of the bishoprics by consolidating them with the remainder. The incomes of some of the richer sees were curtailed, and the surplus thus arising was to be handed over to Ecclesiastical Commissioners. The 'annates,' or first-fruits of livings, had formerly been applied in relief of the 'Church cess.' Instead of these, a graduated tax was to be laid on all livings, and with the money thus accruing the 'Church cess' was to be extinguished. The terms on which lands belonging to the Church were let were to be so altered as to improve the position of the tenant without injuring the clergy. The tenant, it was calculated, would be willing to pay for this advantage, and the sum thus gained would amount to something between two and three millions. This money was to be available for purposes of State.

As soon as this Bill was introduced it was exposed to a double and treble fire of criticism. O'Connell and the Irish party scouted the relief, which consisted only in the abolition of the 'Church cess.' English Radicals declared that, instead of twelve Bishops, the Irish Protestants were not numerous enough to require more than one, or at the most 'two, to keep up the breed.' The Tories raised the cry of confiscation, and loudly declared that all property was imperilled by the Appropriation Clause. The High Church party took up arms to withstand what they regarded as a sacrilegious attack upon a Divine institution. Lord Grey, who, in his insolence towards the Church, was a Whig all over, had told the Bishops to set their house in order. The spoliation begun in Ireland might soon extend to England. The saintly Keble, preaching the Assize sermon at Oxford, uttered a warning note against 'national apostasy.'

The young member for Newark, speaking on the second reading of the Bill, faced the danger with a courageous front. He would not shelter himself, he said, under a silent vote. He admitted the existence of abuses in the Irish Establishment. The Church had slumbered, but, since the Union, had awoke to a new life and fresh energy. It was a popular cry to denounce the Irish Church on account of its 'wealth,' but poverty was no guarantee of efficiency. The churches of the Vaudois were poor enough, but could anyone cite them as models of practical work? It was a social advantage to Ireland that in every parish there should be an educated gentleman and a Christian by profession. The work of the Church was not aggressive: it only required a fair opportunity of setting forth the distinctive doctrines of Protestantism. He could not support the suppression of any of the bishoprics, for, as the work and usefulness of the Church increased, there would be full occupation for all the Bishops of the existing Establishment.

After an animated debate, Lord Althorp withdrew the Appropriation Clause, which asserted the only important principle of the Bill—*i.e.* the right of Parliament to apply ecclesiastical property to the uses of the State—and the Bill, at once lightened and weakened, passed into law without further opposition.

In the following Session, Mr Hume, the Radical member for Middlesex, introduced a 'Universities Admission Bill,' designed to enable Nonconformists of all kinds to enter the Universities, by removing the necessity of subscribing the Thirty-nine Articles at matriculation. Here Mr Gladstone was thoroughly in his element. In defending slavery he had spoken from his father's brief; in defending the Irish Church he had perforce relied on impressive generalities. But in a question affecting the religious character and discipline of the Universities, the member for Newark, who was also a Student of Christ Church, and who had only three years before been a model undergraduate, could speak with the full authority of personal and recent knowledge. His foot, as Rob Roy says, was on his native heath. It was an excellent opportunity excellently used. Mr Gladstone's speech in reply to Mr Hume was skilful and characteristic. It seems that Mr Hume, having no practical acquaintance with the Universities, imagined that if the Vice-Chancellor were no longer empowered to demand subscription as the condition of matriculation, all difficulties in the way of the admission of Dissenters would vanish. Mr Gladstone reminded him that this was not so; that the Vice-Chancellor would still enquire to what college the candidate for matriculation belonged, and the colleges would take good care to admit no one who would not subscribe. The Bill would therefore be inoperative so far as its immediate object was concerned; but still it would lead to great dissensions and confusion. The whole system of the University and of its colleges, both in study and in discipline, aimed at the formation of a moral character, and that aim could not be attained if every student were at liberty to exclude himself from the religious training of the place.

One point which Mr Gladstone incidentally makes speaks volumes for the life which he had lived at Oxford, and the kind of company that he had kept there. Lord Palmerston had expressed a reasonable dislike of a system which compelled the undergraduates to go 'from wine to prayers, and prayers to wine.' But Mr Gladstone had a better opinion of the undergraduates who had so lately been his companions. He did not believe that *even in their most convivial moments they were unfit to enter the House of Prayer.* Oxford produces few men, in any generation, to whom this would suggest itself as a possible vindication of compulsory Chapel.

From a perusal of these speeches, imperfectly reported in the third person, and from contemporary evidence, it is clear that, when due allowance for growth and development is made, Mr Gladstone's early style of oratory was pretty much what it is to-day. His voice was always clear, flexible, and melodious, though his utterance was marked then, even more conspicuously than now, by a Lancastrian 'burr'; his gesture was varied and animated, but not violent. He turned his face and body from side to side, and often wheeled round to face his own party as he appealed for their cheers. The reports of his speeches in the Debating Society at Eton prove that, even in his earliest days, he had an immense command of language. Like Mr Pitt, he showed 'a premature and unnatural dexterity in the combination of words,' and then, as now, he was only too fluent. That brevity could be a merit in composition he seems to have been unaware, for he expresses ingenuous surprise that the examiners for the Ireland scholarship at Oxford had considered it a merit in one Brancker, the winner, that he answered 'all the questions short.' A reporter who had professionally experienced his fluency on the hustings at Newark considered him quite equal to delivering a three-hours' speech to the mob. His style of composition was redundant, involved, and Johnsonese; and his speeches were freely garnished with Horatian and Virgilian citations.

If his early style of public speaking resembled his later style in its faults, it resembled it no less closely in its characteristic excellences. 'Did you ever feel nervous in public speaking?' asked an eminent man. 'In opening a subject, often,' said Mr Gladstone; *'in reply, never.'* A critic of public men, writing in 1838, remarks that Mr Gladstone 'displays considerable acuteness in replying to an opponent; he is quick in his perception of anything vulnerable in the speech to which he replies, and happy in laying the weak points bare to the House ... He is plausible, even when most in error. When it suits himself or his party he can apply himself with the strictest closeness to the real points at issue; when to evade the point is deemed most politic, no man can wander from it more widely.' Later critics, it is believed, have sometimes made a similar observation.

Meanwhile, difficulties were thickening round the Whig Government. The Reform Act had not produced the millennium. Lord Grey's Cabinet had grievously disappointed the expectations of reformers. Occupying a middle position between the Tories and the Radicals, it swayed from time to time in each direction, and of course satisfied no one. No considerable measure of the Government had been passed without important modifications. Every scheme which they propounded bore the marks of compromise.

While the friends of freedom and progress were disappointed by the slackness and indecision of the Government, the forces of tyranny, discovering with joy that the Reform Act had not, after all, demolished them, took heart of grace, and rallied themselves for a struggle to regain their lost ascendancy. 'Conservative reaction' became an accepted formula. On both sides the Ministers were exposed to damaging criticism. In the House of Lords the Duke of Wellington declared that their foreign policy had not produced European peace, that their ecclesiastical concessions had done no good in Ireland, and that they did not know their own minds about the renewal of the Coercion Act. On the other hand, at great public meetings in London and the provincial towns, it was declared that the Whig Government, by violating the Constitution of Ireland, refusing to enquire into public distress, and continuing obnoxious taxation, had betrayed the confidence of the people.

The Trade Unions, which had hitherto worked in isolation, now combined their forces and threatened the security of the Government, and even, as it would seem, plotted a bodily attack upon the Home Secretary. The agricultural labourers rose in organized opposition to their employers. Everywhere the symptoms of discontent were manifest, and the Cabinet, thus beset with external dangers, was torn asunder by internal strife.

Lord Grey's stock of Liberalism, never a very ample one, had been exhausted by the Reform Bill. He was perpetually harassed and disturbed by his imperious son-in-law, Lord Durham, whose fiery temper and impetuous radicalism would be satisfied by no half measures. On the other hand, Mr Stanley had a passion for what is called 'Resolute Government' in Ireland, and this was highly distasteful to the prudent and conciliatory temper of Lord Althorp. A proposal of the Government to issue a Commission to enquire into the Irish Church and the redistribution of its revenues was so abhorrent to the more conservative members of the Cabinet that it led to the resignation of Mr Stanley, Sir James

Graham, the Duke of Richmond, and Lord Ripon. On the other hand, when it became necessary to renew the Coercion Act, a sharp difference of opinion arose in the Cabinet as to the desirability of renewing those clauses which provided for the suppression of Petition and the establishment of martial law, and after some very undignified disclosures in the House of Commons, Lord Althorp, who had favoured the milder course, withdrew from office. This was the last straw. Lord Grey immediately resigned. After a futile attempt to form a joint Government of Whigs and moderate Tories, the former Cabinet was reconstructed under the premiership of Lord Melbourne. But another crisis was close at hand. On November 10 Lord Spencer died, and the accession of his son, Lord Althorp, to the peerage made a vacancy in the Leadership of the House of Commons.

The King was at Brighton. Lord Melbourne waited on him there, to take his pleasure as to the new arrangements which Lord Spencer's death had rendered necessary. He submitted a choice of names for the Chancellorship of the Exchequer and Leadership of the House of Commons. The King took time to consider. Next day he sent for Lord Melbourne again, and handed him a letter announcing his decision. In this letter the King stated that, having lost the services of Lord Althorp as Leader of the House of Commons, he could feel no confidence in the stability of his Government when led by any other member of it; that they were already in a minority in the House of Lords, and he had every reason to believe that the removal of Lord Althorp would speedily put them in the same situation in the other House; that under such circumstances he felt other arrangements to be necessary; and that it was his intention to send for the Duke of Wellington. Nothing could be more peremptory and decisive. The King had dismissed his Ministers. The event had an interest far beyond its immediate consequences. It was the last great act of royal prerogative.

The dismissal of the Whig Ministers threw parties and politicians into unspeakable confusion. No one, it would seem, was less prepared for it than the Duke of Wellington, on whom the King laid the duty of carrying on his government. The Duke's natural affinities were with the High Tory party, but he had sense enough to perceive that the cautious temper and moderate opinions of Sir Robert Peel were more acceptable to the country, and would form an indispensable element in the new Administration. Sir Robert had gone abroad after the Session, and was now in Rome. A messenger (who lived to be famous as the diplomatist Sir James Hudson) was despatched to bring him back. His return was awaited with feverish anxiety, and in the meantime the Duke of Wellington provisionally undertook the offices of First Lord of the Treasury, Home Secretary, Foreign Secretary, and Colonial Secretary. Lord Lyndhurst became Lord Chancellor. The conjuncture was interesting, and an eye-witness has described it with admirable skill:

It was a lively season, that winter of 1834! What hopes, what fears, and what bets! From the day on which Mr Hudson was to arrive at Rome to the election of the Speaker, not a contingency that was not the subject of a wager! People sprang up like mushrooms; town suddenly became full. Everybody who had been in office, and everybody who wished to be in office; everybody who had ever had anything, and everybody who ever expected to have anything, were alike visible. All of course by mere accident; one might meet the same men regularly every day for a month, who were only 'passing through town.'

Now was the time for men to come forward who had never despaired of their country. True, they had voted for the Reform Bill, but that was to prevent a revolution. And now they were quite ready to vote against the Reform Bill, but this was to prevent a dissolution. These are the true patriots, whose confidence in the good sense of their countrymen and in their own selfishness is about equal. In the meantime, the hundred and forty threw a grim glance on the numerous waiters on Providence, and amiable trimmers, who affectionately enquired every day when news might be expected of Sir Robert. Though too weak to form a Government, and having contributed in no wise by their exertions to the fall of the late, the cohort of parliamentary Tories felt all the alarm of men who have accidentally stumbled on some treasure-trove, at the suspicious sympathy of new allies. But, after all, who were to form the Government, and what was the Government to be? Was it to be a Tory Government, or an Enlightened-Spirit-of-the-Age Liberal-Moderate-Reform Government; was it to be a Government of high philosophy or of low practice; of principle or of expediency; of great measures or of little men? A Government of statesmen or of clerks? Of Humbug or of Humdrum? Great questions these, but unfortunately there was nobody to answer them. They tried the Duke; but nothing could be pumped out of him. All that he knew, which he told in his curt, husky manner, was that he had to carry on the King's government. As for his solitary colleague, he listened and smiled, and then in his musical voice asked them questions in return, which is the best possible mode of avoiding awkward enquiries. It was very unfair this; for no one knew what tone to take— whether they should go down to their public dinners and denounce the Reform Act or praise it; whether the Church was to be re-modelled or only admonished; whether Ireland was to be conquered or conciliated ...

At last he came; the great man in a great position, summoned from Rome to govern England. The very day that he arrived he had his audience with the King. It was two days after this audience; the town, though November, in a state of excitement; clubs crowded, not only morning-rooms, but halls and staircases swarming with members eager to give and to receive rumours equally vain; streets lined with cabs and chariots, grooms and horses ...

Here might be marked a murmuring knot of grey-headed privy councillors, who had held fat offices under Perceval and Liverpool, and who looked back to the Reform Act as to a hideous dream; there some middle-aged aspirants might be observed who had lost their seats in the convulsion, but who flattered themselves they had done something for the party in the interval, by spending nothing except their breath in fighting hopeless boroughs, and occasionally publishing a pamphlet, which really produced less effect than chalking the walls. Light as air, and proud as a young peacock, tripped on his toes a young Tory, who had contrived to keep his seat in a Parliament where he had done nothing, but who thought an Under-Secretaryship was now secure, particularly as he was the son of a noble Lord who had also in a public capacity plundered and blundered in the good old time. The true political adventurer, who with dull desperation had stuck at nothing, had never neglected a Treasury note, had been present at every division, never spoke when he was asked to be silent, and was always ready on any subject when they wanted him to open his mouth—who had treated his leaders with servility even behind their backs, and was happy for the day if a future Secretary of the Treasury bowed to him; who had not only discountenanced discontent in the party, but had regularly reported in strict confidence every instance of insubordination which came to his knowledge—might there, too, be detected under all the agonies of the crisis; just beginning to feel the dread misgiving whether being a slave and a sneak were sufficient qualifications for office, without family or connexion. Poor fellow! half the industry he had wasted on his cheerless craft might have made his fortune in some decent trade!

In dazzling contrast with these throes of low ambition, were some brilliant personages who had just scampered up from Melton, thinking it probable that Sir Robert might want some moral lords of the bedchamber. Whatever may have been their private fears or feelings, all, however, seemed smiling and significant, as if they knew something if they chose to tell it, and that something very much to their own satisfaction. The only grave countenance that was occasionally ushered into the room belonged to some individual whose destiny was not in doubt, and who was already practising the official air that was in future to repress the familiarity of his former fellow strugglers.

In the scramble for offices, so delightfully described by Lord Beaconsfield in the foregoing pages, there was one result which was inevitable. Mr Gladstone must be a member of the new Government. When a Prime Minister in difficulties, looking about for men to fill the minor offices of his Administration, sees among his supporters a clever and comely young man, eloquent in speech, ready in debate, with a safe seat, an ample fortune, a high reputation at the University, and a father who wields political influence in an important constituency, he sees a junior Lord of the Treasury made ready to his hand.

On Christmas Eve, Mr Gladstone, having accepted office, issued his address to the electors of Newark. This document was, as it was bound to be, an echo of the manifesto which Sir Robert Peel had addressed to the electors of Tamworth. Sir Robert had declared that the Reform Act was a final and irrevocable settlement of a great constitutional question, and a settlement which no friend to the peace and welfare of the country would attempt to disturb. But he expressed the readiness of the Government to reform real abuses and defects, though they declined to seek 'a false popularity by adopting every popular impression of the day.'

In the same strain Mr Gladstone told the electors of Newark that the best friends of the late Ministry had been alienated from it by its tendency to rash, violent, and indefinite innovation, and that there were even 'those among the servants of the King who did not scruple to solicit the suffrages of their constituents with promises to act on the principles of Radicalism.' Mr Gladstone went on to say: 'The question has then, as it appears to me, become, whether we are to hurry onwards at intervals, but not long ones, through the medium of the ballot, short Parliaments, and other questions called popular, into republicanism or anarchy; or whether, independently of all party distinction, the people will support the Crown in the discharge of its duty to maintain in efficiency and transmit in safety those old and valuable institutions under which our country has greatly flourished ... Let me add shortly, but emphatically, concerning the reform of actual abuses, whether in Church or State, that I regard it as a sacred duty—a duty at all times, and certainly not least at a period like this, when the danger of neglecting it is most clear and imminent—a duty not inimical to true and determined Conservative principle, nor a curtailment or modification of such principle, but its legitimate consequence, or rather an actual element of its composition.'

Parliament was dissolved on December 29. Mr Gladstone was returned unopposed, this time in conjunction with the Liberal lawyer whom he had beaten at the last election. The new Parliament met on February 19, 1835. The elections had given the Liberals a considerable majority. The old House of Commons had been burnt down during the recess. It was, perhaps, a parable of actual and impending changes that the Commons now assembled in the chamber which had been the House of Lords, and that for the first time there was a gallery for reporters in the House. A standing order still existed which forbade the publication of the debates, but the reporters' gallery was a formal and visible recognition of the people's right to know what their representatives were doing in their name.

Immediately after the meeting of Parliament, Mr Gladstone was promoted from his post at the Treasury to the Under-Secretaryship for the Colonies. His official chief was Lord Aberdeen, and thus began a relation which was destined to affect momentously the careers both of the younger and of the older statesman. Both in the House and in his office the new Under-Secretary gave proof of his great capacity and untiring energies. But the Administration was not long-lived. On March 30, Lord John Russell moved his resolution in favour of an enquiry into the temporalities of the Irish Church, with the intention of applying any surplus to general education without distinction of religious creed. This was in fact a revival of the abandoned 'Appropriation Clause,' and it was carried against Ministers by a majority of thirty-three. On April 8, Sir Robert Peel resigned, and the Under-Secretary for the Colonies of course followed his chief into private life.

Released from the labours of office, Mr Gladstone was free to follow the bent of his own inclinations, and to order his life according to his own ideals. Living in chambers in the Albany, he pursued the same even course of steady work, reasonable recreation, and systematic devotion, which he had marked out for himself at Oxford. He went freely into society, dined out constantly, and took his part in musical parties, delighting his hearers with the cultivated beauty of his tenor voice. Mr Monckton Milnes had now established himself in London, and gathered round him a society of young men who were interested in theology and politics. He used to entertain them at parties on Sunday evenings, and this arrangement, he says, writing on March 13, 1838, 'unfortunately excludes the more serious members, Acland, Gladstone, &c. I really think when people keep Friday as a fast, they might make a feast of Sunday.' Mr Gladstone used to receive his friends at his rooms in the Albany, and on one occasion entertained Mr Wordsworth at breakfast in a charmed circle of young adorers.

But, though he found time for occasional relaxation, his days were divided between his parliamentary duties and study. Then, as now, his constant companions were Homer and Dante, and it is recorded that at this time he read the whole of St Augustine, in twenty-two octavo volumes. He was, as always, a diligent attendant on, and a careful critic of, preaching, and used to frequent the services at St James's, Piccadilly, and Margaret Chapel, since better known as All Saints', Margaret Street. At the same time he threw himself with diligence into the duties of a private member, working freely on committees, and taking constant part in debate. In 1836 he spoke with his habitual animation in defence of the East Indian planters, and of the system of apprenticeship which had taken the place of slavery. He spoke also on the government of Canada, strongly supporting the cause of authority and order; and at great length on Church Rates, perorating in a most impressive vein on the necessity of national religion to the security of a State.

On June 20, 1837, King William IV died; and Parliament, having been prorogued by the young Queen in person, was dissolved on the 17th of the following month. Simply on the strength of his parliamentary reputation, Mr Gladstone was nominated, without his consent, for Manchester, and was placed at the bottom of the poll; but, having been at the same time nominated at Newark, was again returned. On August 11, wearied with electioneering, he turned his steps to Scotland, 'to see what grouse he could persuade into his bag.' The new Parliament met on October 20, but no business of importance was transacted till after the Christmas recess. In 1838 Mr Gladstone returned again and again to the championship of the planters, each time with increasing power and success. His impassioned speech of March 30 may be regarded as having placed him high among parliamentary debaters.

On April 20, 1838, the Rev. Samuel Wilberforce, afterwards Bishop of Oxford, and of Winchester, wrote thus to Mr Gladstone: 'It would be an affectation in you, which you are above, not to know that few young men have the weight you have in the House of Commons, and are gaining rapidly throughout the country. Now I do not wish to urge you to consider this as a talent for the use of which you must render an account, for so I know you do esteem it, but what I want to urge upon you is that you should calmly look far before you; see the degree of weight and influence to which you may fairly, if God spares your life and powers, look forward in future years, and thus act *now* with a view to *then*. There is no height to which you may not fairly rise in this country. If it pleases God to spare us violent convulsions and the loss of our liberties, you may at a future day wield the whole government of this land; and if this should be so, of what extreme moment will your *past steps* then be to the real usefulness of your high station. If there has been any compromise of principle before, you will not then be able to rise above it; but if all your steps have been equal, you will not then be expected to descend below them. I say this to you in the sad conviction that almost all our public men act from the merest expediency; and that from this conventional standard it must be most difficult for one living and acting amongst them to keep himself clear; and yet from the conviction, too, that as yet you are wholly uncommitted to any low principles of thought or action. I would have you view yourself as one who may become the head of all the better feelings of this country, the maintainer of its Church and of its liberties, and who must now be fitting himself for this high vocation. Suffer me to add, what I think my father's life so beautifully shows, that a deep and increasing personal religion must be the root of that firm and unwearied consistency in right, which I have ventured thus to press upon you. May you in another walk, and in still higher opportunities of service, as perfectly illustrate the undoubted truth that those, who honour Him, He will honour.'

To this letter Mr Gladstone replied: 'I fear entering on the subject to which you have given the chief part of your letter, because I know how large it is, and how oppressive, how all but intolerably oppressive, are the considerations with which it is connected. I have not to charge myself inwardly with having been used to look forward along the avenues of life rarely or neglectfully; but rather with that weakness of faith, and that shrinking of the flesh, of which at every moment I am mournfully conscious, but most so when I attempt to estimate or conjecture our probable public destinies during the term to which our natural lives may extend—a prospect which I confess fills me with despondency and alarm.

'Not that these feelings are unmixed: they are tempered even as regards the period of which I speak with the confident anticipations of new developments of religious power which have been forgotten in the day of insidious prosperity, and seem to be providentially reserved for the time of our need, for the swelling of Jordan; and of course there lies beyond that period, for those who are appointed to it, a haven of perfect rest; but still the coming years bear to my view an aspect of gloom for the country—not for the Church; she is the land of Goshen. Looking, however, to the former, to the State as such, and to those who belong to it as citizens, I seem unable to discern resources bearing a just proportion to her dangers and necessities. While the art of politics from day to day embraces more and more vital questions, and enters into closer relations with the characters and therefore the destinies of men, there is, I fear, a falling away in the intellectual stature of the generation of men whose office it is to exercise that art for good. While public men are called by the exigencies of their position to do more and more, there seems to be in the accumulation of business, the bewildering multiplication of details, an indication of their probable capacity to do less and less. The principles of civil government have decayed amongst us as much, I suspect, as those which are ecclesiastical; and one does not see an equally ready or sure provision for their revival. One sees in actual existence the apparatus by which our institutions are to be threatened, and the very groundwork of the national character to be broken up; but upon the other hand, if we look around for the masses of principle, I mean of enlightened principle, blended with courage and devotion, which are the human means of resistance, *these* I feel have yet to be organized, almost to be created.'

III

Religious opinions—Book on Church and State—Marriage—Becomes Vice-President of the Board of Trade—Admitted to the Cabinet—Resigns.

This year—1838—claims special note in a record of Mr Gladstone's life, because it witnessed the appearance of his famous work on 'The State in its Relations with the Church.' We have seen that he left Oxford before the beginning of that Catholic revival which has transfigured both the inner spirit and the outward aspect of the Church of England. But the revival was now in full strength. The astonishing genius of Mr Newman had begun to operate. The 'Tracts for the Times' were saturating England with new influences. The passionate, almost despairing, appeal of half-a-dozen gifted and holy men at Oxford had awoke a response in every corner of the kingdom. 'We did,' they said, 'but light a beacon fire on the summit of a lonely hill: and now we are amazed to find the firmament on every side red with the light of some responsive flame.' The Catholic revival now counted no more enthusiastic or more valuable disciple than the young member for Newark. The influence of the revival had reached him through his friendships, notably with Mr James Hope, Fellow of Merton, afterwards Mr Hope-Scott, QC, and with the Rev. H. E. Manning, now Cardinal-Archbishop.

Cardinal Newman, organizing the crusade and reckoning up his actual and possible allies, writes on October 2, 1833: 'As to Gladstone, perhaps it would be wrong to ask a young man so to commit himself.' But on November 13, he records: 'The Duke of Newcastle has joined us ... Gladstone, &c. I suppose these names must not be mentioned.'

Naturally and profoundly religious, and now steeped in the Catholic theology, Mr Gladstone conceived that those who professed the warmest regard for the Church of England, and posed as her most strenuous defenders, were inclined to base their championship on mistaken grounds, and to direct their efforts towards even mischievous ends. To supply a more reasonable basis for action, and to lead this energy into more profitable channels, were the objects which he proposed to himself in his treatise of 1838. The distinctive principle of the book was that the State had a conscience. This being admitted, the issue was this whether the State, in its best condition, has such a conscience as can take cognizance of religious truth and error, and in particular whether the State of the United Kingdom at that time was, or was not, so far in that condition as to be under an obligation to give an active and an exclusive support to the established religion of the country. The work attempted to survey the actual state of the relations between the State and the Church; to show from history the ground which had been defined for the National Church at the Reformation; and to enquire and determine whether the existing state of things was worth preserving and defending against encroachment from whatever quarter. This question it decided emphatically in the affirmative. Faithful to logic and to its theory, the book did not shrink from applying them to the crucial case of the Irish Church. It did not disguise the difficulties of the case, for the author was alive to the paradox which it involved. But the one master idea of the system, that the State as it then stood was capable in this age, as it had been in ages long gone by, of assuming beneficially a responsibility for the inculcation of a particular religion, carried him through all. His doctrine was, that the Church, as established by law, was to be maintained for its truth; that this was the only principle on which it could be properly and permanently upheld; that this principle, if good in England, was good also for Ireland; that truth is of all possessions the most precious to the soul of man; and that to 'remove this priceless treasure from the view and the reach of the Irish people, would be meanly to purchase their momentary favour at the expense of their permanent interests, and would be a high offence against our own sacred obligations.'

In the task of bringing out the book, Mr Gladstone derived great assistance from his friend Mr Hope, who read and criticized the manuscript, and saw the sheets through the press. The following letters refer to this act of friendship:

W. E. Gladstone, Esq., MP, to J. R. Hope, Esq.

House of Commons: July 18, 1838.

I hope in a day or two to get my colonial information sufficiently in form, and then to send you my whole papers. If you let them lie just as they are, turning the leaves one by one, I think you will not find the manuscript very difficult to make out, though it is strangely cut in pieces and patched. I have divided it all through into *sectiuncules*, occupying generally from half a page to a whole one.

I hope that its general tendency will meet your approval; but a point about which I am in great doubt, and to which I request your particular attention is, whether either the work or some of the chapters are not so deficient in clearness and arrangement as to require being absolutely re-written before they can with propriety be published?

Making allowance for any obscurity which may arise from its *physical* state as a MS, I hope you will look vigorously at it in this point of view, and tell me what you think is the amount of the disease, and the proper kind of remedy. I can excuse myself; considering the pressure of other engagements, for having written irregularly and confusedly upon a subject very new in many of its parts, and requiring some abstraction—(at every turn it has brought home the truth of Bacon's observation, that politics are of all sciences the most immersed in matter. One has to go on detaching as it were one's soul from clay all the way through)—but I should be inexcusable if I were to *publish* in such a state: between my eyes and my business I fear it would be hard for me to re-write, but if I could put it into the hands of any other person who could, and who would extract from my papers any thing worth having, that might do. I wish very much that something should be published by somebody on the subject, and that speedily, to begin to draw attention to a subject, on which men's minds are so sadly undisciplined. When set in motion, the ball will roll, as I anticipate.

As regards myself, if I go on and publish, I shall be quite prepared to find some persons surprised, but this, if it should prove so, cannot be helped; I have not knowingly exaggerated anything; and when a man expects to be washed overboard, he must tie himself with a rope to the mast.

I shall trust to your friendship for frankness in the discharge of your irksome task. Pray make verbal corrections without scruple where they are needed.—Sincerely yours,

W. E. GLADSTONE.

July 21, 1838.

My dear Hope,—Behold your rashness!
Please read Nos II, V, and VI first. These, with VIII, are, I think, the most important, and it is about these that I am in great fear and doubt whether they may not require re-writing; as, however, we read that chopping old somebody made him young, I have some hope for my unfortunate papers, which you will find have pretty well undergone that operation. Mind to turn the leaves as they lie.—Ever yours,

W. E.G.

July 26, 1838.

My dear Hope,—I thank you most cordially for your remarks, and I rejoice to find that you act so entirely in the spirit I had anticipated. I trust you will continue to speak with freedom, which is the best compliment as well as the best service you can render me.

I am now likely not to go to Ems, but to have some weeks in this country, which I should wish to employ without any loss of time in going to work as you direct ... As I said before, I think it very probable that you may find that V and VI require quite as rigorous treatment as II, and I am very desirous to set both my mind and eyes at liberty before I go to the Continent, which I can now hardly expect to do before the first week in September. This interval I trust would suffice—unless you find that the other chapters stand in equal need.

Mahon suggested as a title: 'Church and State considered in their connexion.' The defect of this is that I do not *much* consider the Church in its connexion with the State, though partially I do; but it gave me the idea of a modification which I think may do: 'The State viewed in its connexion with the Church.'

I entirely concur with your view regarding the necessity of care, and of not grudging labour in a matter so important and so responsible as an endeavour to raise one of the most momentous controversies which has ever agitated human opinion.—Sincerely yours,

W. E. GLADSTONE.

July 30.

My dear Hope,—Thanks for your letter. I have been pretty hard at work, and have done a good deal, especially on V. Something yet remains. I must make enquiry about the law of excommunication ... I have made a very stupid classification, and have now amended it; instead of faith, discipline, and practice, what I meant was, the rule of faith, discipline, and the bearing of particular doctrines upon practice ... Yours sincerely,

W. E.G.

I send back also I and II that you may see what I have done.

But in spite of various obstacles, the work was brought to a successful issue in the following autumn. Lord Houghton used to say that Sir Robert Peel, on receiving a copy as a gift from his young follower, exclaimed with truly official horror: 'With such a career before him, why should he write books?' But more emotional people took a very different view.

Writing on December 13, 1838, Baron Bunsen says: 'Last night at eleven, when I came from the Duke, Gladstone's book was lying on my table, having come out at seven o'clock. It is the book of the time, a great event—the first book since Burke that goes to the bottom of the vital question; far above his party and his time. I sat up till after midnight, and this morning I continued until I had read the whole... Gladstone is the first man in England as to intellectual power, and he has heard higher tones than anyone else in this land.'

Writing a few days later to Dr Arnold, the Baron again extols the book, and, while lamenting what he conceives to be its author's entanglement in Tractarian traditions, adds: 'His genius will soon free itself entirely, and fly towards Heaven with its own wings.'

On January 9, 1839, Cardinal Newman writes: 'Gladstone's book, you see, is making a sensation.' On the 22nd, '*The Times* is again at poor Gladstone. Really I feel as if I could do anything for him. I have not read his book, but its consequences speak for it. Poor fellow! it is so noble a thing.'

The book soon reached a third edition, and drew from Lord Macaulay that trenchant review in which Mr Gladstone was described, for the infinite gratification of later critics, as the 'rising hope of the stern and unbending Tories.' There ensued some correspondence between the young author, and his distinguished reviewer, who, writing to him on April 11, 1839, said: 'Your book itself, and everything that I heard about you, though almost all my information came—to the honour, I must say, of our troubled times—from people very strongly opposed to you in politics, led me to regard you with respect and goodwill, and I am truly glad that I have succeeded in marking those feelings.' Meanwhile the author's eyesight had been impaired by hard reading. He had eschewed lamps and read entirely by candle-light, and the result was injurious. The doctors recommended him to make a tour in the South of Europe, and he spent the winter in Rome. In the Eternal City he joined his friend, Mr Henry Manning, and together they visited Monsignor (afterwards Cardinal) Wiseman at the English College, on the Feast of the Martyrdom of St Thomas of Canterbury. They attended a solemn Mass in honour of the saint, and their places in the missal were found for them by a young student of the college called Grant, who afterwards became Bishop of Southwark; a curious conjunction of names destined to become famous. Among the visitors at Rome that winter were the widow and daughters of Sir Stephen Richard Glynne, of Hawarden Castle, Flintshire. Mr Gladstone was already acquainted with these ladies, having been a friend of Lady Glynne's eldest son at Oxford, and having visited him at Hawarden in 1835. The visit to Rome threw him much into their society; and he became engaged to the elder of Lady Glynne's daughters. On July 25, 1839, he was married at Hawarden to Miss Catherine Glynne, sister, and in her issue heir, of Sir Stephen Glynne, ninth and last baronet of that name. At the same time and place, Miss Mary Glynne was married to George William, fourth Lord Lyttelton.

It is worthy of note that by his marriage Mr Gladstone became allied with the house of Grenville, a family of statesmen which, directly or in its ramifications, had already supplied England with four Prime Ministers. Baron Bunsen, who made his acquaintance that year, writes that he 'was delighted with the man who is some day to govern England if his book is not in his way.' During the earlier part of their married life Mr and Mrs William Gladstone lived with Sir Thomas Gladstone at 6 Carlton Gardens. Later they lived at 13 Carlton House Terrace, and, when Mr Gladstone was in office, occupied an official residence in Downing Street. In 1856 Mr Gladstone, who had succeeded to his patrimony five years before, bought 11 Carlton House Terrace, which was his London house for twenty years; and he subsequently lived for four years at 73 Harley Street. During the parliamentary recess, Mr and Mrs Gladstone divided their time between Fasque, Sir John Gladstone's seat in Kincardineshire, and Hawarden Castle, which they shared with Mrs Gladstone's brother, Sir Stephen Glynne, till, on his death, it passed into their sole possession.

Marriage and domestic cares (for the blessings of the man who hath his quiver full were not long withheld from him) made little difference in Mr Gladstone's mode of life. He was still the diligent student, the constant debater, and the copious writer that he had been at Eton, at Oxford, and in the Albany. He was one of a committee which met at the lodgings of Mr (now Sir Thomas) Acland, in Jermyn Street, to concert measures for improving and extending the educational machinery of the Church. Among the members of this committee were Lord Ashley, afterwards Lord Shaftesbury, Lord Sandon, afterwards Lord Harrowby, Winthrop Mackworth Praed, and Henry Nelson Coleridge. Their exertions led to the formation of Boards of Education for the different dioceses, and the establishment of training-colleges, with the double aim of securing religious education for the middle classes and the collegiate education of the school masters.

In 1840 he 'completed beneath the shades of Hagley (the home of Lord and Lady Lyttelton), a treatise on 'Church Principles Considered in their Results;' in which he maintained with ingenuity and vigour the visibility and authority of the Church, the mathematical certainty of the Apostolical Succession, and the nature and efficacy of the Sacraments, and vindicated the Church of England as the divinely-appointed guardian of Christian truth, alike against Popish and Puritan innovations. On 'St Stephen's Day,' 1840, Cardinal Newman writes: 'Gladstone's book is not open to the objections I feared; it is doctrinaire, and (I think) somewhat self-confident; but it will do good.'

On the 28th of December, the Rev. Frederick Denison Maurice writes thus of Mr Gladstone and his latest work:

> His Aristotelianism is, it strikes me, more deeply fixed in him than before, and, on that account, I do not see how he can ever enter enough into the feeling and truth of Rationalism to refute it. His notion of attacking the Evangelicals by saying, 'Press your opinions to their results, and they become Rationalistic,' is ingenious, and wrought out, I think, with great skill and an analytical power for which I had not given him credit; but after all it seems to me an argument which is fitter for the Courts than for a theological controversy.

In 1840, in a debate on our relations with China, Mr Gladstone crossed swords with Macaulay, in a speech remarkable for its eloquent expression of anxiety that the arms of England should never be employed in unrighteous enterprises.

At Midsummer, 1840, Mr Gladstone (accompanied by Lord Lyttelton) went down to Eton to examine the candidates for the Newcastle Scholarship, founded by his political patron the fifth Duke. He characteristically set a passage from St Augustine in the paper on divinity; and one of those whom he examined writes: 'I have a vivid and delightful impression of Mr Gladstone sitting in what was then called the Library, on an estrade on which the head master habitually sate, above which was placed, about 1840, the bust of the Duke of Newcastle and the names of the Newcastle Scholars ... When he gave me a Virgil and asked me to translate Georg. ii. 475, *seq.*, I was pleasantly surprised by the beautiful eye turning on me with the question, "What is the meaning of *sacra fero*?" and his look of approval when I said, "Carry the sacred vessels in the procession."

'I wish you to understand that Mr Gladstone appeared not to me only, but to others, as a gentleman wholly unlike other examiners or school people. It was not as a *politician* that we admired him, but as a refined Churchman, deep also in political philosophy (so we conjectured from his quoting Burke on the Continual State retaining its identity though made up of passing individuals), deep also in lofty poetry, as we guessed from his giving us, as a theme for original Latin verse, "the poet's eye in a fine frenzy," &c. When he spoke to us in "Pop" as an honorary member, we were charmed and affected emotionally: his voice was low and sweet, his manner was that of an elder cousin: he seemed to treat us with unaffected respect; and to be treated with respect by a man is the greatest delight for a boy. It was the golden time of "retrograding transcendentalism," as the hard heads called the Anglo-Catholic symphony. He seemed to me then an apostle of unworldly ardour, bridling his life.'

In this examination Mr Gladstone had the satisfaction of awarding the Newcastle medal to Henry Fitzmaurice Hallam, the youngest brother of his own beloved friend.

At the beginning of 1841 troubles were thickening round the Whig Ministry. The Budget showed a deficit of nearly two millions. A proposal to meet this deficit by an alteration in the sugar-duties was defeated in the House of Commons. Then, in despair, Lord John Russell invited the House to consider the state of the law with regard to the trade in corn. He proposed a fixed duty of eight shillings per quarter on wheat, and proportionately diminished rates on rye, barley, and oats. Sir Robert Peel met this proposal by a motion of want of confidence, levelled against the whole financial policy, and especially against this proposal of a fixed duty *in lieu* of a sliding scale. The vote was carried. On June 22 Parliament was dissolved by the Queen in person; the Whig Ministers thus seeking, as Lord Shaftesbury wrote in his diary, to 'hide their own hoary profligacy under her young virtue.'

Their device did not succeed, for the general election resulted in a Tory majority of eighty. Mr Gladstone was again returned for Newark, with the present Duke of Rutland for his colleague. The new Parliament met in August, Ministers were defeated on the Address and resigned, and Sir Robert Peel formed an Administration, in which Mr Gladstone was of course included.

There is a tradition that, having already conceived a lively interest in the ecclesiastical and agrarian problems of Ireland, he had set his affections on the Chief Secretaryship. But Sir Robert Peel, a consummate judge of administrative capacity, had discerned his young friend's financial aptitude, and the member for Newark became Vice-President of the Board of Trade and Master of the Mint, and was sworn of the Privy Council. Speaking from the hustings at his re-election on taking office, he proclaimed that the British farmer might rely on adequate protection for his industry, and that this protection was to be secured by a sliding scale. The duties were to be reduced and the system improved, but the principle was to be maintained.

In the autumn of this year the Anglican Bishopric at Jerusalem was set up. Mr Gladstone dined with Baron Bunsen on the King of Prussia's birthday, when we learn, on the unimpeachable authority of Lord Shaftesbury, that he 'stripped himself of a part of his Puseyite garments, spoke like a pious man, rejoiced in the bishopric of Jerusalem, and proposed the health of Alexander (the new Bishop of that see). This is delightful, for he is a good man, a clever man, and an industrious man.' Baron Bunsen, describing the same occasion, writes 'Never was heard a more exquisite speech. It flowed like a gentle and translucent stream ... We drove back to town in the clearest starlight; Gladstone continuing with unabated animation to pour forth his harmonious thoughts in melodious tone.'

On November 6, 1841, Mr Gladstone writes thus from Whitehall to Mr Hope:

Amidst public business quite sufficient for a man of my compass, I have during the whole of the week perforce been carrying on with the Bishop of London and with Bunsen a correspondence on, and inquisition into, the Jerusalem design, until I almost reel and stagger under it.

On November 20 he writes:

I am ready individually to brave misconstruction for the sake of union with any Christian men, provided the terms of the union be not contrary to sound principle; and perhaps in this respect might go further, at least in one of the possible directions, than you. But to declare the living constitution of a Christian Church to be of secondary moment is of course in my view equivalent to a denial of a portion of the faith—and I think you will say it is a construction which cannot fairly be put upon the design, as far as it exists in fixed rules and articles. It is one thing to attribute this in the way of unfavourable surmise, or as an apprehension of ultimate developments—it is another to publish it to the world as a character ostentatiously assumed.

So even amid the engrossing cares of a new office, the Vice-President of the Board of Trade retained his old interest in ecclesiastical concerns.

On April 6, 1842, he writes thus to Mr Murray the publisher:

> Amidst the pressure of more urgent affairs, I have held no consultation with you regarding my books and the sale or no sale of them. As to the third edition of the 'State in its Relations,' I should think the remaining copies had better be got rid of in whatever summary or ignominious mode you may deem best. They must be dead beyond recall. As to the others, I do not know whether the season of the year has at all revived the demand; and would suggest to you whether it would be well to advertise them a little. I do not think they find their way much into the second-hand shops. With regard to the fourth edition, I do not know whether it would be well to procure any review or notice of it, and I am not a fair judge of its merits even in comparison with the original form of the work; but my idea is, that it is less defective both in the theoretical and in the historical development, and ought to be worth the notice of those who deemed the earlier editions worth their notice and purchase that it would really put a reader in possession of the view it was intended to convey, which I fear is more than can with any truth be said of its predecessors. I am not, however, in any state of anxiety or impatience and I am chiefly moved to refer these suggestions to your judgment from perceiving that the fourth edition is as yet far from having cleared itself.

The position which Mr Gladstone now occupied in the view of his contemporaries is well indicated in the following letter of Sir Stafford Northcote's, written in the same year:

> There is but one statesman of the present day in whom I feel entire confidence, and with whom I cordially agree, and that statesman is Mr Gladstone. I look upon him as the representative of the party, scarcely developed as yet, though secretly forming and strengthening, which will stand by all that is dear and sacred in my estimation, in the struggle which I believe will come ere *very* long between good and evil, order and disorder, the Church and the world, and I see a very small band collecting round him, and ready to fight manfully under his leading.

An inevitable change is from this time to be traced in the topics of Mr Gladstone's parliamentary speaking. Instead of discoursing on the corporate conscience of the State and the endowments of the Church, the importance of Christian education, and the theological unfitness of the Jews to sit in Parliament, he is solving business-like problems about foreign tariffs and the exportation of machinery; waxing eloquent over the regulation of railways, and a graduated tax on corn; subtle on the monetary merits of half-farthings, and great in the mysterious lore of *quassia* and *cocculus indicus*.

In 1842 he had a principal hand in the preparation of the revised tariff, by which duties were abolished or sensibly diminished in the case of twelve hundred duty-paying articles. In defending the new scheme he spoke incessantly, and amazed the House by his mastery of detail, his intimate acquaintance with the commercial needs of the country, and his inexhaustible power of exposition. On March 14 Mr Greville writes: 'Gladstone has already displayed a capacity which makes his admission into the Cabinet indispensable.' A commercial Minister had appeared on the scene, and the shade of Mr Huskisson had revived. Yet amid all the excitements and interests of office, he could turn aside the discourse on social and educational questions with as much earnestness and eloquence as if they, and only they, possessed his mind. In January, 1843, he spoke at the opening of the Collegiate Institution of Liverpool, and delivered a powerful plea for the better education of the middle classes.

This year—1843—was destined to witness a great advance in Mr Gladstone's progress towards the front rank of statesmen. Lord Ripon left the Board of Trade for the Board of Control, and Mr Gladstone, succeeding him as President of the Board of Trade, became a member of the Cabinet at the age of thirty-three. He was now master in name, as he had long been in reality, of his own department. His appointment as President of the Board bears date June 10, 1843, and he has recorded the fact that 'the very first opinion which he ever was called upon to give in Cabinet,' was an opinion in favour of withdrawing the Bill providing Education for Children in Factories: to which vehement opposition was offer by the Dissenters on the ground that it was too favourable to the Established Church.

His position now seemed assured; yet on October 23, 1843, he writes to a friend: 'Uneasy, in my opinion, must be the position of every member of Parliament who thinks independently in these times, or in any that are likely to succeed them; and in proportion as a man's course of thought deviates from the ordinary lines, his seat must less and less resemble a bed of roses.'

The following curious extract from the diary of the late Lord Malmesbury belongs to the period which we are now approaching:

November 7, 1844.—Met Mr Gladstone ... a man who is much spoken of as one who will come to the front. We were disappointed at his appearance, which is that of a Roman Catholic ecclesiastic; but he is very agreeable.

On December 29, 1844, in a letter to his friend Archdeacon (afterwards Bishop) Wilberforce, Mr Gladstone writes thus about the prospects of the Church of England:

'I rejoice to see that your views are on the whole hopeful. For my part I heartily go along with you. The fabric consolidates itself more and more, even while the earthquake rocks it; for, with a thousand drawbacks and deductions, love grows larger, zeal warmer, truth firmer among us. It makes the mind sad to speculate upon the question how much better all might have been; but our mourning should be turned into joy and thankfulness when we think also how much worse it *was*. It seems to be written for our learning and use: "He will be very gracious to thee at the voice of thy cry; when He shall hear it He will answer thee. And though the Lord give you the bread of adversity and the water of affliction, yet shall not thy teachers be removed into a corner any more; but mine eyes shall see thy teachers. And thine ears shall hear a word behind thee, saying, 'This is the way, walk ye in it.'"

This letter was written on the eve of a momentous change in the writer's secular position.

In the Session of 1844 Sir Robert Peel, in response to the requests of Irish members, had given an undertaking that the Government would apply themselves to the question of academical education in Ireland, with a view to bringing it more nearly to the standard of England and Scotland, increasing its amount and improving its quality. In fulfilment of this pledge, the Government, at the opening of the Session of 1845, proposed simultaneously to establish non-sectarian colleges in Ireland, and to increase the grant to Maynooth. The College of Maynooth, intended for the education of Roman Catholic priests and laymen, had fallen into poverty and decay. With a view to propitiating Irish sentiment, the Government proposed to increase the grant already made to the college from £9,000 to £30,000 a year. This grant was not to be subject to an annual vote; and the repairs of the college were to be executed by the Board of Works. These proposals placed Mr Gladstone in a position of great difficulty. The choice before him was to support Sir Robert Peel's measure, or else to retire from his Government into a position of complete isolation, and, what was more than this, subject to a grave and general imputation of political eccentricity. In this strait, Mr Gladstone sought counsel from his friends. Archdeacon Manning and Mr Hope strongly urged him to remain in the Cabinet, where his presence and influence would be of immense value to the Church. Lord Stanley warned him that resignation must be followed by resistance to the proposal of the Government, and that this would involve him in the storms of religious agitation. Mr Gladstone persisted in his intention, but he plainly stated that his resignation would not of necessity be followed by resistance to the proposal about Maynooth.

> My whole purpose was to place myself in a position in which I should be free to consider my course without being liable to any just suspicion on the ground of personal interest. It is not profane if I now say, '*with a great price obtained I this*

freedom.' The political association in which I stood was to me at the time the *alpha* and *omega* of public life. The Government of Sir Robert Peel was believed to be of immovable strength. My place, as President of the Board of Trade, was at the very kernel of its most interesting operations; for it was in progress, from year to year, with continually waxing courage, towards the emancipation of industry, and therein towards the accomplishment of another great and blessed work of public justice. Giving up what I highly prized, aware that

male sarta
Gratia nequicquam coit, et rescinditur,

I felt myself open to the charge of being opinionated, and wanting in deference to really great authorities; and I could not but know that I should inevitably be regarded as fastidious and fanciful, fitter for a dreamer, or possibly a schoolman, than for the active purposes of public life in a busy and moving age.

In January, 1845, Mr Gladstone resigned, not, however, before he had completed a second 'revised tariff,' carrying considerably further the principles on which he had acted in the earlier revision of 1842. In the debate on the Address at the opening of the Session he explained his retirement. He stated that it had reference to the intentions of the Government with respect to Maynooth; that those intentions pointed to a measure at variance with the system which he had maintained, 'in a form the most detailed and deliberate,' in a published treatise; that he thought that those who had borne such solemn testimony to a particular view of a great constitutional question 'ought not to be parties responsible for proposals which involved a material departure from it.' The purpose of his retirement was to place himself in a position to form not only an honest, but likewise an independent and an unsuspected judgment, on the plan to be submitted by the Government.

Mr Gladstone's retirement from the Ministry drew expressions of lively regret, together with flattering testimonies to his character and abilities, alike from his late chief and from the leader of the Opposition. Having, by retiring, established his perfect freedom of action, he met the proposals of the Government in a sympathetic spirit. He defended the grant to Maynooth in a long speech full of ingenious argumentation, and urged with great force that, if the State was to give 'a more indiscriminating support' than previously to various forms of religious opinion, it would be improper and unjust to exclude the Church of Rome in Ireland from participating in its benefits.

No one who has the slightest acquaintance with the tone and temper of the House of Commons needs to he told that Mr Gladstone's resignation was regarded by the mass of his party with angry amazement. Here was a young and successful statesman who had renounced an important post in the Cabinet sooner than be responsible for legislation inconsistent with his earlier opinion, though now, as a private member, he was ready to support the very Bill which he would not be a party to introducing. This was an act of parliamentary Quixotism too eccentric to be intelligible. It argued a fastidious sensitiveness of conscience and a nice sense of political propriety so opposed to the sordid selfishness and unblushing tergiversation of the ordinary place-hunter as to be almost offensive.

The possessor of this kind of supernatural virtue could scarcely be popular with the slaves of party, the docile disciples of the Canton and the Whip, and by them the member for Newark was generally voted whimsical, fantastic, impracticable a man whose 'conscience was so tender that he would never go straight'; a visionary not to be relied on or reckoned with—in brief; exactly that type of character and intellect which is to the political manager a powerful irritant, and to the hacks whom he manipulates a sealed and hopeless mystery. That typical man of the world, Mr Charles Greville, writes on February 6: 'Gladstone's explanation was ludicrous. Everybody said that he had only succeeded in showing that his resignation was quite uncalled for.' This probably expresses the prevailing sentiment, and Mr Gladstone's retirement, by impairing his reputation for common sense, threatened serious and lasting injury to his political career. But the whirligig of time brought its revenges even more swiftly and more unexpectedly than usual. A conjunction of events arose in which he was indispensable. The practical side of his genius was destined to repair the mischief which the speculative side had wrought; but for the moment the speculative side was uppermost, as the following letters show:

The Right Hon. W. E. Gladstone, MP, to J. R. Hope, Esq.

13 Carlton House Terrace:
Thursday night, May 15, '45.

Private

My dear Hope,—In 1838 you lent me that generous and powerful aid in the preparation of my book for the press, to which I owe it that the defects and faults of the work fell short of absolutely disqualifying it for its purpose. From that time I began to form not only high but definite anticipations of the services which you would render to the Church in the deep and searching processes through which she has passed and yet has to pass. These anticipations, however, did not rest only upon my own wishes, or on the hopes which benefits already received might have led me to form. In the commencement of 1840, in the very room where we talked to-night, you voluntarily and somewhat solemnly tendered to me the assurance that you would at all times be ready to co-operate with me in furtherance of the welfare of the Church, and you placed no limit upon the extent of such co-operation. I had no title to expect and had not expected a promise so heart-stirring, but I set upon it a value scarcely to be described, and it ever after entered as an element of the first importance into all my views of the future course of public affairs in their bearing upon religion.

After speaking of the 'gigantic opportunities of good or evil to the Church which the course of events seems certain to open up,' Mr Gladstone continues:

If the time shall ever come (which I look upon as extremely uncertain, but I think if it comes at all it will be before the lapse of many years) when I am called upon to use any of those opportunities, it would be my duty to look to you for aid, under the promise to which I have referred, unless in the meantime you shall as deliberately and solemnly withdraw that promise as you first made it. I will not describe at length how your withdrawal of it would increase that sense of desolation which, as matters now stand, often approaches to being intolerable. I only speak of it as a matter of fact, and I am anxious you should know that I look to it as one of the very weightiest kind, under a title which you have given me. You would of course cancel it upon the conviction that it involved sin upon your part with anything less than that conviction I do not expect that you will cancel it; and I am, on the contrary, persuaded that you will struggle against pain, depression, disgust, and even against doubt touching the very root of our position, for the fulfilment of any actual *duties* which the post you actually occupy in the Church of God, taken in connexion with your faculties and attainments, may assign to you.

* * * * *

You have given me lessons that I have taken thankfully. Believe I do it in the payment of a debt, if I tell you that your mind and intellect, to which I look up with reverence under a consciousness of immense inferiority, are much under the dominion, whether it be known or not known to yourself, of an agency lower than their own, more blind, more variable, more difficult to call inwardly to account and make to answer for itself—the agency, I mean, of painful and disheartening impressions—impressions which have an unhappy and powerful tendency to realise the very worst of what they picture. Of this fact I have repeatedly noted the signs in you.

* * * * *

I should have been glad to have got your advice on some points connected with the Maynooth question on Monday next, but I will not introduce here any demand upon your kindness; the claims of this letter on your attention, be they great or small, and you are their only judge, rests upon wholly different grounds. God bless and guide you, and prosper the work of your hands.—

Ever your affectionate friend,
W. E. GLADSTONE.

On July 23, 1845, Mr Gladstone writes thus to the same friend:

Ireland is likely to find this country and Parliament so much employment for years to come, that I feel rather oppressively an obligation to try and see it with my own eyes instead of using those of other people, according to the limited measure of my means. Now your company would be so very valuable as well as agreeable to me, that I am desirous to know whether you are at all inclined to entertain the idea of devoting the month of September, after the meeting in Edinburgh, to a working tour in Ireland with me—eschewing all grandeur, and taking little account even of scenery, compared with the purpose of looking from close quarters at the institutions for religion and education of the country, and at the character of the people. It seems ridiculous to talk of supplying the defects of second-hand information by so short a trip; but though a longer time would be much better, yet even a very contracted one does much when it is added to an habitual though indirect knowledge.

Subsequent events make it a matter of regret that this projected tour never took place.

Meanwhile it is worthy of remark that while he was ready to deal more generously than before with the Roman Catholics in Ireland, his faith in the Irish Establishment was becoming less robust. On August 16 in this year he wrote to his friend Bishop Wilberforce: 'I am sorry to express my apprehension that the Irish Church is not in a large sense efficient; the working results of the last ten years have disappointed me. It may be answered, Have faith in the ordinance of God; but then I must see the seal and signature, and these how can I separate from ecclesiastical descent? The title, in short, is questioned, and vehemently, not only by the Radicalism of the day, but by the Roman Bishops, who claim to hold the succession of St Patrick, and this claim has been alive all along from the Reformation, so that lapse of years does nothing against it.'

In the autumn of this year Mr Gladstone went to Munich and paid his first visit to Dr Döllinger. He remained there a week, in daily converse with the great theologian, and laid the foundation of a friendship which was sustained by correspondence and repeated visits, and was interrupted only by the doctor's death in 1890.

On October 30, 1845, he writes from Baden-Baden:

'No religion and no politics until we meet,' and that more than ever uncertain! Hard terms, my dear Hope; do not complain if I devote to them the scraps or ends of my fourth page. But now let me rebuke myself, and say, No levity about great and solemn things. There are degrees of pressure from within that it is impossible to resist. The Church in which our lot has been cast has come to the birth, and the question is, will she have strength to bring forth? I am persuaded it is written in God's decrees that she shall; and that after deep repentance and deep suffering a high and peculiar part remains for her in healing the wounds of Christendom. Nor is there any man—I cannot be silent—whose portion in her work is more clearly marked out for him than yours. But you have, if not your revenge, your security. I must keep my word, God bless and guide you.

Yours affectionately,
W. E. G.

13 C. H. Terrace:
Dec. 7, Second Sunday in Advent, 1845.

My dear Hope,—I need hardly tell you I am deeply moved by your note, and your asking my prayers. I trust you give what you ask. As for them, you have long had them; in private and in public, and in the hour of Holy Communion. But you must not look for anything from them; only they cannot do any harm. Under the merciful dispensation of the Gospel, while the prayer of the righteous availeth much, the petition of the unworthy does not return in evils on the head, of those for whom it is offered.

Your speaking of yourself in low terms is the greatest kindness to me. It is with such things before my eyes that I learn in some measure by comparison my own true position.

*   *   *   *   *

Now let me use a friend's liberty on a point of practice. Do you not so far place yourself in rather a false position by withdrawing in so considerable a degree from those active external duties in which you were so conspicuous? Is rest in that department really favourable to religious enquiry? You said to me you preferred at this time selecting temporal works are we not in this difficulty, that temporal works, so far as mere money is concerned, are nowadays relatively overdone? But if you mean temporal works otherwise than in money, I would to God we could join hands upon a subject of the kind which interested you much two years ago. And now I am going to speak of what concerns myself more than you, as needing it more.

The desire we then both felt passed off as far as I am concerned, into a plan of asking only a donation and subscription. Now it is very difficult to satisfy the demands of duty to the poor by money alone. On the other hand, it is extremely hard for me (and I suppose possibly for you) to give them much in the shape of time and thought, for both with me are already tasked up to and beyond their powers, and by matters which I cannot displace. I much wish we could execute some plan which, without demanding much time, would entail the discharge of some humble and humbling offices … If you thought with me—and I do not see why you should not, except that to assume the reverse is paying myself a compliment—let us go to work, as in the young days of the college plan, but with a more direct and less ambitious purpose … In answer give me advice and help if you can; and when we meet to talk of these things, it will be more refreshing than metaphysical or semi-metaphysical argument. All that part of my note which refers to questions internal to yourself is not meant to be answered except in your own breast.

And now may the Lord grant that, as heretofore, so ever we may walk in His holy house as friends, and know how good a thing it is to dwell together in unity! But at all events may He, as He surely will, compass you about with His presence and by His holy angels, and cause you to awake up after His likeness, and to be satisfied with it.

Ever your affectionate friend,
W. E. GLADSTONE.

In the winter of this year Mr Gladstone sustained a slight but permanent injury. Though not a passionate sportsman, he was fond of shooting. His gun exploded while he was loading it, and so shattered the first finger of his left hand that amputation was necessary.

IV

Free Trade—The Repeal of the Corn Laws—Retires from the representation of Newark—Returned for the University of Oxford—Growth and transition—Loss of a child—The Gorham judgment—Secession of friends

How patient of inevitable ill,
Yet how determinate in their righteous will!

Such was a poet's most just description of the English people at a crisis when their patience had been strained to bursting-point. Towards the year 1845 Englishmen were awaking to the fact that a great part of the 'ill' under which they laboured was in no sense 'inevitable,' but was the direct and necessary consequence of legislation which made their principal form of food dear and difficult to procure, even when nature and Providence supplied it with the utmost bounty. What Lord Beaconsfield called the 'clear perception and terse eloquence' of Mr Charles Villiers enforced this truth upon the attention of Parliament; and the Anti-Corn-Law League, working by an admirable organization, and teaching by the mouth of two of the greatest orators who ever spoke the English language, drove the lesson home to the conscience and intellect of their countrymen, already well prepared for it by the sharp discipline of physical privation. The agitation had now been progress for some ten years, and for the moment it seemed to be losing energy. Its fertility of resource was a little exhausted; its reiterated appeals fell with less than their former effect upon the public ear. A series of good harvests had rendered the evils of restrictive legislation more endurable.

Sir Robert Peel had closed the Session of 1845 with an overwhelming majority in both Houses. True it is that, in the four years during which he had conducted affairs, he had frequently strained the patience of his supporters; but then passive murmurs only proved how necessary he was to their interests, and how accurately he had calculated their faculty of sufferance. True it is that, towards the end of the Session of '45, a solitary voice from the Tory benches had presumed to prophesy that protection was then in about the same condition as Protestantism was in 1828, and amid tumultuous sympathy a Conservative Government had been denounced as 'an organized hypocrisy'; but the cheers of mutual sensibility were in a great degree furnished by the voices opposite, and the Tory gentlemen beneath the gangway who swelled the chorus did so with downcast eyes as if they yet hesitated to give utterance to feelings too long and too painfully suppressed. Practically speaking, the Conservative Government at the end of the Session of '45 was far stronger than even at the commencement of the Session of '42. If they had forfeited the hearts of their adherents, they had not lost their votes; while, both in Parliament and the country, they had succeeded in appropriating a mass of loose, superficial opinion not trammelled by party ties, and which complacently recognized in their measures the gradual and moderate fulfilment of a latitudinarian policy both in Church and State. This position was also aggrandized and confirmed by a conviction then prevalent, and which it is curious to observe is often current on the eve of great changes, that the Ministry of Sir Robert Peel was the only body of men then competent to carry on affairs.*

Thus all seemed to be going well with the Government when an unusual phenomenon was noted by readers of the newspapers. Four Cabinet Councils were held in one week. Obviously the Government were in difficulties. What those difficulties were it was not hard to guess. In the previous autumn it had become known that, after a long season of sunless wet, the potatoes had everywhere been attacked by an obscure disease. The failure of this crop meant an Irish famine. The steps suggested to meet this impending calamity were strange enough. The head of the English peerage recommended the poor to rely on curry-powder as a nutritious and satisfying food. Another duke thought that the Government could show no favour to a population almost in a state of rebellion, but that individuals might get up a subscription. A noble lord, harmonizing materialism and faith, urged the Government to encourage the provision of salt-fish, and at the same time to appoint a day of public acknowledgment of our dependence on Divine goodness. The council of the Royal Agricultural Society, numbering some of the wealthiest noblemen and squires in England, were not ashamed to lecture the labourers on the sustaining properties of thrice-boiled bones.

Amid these Conflicting counsels, Sir Robert Peel took a bold and sagacious line. He urged upon his colleagues that all restrictions on the importation of food should be at once suspended. He was supported by only three members of

---

* *Lord George Bentink*, by B. Disraeli, chapter 1.

his Cabinet. All that the rest would consent to do was to appoint a commission, consisting of heads of Irish departments, with powers to relieve distress and provide employment in the event of a sudden outbreak of famine.

The decisive step came from the opposite camp. Writing from Edinburgh, on November 22, to the electors of the City of London, Lord John Russell announced his conversion to total and immediate repeal of the Corn Laws. This letter of course confirmed Sir Robert Peel in his views as to the duty of the Government; but he had to cope with incurable dissensions in his Cabinet. Lord Stanley and the Duke of Buccleuch resigned; and on December 5 Sir Robert apprised the Queen that he could no longer carry on the Government. The task of forming an Administration was offered to, and after a struggle declined by, Lord John Russell, and on December 20 Sir Robert Peel resumed office. Lord Stanley declined to re-enter the Government, and his place as Secretary of State for the Colonies was offered to and accepted by Mr Gladstone.

His return to the Cabinet cost the young Minister his seat. Hitherto he had sat for Newark as the Duke of Newcastle's nominee. The Duke was the staunchest of Protectionists. He turned his own son, Lord Lincoln, out of the representation of Nottinghamshire for accepting office under Sir Robert Peel, and he naturally showed no mercy to the brilliant but wayward politician whom his favour had made member for Newark. Mr Gladstone therefore did not offer himself for re-election on taking office, and he remained outside the House of Commons during the great struggle of the coming year. It was a curious irony of fate which excluded him from Parliament at this crisis; for it seems unquestionable that he was the most advanced Free-Trader in Sir Robert Peel's Cabinet. There are indeed some who believe that Sir Robert's conversion was in some measure accelerated by the representations of his younger colleague.

Mr Gladstone's keen intelligence, no longer concerned exclusively with theological problems, but exercised in the commonplace business of the Board of Trade, had long been tending towards freedom of commerce. After resigning office at the beginning of 1845, he had published a pamphlet on 'Recent Commercial Legislation,' in which he deduced from a survey of recent reductions of duties, and their results on revenue and trade, the conclusion that all materials of industry should, as far as possible, be set free from legal charges. The doctrine thus applied to the raw material of labour gained cogency and impressiveness when applied to food. Throughout the Session of 1846, in spite of departmental duties at the Colonial Office, he was constantly employed in the preparation and completion of the great measure of the year. His singular combination of intellectual shrewdness with commercial knowledge did much to conduct the repeal of the Corn Laws through a desperate struggle to a successful issue. On June 25, 1846, the Corn Bill was read a third time in the House of Lords.

On the same day the Government was beaten in the House of Commons on the second reading of a Coercion Bill for Ireland. Sir Robert Peel quitted office for ever, 'leaving a name execrated,' as he said, 'by every monopolist, but remembered with expressions of good will in those places which are the abodes of men whose lot it is to labour and to earn their daily bread by the sweat of their brow.' He was succeeded by Lord John Russell at the head of a Whig Administration.

Early in 1847, it was announced that one of the two members for the University of Oxford intended to retire at the general election. Mr Gladstone, who was regarded alike by his contemporaries at Oxford, by men senior to himself in the University, and by those who had come after him, with feelings of enthusiastic admiration, was proposed for the vacant seat. The representation of the University had been pronounced by Mr Canning to be the most coveted prize of public life, and Mr Gladstone has himself confessed that he 'desired it with an almost passionate fondness.' In his address to the electors, he avowed that in the earlier part of his public life he had been an advocate for the exclusive support of the national religion by the State. But it had been in vain. 'I found that scarcely a year passed without the adoption of some fresh measure involving the national recognition and the national support of various forms of religion, and, in particular, that a recent and fresh provision had been made for the propagation from a public chair of Arian or Socinian doctrines. The question remaining for me was whether, aware of the opposition of the English people, I should set down as equal to nothing, in a matter primarily connected not with our own but with their priesthood, the wishes of the people of Ireland; and whether I should avail myself of the popular feeling in regard to the Roman Catholics for the purpose of enforcing against them a system which we had ceased by common consent to enforce against Arians—a system, above all, of which I must say that it never can be conformable to policy, to justice, or even to decency, when it has become avowedly partial and one-sided in its application.' On the eve of the election he wrote to his old friend and tutor, Dr Charles Wordsworth, whom he had just induced to take the Wardenship of Trinity College, Glenalmond:

'I am desirous, and by God's help determined, to leave at least a recollection upon the minds of men in your position; and the more so because I see plainly that this is nearly, if it be not quite, the last election at which you will have the power to exercise a choice as to prospective Church policy.'

Dr Moberly, afterwards Bishop of Salisbury, wrote thus, on July 8, to a doubtful voter:

> For my own part, I certainly disapprove of Gladstone's vote on 'the Godless colleges' (in Ireland); and I am not sure, even though I acknowledge the difficulties of the case, whether I approve of that respecting Maynooth; but I feel that I am not specifically called on to reward or punish individual votes, as to select *the*

deepest, truest, most attached, most effective advocate for the church and Universities in coming, and, probably, very serious dangers. I think your correspondence with Gladstone's committee has probably done great good. It is very useful that Gladstone should know that there are those who are not satisfied with some of his past acts; but surely you will not press this hitherto useful course to the extreme result of refraining from voting.

Again, on July 20:

At this moment, I believe it to be *the question* whether Gladstone shall be placed in a position of political strength and independence, by being elected for the University, or whether he shall cease to be a public man altogether … If Oxford will not have him, none will; and we shall simply have discarded, not from our own representation only, but from the political service of the Church and country, the man who, in this generation, has most ability, and willingness, and credit to serve them effectually. But I do not despair of you yet. The election will certainly be a very narrowly decided one.

To the same effect the Rev. F. D. Maurice:

If I had a vote for the University I should certainly give it to Mr Gladstone. I do not express this opinion hastily; but after endeavouring to consider the subject on all sides, and with some inclinations towards a different conclusion … Mr Gladstone supported the Dissenting Chapels Bill, supported the grant to Maynooth even against the doctrines of his own book. Both charges are true; and hereby I think he showed, whether he was right or wrong, that he was an honest man, no disciple of expediency; and that he really could distinguish, and had courage to own the distinction, between the temporary and the eternal, between that which is of Heaven and that which is of earth … Mr Gladstone gave up place that he might confess what he need not have confessed, what it would have done him good with his Oxford constituents not to have confessed. Whether he was right or wrong about Maynooth, this was the reverse of following expediency; it was acting upon principle. It is a kind of principle which you have need of at Oxford; it is the very principle which saves a man from becoming the slave of circumstances.

Parliament was dissolved on July 23, 1847. The nomination at Oxford took place on July 29. The present Lord Chief Justice of England was the indefatigable secretary of Mr Gladstone's committee. Mr Hope-Scott has left it on record that Mrs Gladstone was a potent canvasser. Sir Robert Peel went down to vote for his colleague. The venerable Dr Routh, then nearly ninety-two years old, emerged from his seclusion at Magdalen College to support a candidate whose theology was congenial to his own. At the close of the poll, Sir Robert Inglis, that fine type of prehistoric Toryism, stood at the head, and Mr Gladstone next to him with a majority of 173 over his Ultra-Protestant opponent.

Mr Gladstone's career naturally divides itself into three main parts. The first of them ends with his retirement from the representation of Newark. The central part ranges from 1847 to 1868. Happily, the third is still incomplete.

We have thus brought him through the preparatory stages of his course. We have carefully followed his early education; the influences which formed his character and mind; the political and theological controversies in which he shared, and the part which he bore in each. Wherever it was possible, his very words have been recorded. All this has been done in the hope of bringing vividly before the mind the scenes and acts of a past so distant that it is almost forgotten. A few contemporary observers survive; and it is only by their kindness that the writer has been enabled to present even this imperfect record of the circumstances amid which the greatest of our living countrymen reached maturity; the processes by which he was prepared for his destined work; and the forces which determined the course and complexion of his magnificent career.

We now see him in his thirty-ninth year, with a record of signal and unbroken success, in the enjoyment of all that health, intellect, fortune, and high character can give; eloquent, cultivated, accomplished, and now experienced in public life; standing well with his party and not ill with his opponents; admired, respected, and palpably destined to bear again, as he had borne before, a leading part in the highest tasks of Imperial Government. It is an interesting moment in an interesting career; but the subject expands before us, and for the remainder of the narrative we must be content with a more general view and a less detailed presentment than were applicable to the earlier stages.

A careful study of Mr Gladstone's votes and speeches during the next three years would lead the student, even if he had no other knowledge of the facts to guide him, to the conclusion that the subject of his study had arrived at a period of transition. On one side the Conservative Free-trader clings firmly and tenaciously to the Toryism of his youth; on another, he is reaching out towards new realms of Liberal thought and action. He opposes marriage with a deceased wife's sister on theological and social grounds, asserting roundly that such marriage is 'contrary to the law of God, declared for three thousand years and upwards.' He deprecates the appointment of a Commission to enquire into the Universities, because it will deter intending benefactors from effecting their munificent intentions. He argues for a second chamber in Australian legislatures, citing, perhaps a little unfortunately, the constitutional example of contemporary France. In all these utterances it is not hard to read the influence of the traditions in which he was reared, or of the ecclesiastical community which he represents in Parliament.

Yet even in the theological domain a tendency towards Liberalism shows itself. His hatred of Erastianism is evinced in his gallant but unsuccessful attempt to secure for the clergy and laity of each colonial diocese the power of self-government. Amid the indignant protests of his Tory allies, and in opposition to his own previous speech and vote, he vindicates the policy of admitting the Jews to Parliament. He defends the establishment of diplomatic relations with the Court of Rome; he supports the alteration of the parliamentary oath; and, though he will not abet an abstract attack on Church rates, he contends that their maintenance involves a corresponding duty to provide accommodation in the church for the very poorest of the congregation.

On the commercial side his Liberalism is rampant. With even fanatical faith he clings to Free Trade, as the best guarantee for our national stability amid the crash of the dynasties and constitutions which went down in '48. He thunders against the insidious dangers of reciprocity. He desires, by reforming the laws which govern navigation, to make the ocean, 'that great highway of nations, as free to the ships that traverse its bosom as to the winds that sweep it.'

And so the three years—1847, 1848, 1849—rolled by, full of stirring events in Europe and in England, in Church and in State, but marked by no special incidents in the life of Mr Gladstone. For him these years were a period of mental growth, of transition, of development. A change was silently proceeding, which was not completed for twenty years—if, indeed, it has been completed yet. 'There have been,' he wrote in later days to Bishop Wilberforce, 'two great deaths, or transmigrations of spirit, in my political existence—one, very slow, the breaking of ties with my original party.' This was now in progress. The other will be narrated in due course.

The year 1850 was destined to bring into this brilliant and prosperous life the new and bitter element of personal sorrow. This sorrow was twofold. In the first place it took the form of domestic bereavement. On April 9 Mr and Mrs Gladstone lost a little daughter, Catherine Jessy, between four and five years old. The illness was long and painful, and Mr Gladstone bore his part in the nursing and watching. It is said by those who remember him in those days that he was tenderly fond of his little children, and the sorrow had therefore a peculiar bitterness. It was the first time that death had entered his married home.

The other trial of the year, scarcely less searching, though unlike in all its circumstances, had its origin in the religious sphere. An Evangelical clergyman, the Rev. J. C. Gorham, had been presented to a living in the diocese of Exeter; and that truly formidable prelate, Bishop Phillpotts, refused to institute him, alleging that he held heterodox views on the subject of Holy Baptism. After complicated litigation, the Judicial Committee of the Privy Council decided, on March 8, 1850, that the doctrine held by the incriminated clergyman was not such as to bar him from preferment in the Church of England. This decision naturally created great commotion in the Church. Men's minds were rudely shaken. The orthodoxy of the Church of England seemed to be jeopardized, and the supremacy of the Privy Council in a matter touching religious doctrine was felt to be an intolerable burden.

Mr Gladstone was one of those whom these events profoundly agitated, and on June 4 he liberated his soul in an elaborate and important letter addressed to Dr Blomfield, Bishop of London. The subject of this letter was 'The Royal Supremacy, viewed in the light of Reason, History, and the Constitution.' It sought to prove that, as settled at the Reformation, the Royal Supremacy was not inconsistent with the spiritual life and inherent jurisdiction of the Church, but that the recent establishment of the Privy Council as the ultimate court of appeal in religious causes was 'an injurious, and even dangerous, departure from the Reformation Settlement.'

Mr. Gladstone thus sums up his contention:

I find it no part of my duty, my Lord, to idolize the Bishops of England and Wales, or to place my conscience in their keeping. I do not presume or dare to speculate upon their particular decisions; but I say that, acting jointly; publicly, solemnly, responsibly, they are the best and most natural organs of the judicial office of the Church in matters of heresy, and, according to reason, history, and the Constitution, in that subject-matter the fittest and safest counsellors of the Crown.

* * * *

We should, indeed, have a consolation, the greatest perhaps which times of heavy trouble and affliction can afford, in the reduction of the whole matter to a short, clear, and simple issue; because such a resolution, when once unequivocally made clear by acts, would sum up the whole case before the Church to the effect of these words; 'You have our decision; take your own; choose between the mess of pottage, and the birthright of the Bride of Christ.'

Those that are awake might hardly require a voice of such appalling clearness; those that sleep, it surely would awaken of those that would not hear, it must be said, 'Neither would they hear, though one rose from the dead.'

But She that, a stranger and a pilgrim in this world, is wedded to the Lord, and lives only in the hope of His Coming, would know her part; and while going forth to her work with steady step and bounding heart, would look back with deep compassion upon the region she had quitted—upon the slumbering millions, no less blind to the Future, than ungrateful to the Past.

After citing De Maistre's famous eulogy of the Church of England as *'très-précieuse,'* Mr Gladstone thus concludes:

It is nearly sixty years since thus a stranger and an alien, a stickler to the extremest point for the prerogatives of his Church, and nursed in every prepossession against ours, nevertheless turning his eye across the Channel, though he could then only see her in the lethargy of her organization, and the dull twilight of her learning, could nevertheless, discern that there was a special work written of God for her in Heaven, and that she was VERY PRECIOUS to the Christian world. Oh! how serious a rebuke to those who, not strangers but suckled at her breast, not two generations back, but the witnesses now of her true and deep repentance, and of her reviving zeal and love, yet (under whatever provocation) have written concerning her even as men might write that were hired to make a case against her, and by an adverse instinct in the selection of evidence, and a severity of construction, such as no history of the deeds of man can bear, have often, too often in these last years, put her to open shame! But what a word of hope and encouragement to everyone who, as convinced in his heart of the glory of her providential mission, shall unshrinkingly devote himself to defending within her borders the full and whole doctrine of the Cross, with that mystic symbol now as ever gleaming down on him from Heaven, now as ever showing forth its inscription: *in hoc signo vinces.*

Unhappily for Mr Gladstone's peace of mind, the view of the Church of England, thus boldly and beautifully set forth, did not commend itself to all those with whom up to this time he had acted in religious matters. Among those whom the troubles of the Church most powerfully affected were his two most intimate friends, the godfathers of his eldest son. These were the Archdeacon of Chichester, now Cardinal Manning, and the late Mr Hope-Scott, QC. Archdeacon Manning was a man who, from his undergraduate days, had exercised a powerful influence over his contemporaries. This influence was due to a early maturity of intellect and character. He had great shrewdness, tenacious will, a cogent and attractive style, and an impressive air of authority, enforced by natural advantages of person and bearing. As years went on, to these qualifications for leadership were added an increasing fervour of devotion, an enlarged acquaintance with life and men, and an unequalled gift of administration. Tradition says that the future Cardinal had once contemplated a political career, and, though a priest, he was essentially a statesman. He was on terms of affectionate intimacy with Mr Gladstone, and was his trusted counsellor in all that concerned the welfare and efficiency of the Church of England.

The character of Mr Hope (who became Hope-Scott on succeeding to the estate of Abbotsford) and the sentiments which Mr Gladstone entertained towards him, have been partially indicated by letters quoted in previous chapters. A fuller view of him is given in the following letter addressed by Mr Gladstone in 1873 to his friend's daughter, now Mrs Maxwell-Scott of Abbotsford:

Few men, perhaps, have had a wider contact with their generation, or a more varied experience of personal friendships, than myself. Among the large number of estimable and remarkable people whom I have known, and who have now passed away, there is in my memory an inner circle, and within it are the forms of those who were marked off from the comparative crowd even of the estimable and remarkable by the peculiarity and privilege of their type. Of these very few—some four or five I think only—your father was one: and with regard to them it always seemed to me as if the type in each case was that of the individual exclusively, and as if there could be but one such person in our world at a time. After the early death of Arthur Hallam, I used to regard your father distinctly as at the head of all his contemporaries in the brightness and beauty of his gifts.

We were at Eton at the same time, but he was considerably my junior, so that we were not in the way of being drawn together. At Christ Church we were again contemporaries, but acquaintances only, scarcely friends. I find he did not belong to the 'Oxford Essay Club,' in which I took an active part, and which included not only several of his friends, but ones with whom, unless my memory deceives me, he was most intimate—I mean Mr Leader.

* * * *

The next occasion on which I remember to have seen him was in his sitting-room at Chelsea Hospital. There must, however, have been some shortly preceding contact, or I should not have gone there to visit him. I found him among folios and books of grave appearance. It must have been about the year 1836. He opened a conversation on the controversies which were then agitated in the Church of England, and which had Oxford for their centre. I do not think I had paid them much attention but I was an ardent student of Dante, and likewise of Saint Augustine; both of them had acted powerfully upon my mind; and this was in truth the best preparation I had for anything like mental communion with a person of his elevation. He then told me that he had been seriously studying the controversy, and that in his opinion the Oxford authors were right. He spoke not only with seriousness, but with solemnity, as if this was for him a great epoch; not merely the adoption of a speculative opinion, but the reception of a profound and powerful religious impulse. Very strongly do I feel the force of Dr Newman's statements as to the religious character of his mind. It is difficult in retrospect to conceive of this, except as growing up with him from infancy. But it appeared to me as if at this period, in some very especial manner, his attention had been seized, his intellect exercised and enlarged in a new field; and as if the idea of the Church of Christ had then once for all dawned upon him as the power which, under whatever form, was from thenceforward to be the central object of his affections, in subordination only to Christ Himself, and as His continuing representative.

From that time I only knew of his career as one of unwearied religious activity, pursued with an entire abnegation of self, with a deep enthusiasm, under a calm exterior, and with a grace and gentleness of manner, which, joined to the force of his inward motives, made him, I think, without doubt the most winning person of his day. It was for about fifteen years, from that time onwards, that he and I lived in close, though latterly rarer intercourse. Yet this was due, on my side, not to any faculty of attraction, but to the circumstance that my seat in Parliament, and my rather close attention to business, put me in the way of dealing with many questions relating to the Church and the universities and colleges, on which he desired freely to expand his energies and his time.

* * * * *

His correspondence with me, beginning in February 1837, truly exhibits the character of our friendship, as one founded in common interests, of a kind that, gradually commanded more and more of the public attention, but that with him were absolutely paramount. The moving power was principally on his side. The main subjects on which it turned, and which also formed the basis of general intercourse, were as follows: First, a missionary organization for the province of Upper Canada. Then the question of the relations of Church and State, forced into prominence at that time by a variety of causes, and among them not least by a series of lectures, which Dr Chalmers delivered in the Hanover Square Rooms, to distinguished audiences, with a profuse eloquence, and with a noble and almost irresistible fervour. Those lectures drove me upon the hazardous enterprise of handling the same subject upon what I thought a sounder basis. Your father warmly entered into this design and bestowed upon a careful and prolonged examination of this work in MS, and upon a searching yet most tender criticism of its details, an amount of thought and labour which it would, I am persuaded, have been intolerable to any man to supply, except for one for whom each and every day as it arose was a new and an entire sacrifice to duty. As in the year 1838, when the manuscript was ready, I had to go abroad on account mainly of some overstrain upon the eyes, he undertook the whole labour of carrying the work through the press; and he even commended me, as you will see from the letters, because I did not show an ungovernable impatience of his aid.

The general frame of his mind at this time, in October 1838, will be pretty clearly gathered from a letter of that month ... written when he had completed that portion of his labours. He had full, unbroken faith in the Church of England, as a true portion of the Catholic Church; to her he had vowed the service of his life; all his desire was to uphold the framework of her institutions, and to renovate their vitality. He pushed her claims, you may find from the letters, further than I did; but the difference of opinion between us was not such as to prevent our cordial co-operation then and for years afterwards; though in using such a term I seem to myself guilty of conceit and irreverence to the dead, for I well know that he served her from an immeasurably higher level.

* * * *

I do not know whether the one personal influence, which alone, I think, ever seriously affected his career, was brought to bear upon him at this time (1841). But the movement of his mind, from this juncture onwards, was traceably parallel to, though at a certain distance from, that of Dr Newman. My opinion is (I put it no higher) that the Jerusalem Bishopric snapped the link which bound Dr Newman to the English Church. I have a conviction that it cut away the ground on which your father had hitherto most firmly and undoubtingly stood. Assuredly, from 1841 or 1842 onwards, his most fond, most faithful, most ideal love progressively decayed, and doubt nestled and gnawed in his soul. He was, however, of a nature in which levity could find no place. Without question, he estimated highly, as it deserves to be estimated, the tremendous nature of a change of religious profession, as between the Church of England and the Church of Rome; a change dividing asunder bone and marrow. Nearly ten years passed, I think, from 1841, during which he never wrote or spoke to me a *positive* word indicating the possibility of the great transition. Long he harboured his misgivings in silence, and ruminated upon them. They even, it seemed to me, weighed heavily upon his bodily health. I remember that in 1843 I wrote an article in a Review which referred to the remarkable words of Archbishop Laud respecting the Church of Rome as it was; and applied to the case those other remarkable words of Lord Chatham respecting America, 'Never, never, never.' He said to me, half-playfully (for the article took some hold upon his sympathies), 'What, Gladstone, *never, never, never?*'

It must have been about this time that I had another conversation with him about religion, of which, again, I exactly recollect the spot. Regarding (forgive me) the adoption of the Roman religion by members of the Church of England as nearly the greatest calamity that could befall Christian faith in this country, I rapidly became alarmed when these changes began; and very long before the great luminary, Dr Newman, drew after him, it may well be said, 'the third part of the stars of Heaven.' This alarm I naturally and freely expressed to the man upon whom I most relied, your father.

On the occasion to which I refer he replied to me with some admission that they were calamitous; 'but,' he said, 'pray remember an important compensation, in the influence which the English mind will bring to bear upon the Church of Rome itself. Should there be in this country any considerable amount of secession to that Church, it cannot fail to operate sensibly in mitigating whatever gives most offence in its practices or temper.' I do not pretend to give the exact words, but their spirit and effect I never can forget. I then thought there was great force in them.

When I learned that he was to be married, my opinion was that he had only allowed his thoughts to turn in the direction of the bright and pure attachment he had formed, because the object to which they had first been pledged had vanished or been hidden from his view.

* * * * *

I have just spoken of your father as the man on whom I most relied; and so it was. I relied on one other, also a remarkable man, who took the same course, at nearly the same time; but on him most, from my opinion of his sagacity. From the correspondence of 1838 you might suppose that he relied upon me, that he had almost given himself to me. But whatever expressions his warm feelings combined with his humility may have prompted, it really was not so; or ought it to have been so, for I always felt and knew my own position beside him to be one of mental as well as moral inferiority. I cannot remember any occasion on which I exercised an influence over him. I remember many on which I tried; and especially when I saw his mind shaken, and, so to speak, on the slide. But these attempts (of which you may possibly have some written record) completely failed, and drove him into reserve. Never, on any one occasion, would he enter freely into the question with me. I think the fault lay much on my side. My touch was not fine enough for his delicate spirit. But I do not conceal from you that I think there was a certain amount of fault on his side also. Notwithstanding what I have said of his humility, notwithstanding what Dr Newman has most truly said of his self-renouncing turn, and total freedom from ambition, there was in him, I think, a subtle form of self-will, which led him, where he had a foregone conclusion or a latent tendency, to indulge it, and to refuse to throw his mind into free partnership with others upon questions of doubt and difficulty. Yet I must after all admit his right to be silent, unless where he thought he was to receive real aid; and of this he alone could be the judge.

* * * * *

Whatever may have been the precise causes of the reticence to which I have referred (and it is possible that physical weakness was among them), the character of our friendship had during these later years completely changed. It was originally formed in common and very absorbing interests. He was not of those shallow souls which think, or persuade themselves they think, that such a relation can continue in vigour and in fruitfulness when its daily bread has been taken away. The feeling of it indeed remained on both sides, as you will see. On my side, I may say that it became more intense; but only according to that perversity, or infirmity, of human nature, according to which we seem to love truly only when we lose. My affection for him, during those later years before his change, was, I may almost say, intense; and there was hardly anything, I think, which he could have asked me to do, and which I would not have done. But as I saw more and more through the dim light what was to happen, it became more and more like the affection which is felt for one departed.

As far as narrative is concerned, I am now at the close. In 1850 came the discussions and alarms connected with the Gorham judgment; and came also the last flickering of the flame of his attachment to the Church of England. Thereafter I never found myself able to turn to account as an opening any word he spoke or wrote to me.

It will be easily seen, from the foregoing extracts, that the change which was now impending cut Mr Gladstone to the quick. 'I should say,' writes one who knows him well, 'that it touched the depths of his soul almost more than anything which has happened since.' And, as so often happens in human life, the sorrow did not come alone. Throughout this period of transition Mr Hope was in close association with Archdeacon Manning, who shared his worst misgivings about the character and destinies of the Church of England. They advanced with even steps towards the inevitable goal. In November the Archdeacon resigned his preferments, and on the Passion Sunday next ensuing he and Mr Scott were together received into the Roman Church. To their friend who remained behind, this twofold secession was an overwhelming grief. Mr Gladstone said, 'I felt as if I had lost my two eyes.' It was by no wish of his that his intimacy with Mr Hope now came to an end. The decision was taken by the other. In reply to a letter expressing Mr Gladstone's unchanged feelings, Mr Hope writes: 'It would be hardly possible for either of us to attempt (except under one condition, for which I daily pray) the restoration of entire intimacy.' This letter was acknowledged by Mr Gladstone in these beautiful and moving words:

> 6 Carlton Gardens: June 22, 1851.
>
> My dear Hope,—Upon the point most prominently put in your welcome letter I will only say you have not misconstrued me. Affection which is fed by intercourse, and above all by co-operation for sacred ends, has little need of verbal expression, but such expression is deeply ennobling when active relations have changed. It is no matter of merit to me to feel strongly on the subject of that change. It maybe little better than pure selfishness. I have too good reason to know what this year has cost me; and so little hope have I that the places now vacant can be filled up for me, that the marked character of these events in reference to myself rather teaches me this lesson—the work to which I had aspired is reserved for other and

better men. And if that be the Divine will, I so entirely recognize its fitness that the grief would so far be small to me were I alone concerned. The pain, the wonder, and the mystery is this—that you should have refused the higher vocation you had before you. The same words, and all the same words, I should use of Manning too. Forgive me for giving utterance to what I believe myself to see and know; I will not proceed a step further in that direction.

There is one word, and one only in your letter that I do not interpret closely. Separated we are, but I hope and think not yet estranged. Were I more estranged I should bear the separation better. If estrangement is to come I know not, but it will only be, I think, from causes the operation of which is still in its infancy—causes not affecting me. Why should I be estranged from you? I honour you even in what I think your error; why, then, should my feelings to you alter in anything else? It seems to me as though, in these fearful times, events were more and more growing too large for our puny grasp, and that we should the more look for and trust the Divine purpose in them, when we find they have wholly passed beyond the reach and measure of our own. 'The Lord is in His holy temple: let all the earth keep silence before Him.' The very afflictions of the present time are a sign of joy to follow. Thy kingdom come, Thy will be done, is still our prayer in common: the same prayer, in the same sense; and a prayer which absorbs every other. That is for the future: for the present we have to endure, to trust, and to pray that each day may bring its strength with its burden, and its lamp for its gloom.

Ever yours with unaltered affection,
W. E. GLADSTONE.

Writing twenty-two years afterwards to Mrs Maxwell-Scott, Mr Gladstone says of the letter to which this was the reply:

It was the epitaph of our friendship, which continued to live, but only, or almost only, as it lives between those who inhabit separate worlds. On no day since that date, I think, was he absent from my thoughts; and now I can scarcely tear myself from the fascination of writing about him. And so, too, you will feel the fascination of reading about him; and it will serve to relieve the weariness with which otherwise you would have toiled through so long a letter ... If anything which it contains has hurt you, recollect the chasm which separates our points of view; recollect that what came to him as light and blessing and emancipation, had never offered itself to me other wise than as a temptation and a sin; recollect that when he found what he held his 'pearl of great price,' his discovery was to me beyond what I could describe, not only a shock and a grief but a danger too. I having given you my engagement, you having accepted it, I have felt that I must above all things be true, and that I could only be true by telling you everything. If I have traversed some of the ground in sadness, I now turn to the brighter thought of his present light and peace and progress; may they be his more and more abundantly, in that world where the shadows that our sins and follies cast no longer darken the aspect and glory of the truth; and may God ever bless you, the daughter of my friend!

But it is time to return to the secular sphere.

V

Don Pacifico—Civis Romanus—The Neapolitan prisons—The Papal aggression—Triumph over Mr Disraeli—The Coalition Government—Chancellor of the Exchequer—First Budget

THIS YEAR—1850—WAS MARKED by the memorable debate which is associated with the name of Don Pacifico. The circumstances from which that debate ultimately proceeded were as little dignified or striking as could easily be supposed. Don Pacifico was a Maltese Jew, a British subject domiciled at Athens. He happened to become obnoxious to the Athenian mob, who on April 4, 1847, wrecked and robbed his house. Don Pacifico appealed to the Greek Government for compensation. He claimed nearly thirty-two thousand pounds for the loss of his effects, among which a peculiarly sumptuous bedstead figured largely in the public view. The Greek Government were poor and were dilatory, and Don Pacifico's claim remained unheeded. At the same time the English Government, or at any rate the Foreign Secretary, Lord Palmerston, had other quarrels with the Greek Government. Some land belonging to an Englishman resident in Athens had been taken by the Government, and they had offered the owner what he considered an insufficient compensation. Some Ionian subjects of the Queen had suffered hardship at the hands of the Greek authorities. A midshipman belonging to one of her Majesty's ships had been arrested by mistake at Patros. None of the incidents, taken by themselves, were of the least importance; but, unfortunately, Lord Palmerston had persuaded himself that the French Minister at Athens was plotting against English interests there, and was egging on the Greek Government to disregard our claims. This was enough. The outrage on Don Pacifico's bedstead remained the head and front of Greek offending, but Lord Palmerston included all the other slights, blunder and delays of justice in one sweeping indictment; made the private claims into a national demand; and peremptorily informed the Greek Government that they must pay what was demanded of them within a given time. The Government hesitated, and the British fleet was ordered to the Piraeus, and seized all the Greek vessels which were found in the waters. Russia and France took umbrage at this high-handed proceeding, and championed Greece. Lord Palmerston informed them that it was none of their business, and stood firm. The French Ambassador was withdrawn from London, and for a while the peace of Europe was menaced.

The Tories, always ready to assail in opposition the blustering policy which they practise in office, made a violent attack upon Lord Palmerston. In the House of Lords, Lord Stanley carried a resolution expressing regret that 'various claims against the Greek Government, doubtful in point of justice or exaggerated in amount, have been enforced by coercive measures, directed against the commerce and people of Greece, and calculated to endanger the continuance of our friendly relations with foreign Powers.' It was necessary to meet the advance vote of the Lords by a counterblast in the Commons, and Mr Roebuck, an independent Liberal, was put up to move that the principles which had governed the foreign policy of the Government were 'calculated to maintain the honour and dignity of this country, and in times of unexampled difficulty to preserve peace between England and the various nations of the world.' The debate began on June 24, 1850. In reply to Mr Roebuck, Lord Palmerston spoke with extraordinary force and skill. His speech lasted nearly five hours. 'He spoke,' Mr Gladstone said, 'from the dusk of one day to the dawn of the next.' He defended his policy at every point. He declared that in every step which he had taken, however high-handed it might seem, he had been influenced by the sole desire that the meanest, the poorest, even the most disreputable, subject of the English Crown should be defended by the whole might of England against foreign oppression. He reminded the House of all that was implied in the Roman boast, *Civis Romanus sum*, and he urged the House to make it clear that a British subject, in whatever land he might be, should feel confident that the watchful eye and the strong arm of England would protect him. This was irresistible. *Civis Romanus* settled the business. It was in vain that Mr Gladstone, after reviewing the legal and constitutional aspects of the case, fastened upon this phrase with all his rhetorical force, and demonstrated its 'inapplicability to the condition and claims of an English citizen.'

> 'Sir, great as is the influence and power of Britain, she cannot afford to follow, for any length of time, a self-isolating policy. It would be a contravention of the law of nature and of God, if it were possible for any single nation of Christendom to emancipate itself from the obligations which bind all other nations, and to arrogate, in the face of mankind, a position of peculiar privilege. And now I will

grapple with the noble lord on the ground which he selected for himself, in the most triumphant portion of his speech, by his reference to those emphatic words, *Civis Romanus sum*. He vaunted, amidst the cheers of his supporters, that under his Administration an Englishman should be, throughout the world, what the citizen of Rome had been. What, then, sir, was a Roman citizen? He was the member of a privileged caste; he belonged to a conquering race, to a nation that held all others bound down by the strong arm of power. For him there was to be an exceptional system of law; for him principles were to be asserted, and by him rights were to be enjoyed, that were denied to the rest of the world. Is such, then, the view of the noble lord as to the relation which is to subsist between England and other countries? Does he make the claim for us that we are to be uplifted upon a platform high above the standing-ground of all other nations? It is, indeed, too clear, not only from the expressions but from the whole tone of the speech of the noble viscount, that too much of this notion is lurking in his mind; that he adopts, in part, that vain conception that we, forsooth, have a mission to be the censors of vice and folly, of abuse and imperfection, among the other countries of the world; that we are to be the universal schoolmasters; and that all those who hesitate to recognize our office can be governed only by prejudice or personal animosity, and should have the blind war of diplomacy forthwith declared against them. And certainly, if the business of a Foreign Secretary properly were to carry on diplomatic wars, all must admit that the noble lord is a master in the discharge of his functions. What, sir, ought a Foreign Secretary to be? Is he to be like some gallant knight at a tournament of old, pricking forth into the lists, armed at all points, confiding in his sinews and his skill, challenging all comers for the sake of honour, and having no other duty than to lay as many as possible of his adversaries sprawling in the dust? If such is the idea of a good Foreign Secretary, I, for one, would vote to the noble lord his present appointment for his life. But, sir, I do not understand the duty of a Secretary for Foreign Affairs to be of such a character. I understand it to be his duty to conciliate peace with dignity. I think it to be the very first of all his duties studiously to observe, and to exalt in honour among mankind, that great code of principles which is termed the law of nations, which the honourable and learned member for Sheffield has found, indeed, to be very vague in their nature, and greatly dependent on the discretion of each particular country, but in which I find, on the contrary, a great and noble monument of human wisdom, founded on the combined dictates of reason and experience, a precious inheritance bequeathed to us by the generations that have gone before us, and a firm foundation on which we must take care to build whatever it may be our part to add to their acquisitions, if, indeed; we wish to maintain and to consolidate the brotherhood of nations and to promote the peace and welfare of the world.

* * * * *

Sir, I say the policy of the noble lord tends to encourage and confirm in us that which is our besetting fault and weakness, both as a nation and as individuals. Let an Englishman travel where he will as a private person, he is found in general to be upright, high-minded, brave, liberal, and true; but, with all this, foreigners are too often sensible of something that galls them in his presence, and I apprehend it is because he has too great a tendency to self-esteem—too little disposition to regard the feelings, the habits, and the ideas of others. Sir, I find this characteristic too plainly legible in the policy of the noble lord. I doubt not that use will be made of our present debate to work upon this peculiar weakness of the English mind. The people will be told that those who oppose the motion are governed by personal motives, have no regard for public principles, no enlarged ideas of national policy. You will take your case before a favourable jury, and you think to gain your verdict; but, sir, let the House of Commons be warned—let it warn itself—against all illusions. There is in this case also a course of appeal. There is an appeal, such as the honourable and learned member for Sheffield has made, from the one House of Parliament to the other. There is a further appeal from this House of Parliament to the people of England; but, lastly, there is also an appeal from the people of England to the general sentiment of the civilized world; and I, for my part, am of opinion that England will stand shorn of a chief part of her glory and pride if she shall be found to have separated herself, through the policy she pursues abroad, from the moral support which the general and fixed convictions of mankind afford—if the day shall come when she may continue to excite the wonder and the fear of other nations, but in which she shall have no part in their affection and regard.

No, sir, let it not be so; let us recognize, and recognize with frankness, the equality of the weak with the strong; the principles of brotherhood among nations, and of their sacred independence. When we are asking for the maintenance of the rights which belong to our fellow-subjects resident in Greece, let us do as we would be done by, and let us pay all respect to a feeble State, and to the infancy of free institutions, which we should desire and should exact from others towards their maturity and their strength. Let us refrain from all gratuitous and arbitrary meddling in the internal concerns of other States, even as we should resent the same interference, if it were attempted to be practised towards ourselves. If the noble lord has indeed acted on these principles, let the Government to which he belongs have your verdict in its favour; but if he has departed from them, as I contend, and as I humbly think and urge upon you that it has been too amply proved, then the House of Commons must not shrink from the performance of its duty under whatever expectations of momentary obloquy or reproach, because we shall have done what is right; we shall enjoy the peace of our own consciences, and receive, whether a little sooner or a little later, the approval of the public voice for having entered our solemn protest against a system of policy which we believe, nay, which we know, whatever may be its first aspect, must, of necessity, in its final results be unfavourable even to the security of British subjects resident abroad, which it professes so much to study—unfavourable to the dignity of the country, which the motion of the honourable and learned member asserts it preserves—and equally unfavourable to that other great and sacred object, which also it suggests to our recollection, the maintenance of peace with the nations of the world.

The speech from which these citations are made deserves careful study. Lord Palmerston himself admitted that it was 'a first-rate performance.' In width and accuracy of information, debating skill, logical grip, and force of rhetoric it seems to mark a distinct advance upon the speaker's previous efforts. It is indeed a remarkably perfect composition, finely conceived and finely executed. But, apart from its merits as a work of art, is notable as exemplifying at a comparatively early period, and in high perfection, two of Mr Gladstone's most conspicuous qualities, which have grown with his growth and strengthened with his strength, and have been attended by important and opposing consequences. The first of these is his high and even austere morality. He appeals to the most august of all tribunals, to 'the law of nature and of God.' As a test of a foreign policy he asks, not whether it is striking, or brilliant, or successful, but whether it is right. Is it consistent with moral principle and public duty; with the chivalry due from the strong to the weak; with the 'principles of brotherhood among nations, and of their sacred independence'? It is this habit of Mr Gladstone's mind which has done so much to secure him the enthusiastic veneration of his followers, who loathe the savage law of brute force, who recognize the operation of moral principle in international relations, and, who feel it a personal pain and degradation when England is forced to figure as the swashbuckler of Europe.

But if this element has been a main factor in Mr Gladstone's hold over the affections of his disciples, and thereby of his public success, it is not difficult to discern, in the second of the citations given above, the operation of another element which has done much to mar his popularity, to limit his range of influence, and to set great masses of his countrymen in opposition to his policy. This is his tendency to belittle England, to dwell on the faults and defects of Englishmen, to extol and magnify the virtues and graces of other nations, and to ignore the homely prejudice of patriotism. He has frankly told us that he does not know the meaning of 'prestige,' and an English Minister who makes that confession has yet to learn one of the governing sentiments of

'An old and haughty nation proud in arms.'

Whether this peculiarity of Mr Gladstone's mind can be referred to the fact that he has not a drop of English blood in his body is perhaps a fanciful enquiry, but its consequences are palpable enough in the vulgar belief that he is indifferent to the interests and honour of the country which he has three times ruled, and that his love of England is swamped and lost in the enthusiasm of humanity—unquestionably a nobler sentiment, but unfortunately one which has little power to sway the average Englishman. As it has been since seen in, the disputes about the *Alabama*, and the Eastern question, and in the controversy about Home Rule, so it was in the debate on Don Pacifico. For the moment, *Civis Romanus* carried all before it. Brotherhood, humanity, and chivalry went to the wall, and Lord Palmerston secured a majority of forty-six.

Sir Robert Peel had spoken in the debate. He praised Palmerston's speech as a parliamentary performance, but gravely rebuked the policy which that speech defended. The division was taken in the early morning of June 29. In the afternoon of the same day he had a fall from his horse, and received injuries which proved fatal. He died on July 2. It fell to Mr Gladstone's lot to pronounce in the House of Commons a eulogy of his departed chief. His speech is full of pathos and eloquence, and, with its appropriate quotation from 'Marmion' is a favourable specimen of that style of memorial oratory, at once dignified and moving, in which he excels. He spoke of the hope and expectation which had been generally entertained that Sir Robert Peel would 'still have been spared to render to his country the most essential services.' One of those services would have been the consolidation and guidance of that brilliant group of gifted and high-minded men who had followed him in his momentous transition from Protection to Free Trade. The death of Sir Robert Peel dissolved the Peelite party. With the other members of that party we need not concern ourselves; Mr Gladstone is our business. Another stage had been reached in the process which was to convert him into a Liberal.

In the winter of 1850-1, Mr Gladstone spent between three and four months at Naples. He was taken there by the illness of one of his children, for whom a southern climate had been recommended. It is not a little remarkable that the statesman who had so lately and so vigorously denounced the 'vain conception that we, forsooth, have a mission to be the censors of vice and folly, of abuse and imperfection, among the other countries of the world,' should now have found himself irresistibly impelled by conscience and humanity to undertake a signal and effective crusade against the domestic administration of a friendly Power. During his residence at Naples, he learned that more than half the Chamber of Deputies, who had followed the party of opposition, had been banished or imprisoned; that a large number, probably not less than twenty thousand, of the citizens had been imprisoned on charges of political disaffection, and that in prison they were subjected to the grossest cruelties. Mr Gladstone's humanity was deeply stirred by these tales of oppression and wrong, and he determined to examine them at first hand. So, to quote Lord Palmerston's phrase, 'instead of confining himself to those amusements that abound in Naples; instead of diving into volcanoes and exploring excavated cities, we see him going to courts of justice, visiting prisons, descending into dungeons, and examining great numbers of the cases of unfortunate victims of illegality and injustice, with a view afterwards to enlist public opinion in the endeavour to remedy those abuses.'

The result of these investigations Mr Gladstone gave to the world in a letter which, on April 7, 1851, he addressed to Lord Aberdeen. In this letter he brings an elaborate, detailed, and horrible indictment against the rulers of Naples, and especially as regards the arrangements of their prisons and the treatment of persons confined in them for political offences. He denounces the Neapolitan Government, in indignant words which he had heard on the spot, as *la negazione di Dio eretta a sistema di governo*. The publication of this letter caused a wide sensation in England and abroad, and profoundly agitated the court of Naples. In reply to a question in the House of Commons, Lord Palmerston accepted and adopted Mr Gladstone's statement, expressed keen sympathy with the cause which he had espoused, and sent a copy of his letter to the Queen's representative at every court of Europe. A second letter and a third followed, and their effect, though for a while retarded, was unmistakably felt in the subsequent revolution which created a free and united Italy.

When Mr Gladstone returned from Italy to England at the beginning of the Session of 1851, he found the country in convulsions of Protestant fury. In the preceding September the Pope had issued Letters Apostolic, establishing a Roman Hierarchy in England, and purporting to map out the country into papal dioceses. This act of aggression was met by a storm of public indignation. People who had no particular religion of their own found a certain satisfaction to their conscience in denouncing the religion of others. Honest Protestants were genuinely indignant at what they regarded as an attack upon the Reformed Faith. Well-instructed Anglicans resented an act which practically denied the jurisdiction and authority of the Church of England. Devotees of the British Constitution were irritated by an interference with the royal prerogative; and fervent patriots were enraged by the gratuitous intrusion of a foreign potentate. No element of combustion was wanted. Public meetings were held everywhere, fiery speeches made, and heroic resolutions passed. Every platform and every pulpit rang with variations on the fine old British air of 'No Popery!' and even Covent Garden Theatre and the Lord Mayor's banquet at the Guildhall re-echoed the strain in Shakespearian quotations.

The Prime Minister, Lord John Russell, had published one of his celebrated letters, addressed this time to the Bishop of Durham, and, not content with rebuking and defying the Pope, had gone out of his way to denounce and insult the whole High Church party as the secret allies and fellow-workers of Rome. As soon as Parliament met, he introduced the Ecclesiastical Titles Bill, designed to prevent the assumption by Roman Catholic prelates of titles taken from any territory or place in the United Kingdom. Penalties were attached to the use of such titles, and all acts done by, and bequests made to, persons under them were to be void. The Bill was not well received; it was airily lampooned by Mr Disraeli, and solemnly denounced by Mr Gladstone. It was condemned on one side as too stringent, on another as too mild. The difficulty of applying it to Ireland, where the system which it condemned had long been in full force, necessitated material alterations in it, and each alteration added force to the criticisms of opponents. Those who thought the Bill too mild were indignant at concessions which made it milder; those who resented it as a violation of religious liberty pointed out triumphantly that it could no longer be justified even as a temporary expedient designed to serve a practical end. Somehow the Bill scrambled through Parliament, and became simultaneously a law and a dead letter. Nobody obeyed it, or suffered for disobeying it, and twenty years afterwards it was quietly repealed at Mr Gladstone's instance. But the difficulty which the Government encountered in this ecclesiastical legislation was only one among many. Their budget was unpopular; their majority declined; they were beaten on a motion in favour of assimilating the county to the borough franchise; and, after a variety of petty defeats, they resigned: but when Lord Stanley (who, it is said, offered Mr Gladstone the Foreign Office) and Lord Aberdeen had both declined the task of forming an administration, Lord John Russell and his colleagues resumed office. This reconstructed Ministry very soon received a fatal blow. Lord Palmerston was one of the most independent and most masterful of men. He was intensely interested in foreign affairs, understood them thoroughly, and had absolute reliance on his own judgment. Again and again, in spite of repeated warnings from Lord John Russell and an imperative memorandum from the Queen herself, he had taken his own line in important transactions, without even formal reference to his Sovereign or the Prime Minister. His crowning indiscretion was committed in December, 1851. On the 2nd of the month Louis Napoleon, Prince President of the French Republic, by a single act of lawless violence, abolished the Constitution, and made himself practically Dictator. The details of that monstrous act, and of the bloodshed which accompanied it, are written by the hand of a master in the *'Histoire d'un Crime.'* The news created a profound sensation in England, and the Queen was rightly and keenly anxious that no step should be taken and no word said which would convey the impression that the English Government approved of what had been done.

But it soon leaked out that Lord Palmerston had expressed to Count Walewski, the French Ambassador in London, his entire approval of the Prince President's act. This was too much for the patience of even a gracious Queen and a long-suffering Premier. After some rather complicated explanations which explained nothing, Lord John Russell dismissed Lord Palmerston from office on Christmas Eve, 1851.

In the Christmas recess of 1851, Mr Gladstone found time to write a letter to Dr Skinner, Bishop of Aberdeen and Primus (whom he addressed as 'Right Reverend

Father') on the position and functions of the laity in the Church. This letter is remarkable because, as was detected at the time by Dr Charles Wordsworth, Bishop of St Andrew's, it 'contained the germ of Liberation, and the political equality of all religions.' The Bishop published a controversial rejoinder, which drew from Dr Gaisford, Dean of Christ Church, these emphatic words 'You have proved to my satisfaction that this gentleman is unfit to represent the University.'

In the following February, Lord Palmerston enjoyed, in his own jaunty phrase, his 'tit-for-tat with Johnny Russell,' and helped the Tories to defeat his late chief on a Bill for reorganizing the militia as a precaution against possible aggression from France.

Lord John Russell was succeeded by Lord Derby, with Mr Disraeli (who now entered office for the first time) as Chancellor of the Exchequer and Leader of the House of Commons; with a string of nonentities in the other offices of State; and with a scarcely-disguised intention to revive protection. Mr Disraeli introduced and carried a makeshift Budget, and the Government tided over the Session, and dissolved Parliament on July 1, 1852. Mr Gladstone's majority at Oxford was largely increased, but the general election did not materially disturb the balance of parties. There was now some talk of inducing Mr Gladstone to join the Tory Government, and, on November 28, Lord Malmesbury dubiously remarks, 'I cannot make out Gladstone, who seems to me a dark horse.' In the following month the Chancellor of the Exchequer produced his second Budget. It was an ambitious and a skilful attempt to reconcile conflicting interests, and to please all while offending none. The Government had come into office pledged to do something for the relief of the agricultural interest. They redeemed their pledge by reducing the duty on malt. This reduction created a deficit; and they repaired the deficit by doubling the duty on inhabited houses. Unluckily, the agricultural interest proved, as usual, ungrateful to its benefactors, and made light of the reduction on malt; while those who were to pay for it in double taxation were naturally indignant. The voices of criticism, 'angry, loud, discordant voices,' were heard simultaneously on every side. The debate waxed fast and furious. In defending his hapless proposals, Mr Disraeli gave full scope to his most characteristic gifts; he pelted his opponents right and left with sarcasms, taunts, and epigrams, and went as near personal insult as the forms of Parliament permit. He sat down late at night, and Mr Gladstone rose in a crowded and excited House to deliver an unpremeditated reply which has ever since been celebrated. Even the cold and colourless pages of *Hansard* show signs of the excitement under which he laboured, and of the tumultuous applause and dissent by which his opening sentences were interrupted. The speech of the Chancellor of the Exchequer, he said, must be answered 'on the moment.' It must be 'tried by the laws of decency and propriety.' He indignantly rebuked his rival's language and demeanour. He reminded him of the discretion and decorum due from every member, but pre-eminently due from the Leader of the House. He tore his financial scheme to ribbons. It was the beginning of a duel which lasted till death removed one of the combatants from the political arena. 'Those who had thought it impossible that any impression could be made upon the House after the speech of Mr Disraeli had to acknowledge that a yet greater impression was produced by the unprepared reply of Mr Gladstone.' The House divided and the Government were left in a minority of nineteen. This happened in the early morning of December 17, 1852. Within an hour of the division Lord Derby wrote to the Queen a letter announcing his defeat and the consequences which it must entail, and that evening at Osborne he placed his formal resignation in her Majesty's hands.

It was a moment of intense excitement. Some notion of the frenzy which prevailed may be gathered from the following circumstance. On December 20 'twenty ruffians of the Carlton Club' as Mr Greville calls them, gave a dinner to Major Beresford, who had been charged with bribery at the Derby election, and had escaped with nothing worse than a censure. 'After dinner,' continues Mr Greville, 'when they got drunk, they went up stairs and, finding Gladstone alone in the drawing-room, some of them proposed to throw him out of the window. This they did not quite dare do, but contented themselves with giving some insulting message or order to the waiter, and then went away.' In spite of these amenities Mr Gladstone still remained a member of the club (though he seldom used it) until he joined the Whig Government in 1859.

The new Government was a coalition of Whigs and Peelites, with Sir Willam Molesworth thrown in to represent the Radicals. Lord Aberdeen became Prime Minister, and Mr Gladstone Chancellor of the Exchequer. The other Peelites in the Cabinet were the Duke of Newcastle, Sir James Graham, and Mr Sidney Herbert. Mr Gladstone's seat at Oxford was fiercely contested. The poll was kept open for fifteen days. It may possibly account for the bitterness of the contest that Lord Derby, whom Mr Gladstone had just helped to oust from office, had been elected Chancellor of the University, on the death of the Duke of Wellington, in the previous autumn. Various members of the University had probably hoped to suck no small advantage out of the rule of a Minister who was also chief of their academical body. Mr Gladstone fought the battle on ecclesiastical lines. He laid great stress on Lord Aberdeen's friendliness to the Church, and vehemently protested his own continued loyalty to those principles of Churchmanship of which he had been for twenty years a distinguished exponent. But the more fiery spirits of the High Church party, headed by Arch-deacon Denison, mistrusted and opposed him, mainly on account of his attitude towards religious education, and they succeeded in materially reducing his majority. He was, however, returned again, and entered on the active duties of a great office for which he was pre-eminently and uniquely fitted by an unequalled combination of financial, administrative, and rhetorical gifts. If one can conceive of a heaven-born Chancellor of the Exchequer, Mr Gladstone was that celestial product.

His first Budget, which was awaited with intense interest, was introduced on April 18, 1853. It tended to make life easier and cheaper for large and numerous classes; it promised wholesale remissions of taxation; it lessened the charges on common processes of business, on locomotion, on postal communication, and on several articles of general consumption. The deficiency thus created was to be met by the application of the legacy duty to real property, by an increase of the duty on spirits, and by the extension of the income-tax, at 5*d.* in the pound, to all incomes between £100 and £150.

The speech, five hours long, in which these proposals were introduced, held the House spell-bound. Here was an Orator who could apply all the resources of a burnished rhetoric to the elucidation of figures; who could make pippins and cheese interesting, and tea serious; who could sweep the widest horizon of the financial future, and yet stoop to bestow the minutest attention on the microcosm of penny stamps and post-horses. Above all, the Chancellor's mode of handling the income-tax attracted interest and admiration. It was no nicely-calculated less or more, no tinkering or top-dressing, no mere experimenting with results, but a searching analysis of the financial and moral grounds on which the impost rested, and an historical justification and eulogy of it couched in language worthy of a more majestic theme. 'It was in the crisis of the revolutionary war that, when Mr Pitt found the resources of taxation were failing under him, his mind fell back upon the conception of the income-tax; and, when he proposed it to Parliament, that great man, possessed with his great idea, raised his eloquence to an unusual height and power.' Yet, great as had been the services of the income-tax at a time of national danger, and great as they would prove again should such a crisis recur, Mr Gladstone could not consent to retain it as a part of the permanent and ordinary finances of the country. It was objectionable on account of its unequal incidence, of the harassing investigation into private affairs which it entailed, and of the frauds to which it inevitably led. Therefore, having served its turn, it was to be extinguished in 1860.

> Depend upon it, when you come to close quarters with this subject, when you come to measure and see the respective relations of intelligence and labour and property, and when you come to represent these relations in arithmetical results, you are undertaking an operation which I should say it was beyond the power of man to conduct with satisfaction, but which, at any rate, is an operation to which you ought not constantly to recur; for if, as my hon. friend once said very properly, this country could not bear a revolution once a year, I will venture to say that it could not bear a reconstruction of the income-tax once a year. Whatever you do in regard to the income-tax you must be bold, you must be intelligible, you must be

decisive. You must not palter with it. If you do, I have striven at least to point out as well as my feeble powers will permit, the almost desecration I would say, certainly the gross breach of duty to your country, of which you will be found guilty, in thus jeopardizing one of the most valuable among all its material resources. I believe it to be of vital importance, whether you keep this tax or whether you part with it, that you should either keep it or leave it in a state in which it would be fit for service in an emergency, and that it will be impossible to do if you break up the basis of your income-tax.

* * * *

If the Committee have followed me, they will understand that we stand on the principle that the income-tax ought to be marked as a temporary measure; that the public feeling that relief should be given to intelligence and skill as compared with property ought to be met, and may be met; that the income-tax in its operation ought to be mitigated by every rational means, compatible with its integrity; and, above all, that it should be associated in the last term of its existence, as it was in the first, with those remissions of indirect taxation which have so greatly redounded to the profit of this country, and have set so admirable an example—an example that has already in some quarters proved contagious to other nations of the earth. These are the principles on which we stand, and the figures. I have shown you that if you grant us the taxes which we ask, the moderate amount of £2,500,000 in the whole, and much less than that sum for the present year, you, or the Parliament which may be in existence in 1860, will be in the condition, if you so think fit, to part with the income-tax. I am almost afraid to look at the clock, shamefully reminding me, as it must, how long I have trespassed on the time of the House. All I can say in apology is that I have endeavoured to keep closely to the topics which I had before me—

—immensum spatiis confecimus aequor,
Et jam tempus equum fumantia solvere colla.

These are the proposals of the Government. They may be approved or they may be condemned, but I have this full confidence, that it will be admitted that we have not sought to evade the difficulties of the position; that we have not concealed those difficulties either from ourselves or from others; that we have not attempted to counteract them by narrow or flimsy expedients; that we have prepared plans which, if you will adopt them, will go some way to close up many vexed financial questions which, if not now settled, may be attended with public inconvenience, and even with public danger, in future years and under less favourable circumstances; that we have endeavoured, in the plans we have now submitted to you, to make the path of our successors in future years not more arduous but more easy: and I may be permitted to add that, while we have sought to do justice to the great labour community of England by furthering their relief from indirect taxation, we have not been guided by any desire to put one class against another. We have felt we should best maintain our own honour, that we should best meet the views of Parliament, and best promote the interests of the country, by declining to draw any invidious distinction between class and class, by adopting it to ourselves as a sacred aim to diffuse and distribute the burdens with equal and impartial hand; and we have the consolation of believing that by proposals such as these we contribute, as far as in us lies, not only to develop the material resources of the country, but to knit the various parts of this great nation yet more closely than ever to that Throne and to those institutions under which it is our happiness to live.

Here indeed was an orator who could reconcile the spiritual and material interests of the age, and give a moral significance to dry details of finance and commerce. The scheme thus introduced astonished, interested, and attracted the country. The Queen and Prince Albert wrote to congratulate the Chancellor of the Exchequer. Public authorities and private friends joined in the chorus of eulogy. The Budget demonstrated at once its author's absolute mastery over figures, the persuasive force of his expository gift, his strange power of clothing the dry bones of customs and tariffs with the flesh and blood of human interest, and even something of the warm glow of poetic colour. It established the Chancellor of the Exchequer as the paramount financier of his day, and it was only the first of a long series of similar performances, different, of course, in detail, but alike in their bold outlines and brilliant handling. Probably Mr Gladstone's financial statements, taken as a whole, constitute the most remarkable testimony to his purely intellectual qualities which will be available for the guidance of posterity when it comes to assign his permanent place in the ranks of human greatness.

Looking back on a long life of strenuous exertion, Mr Gladstone declares that the work of preparing his proposals about the Succession Duty and carrying them through Parliament was by far the most laborious task which he ever performed.

Writing on May 22, 1853, Mr Greville records an interview with Sir James Graham, and a curious conversation:

Graham seemed in excellent spirits about their political state and prospects, all owing to Gladstone and the complete success of his Budget. The long and numerous Cabinets, which were attributed by the *Times* to disunion, were occupied in minute consideration of the Budget, which was there fully discussed; and Gladstone spoke in the Cabinet one day for three hours rehearsing his speech in the House of Commons, though not quite at such length ... He talked of a future head, as Aberdeen is always ready to retire at any moment; but it is very difficult to find anyone to succeed him. I suggested Gladstone. He shook his head and said it would not do … He spoke of the grand mistakes Derby had made. Gladstone's object certainly was for a long time to be at the head of the Conservative party in the House of Commons, and to join with Derby, who might, in fact, have had all the Peelites if he would have chosen to ally himself with them, instead of with Disraeli; thus the latter had been the cause of the ruin of the party. Graham thought that Derby had committed himself to Disraeli in George Bentinck's lifetime in some way which prevented his shaking him off, as it would have been his interest to do. The Peelites would have united with Derby, but would have nothing to do with Disraeli.

On November 3, 1853, Bishop Wilberforce, after a conversation with Mr (now Sir) Arthur Gordon, writes: 'Lord Aberdeen now growing to look upon Gladstone as his successor, and so told Gladstone the other day. Cabinet shaky.'

That the Budget of 1853 did not in the result secure for the public all the boons which it promised, was due to circumstances which, if not wholly unforeseen, were not generally foreseen in all the awful possibilities of evil which they opened to the gaze of a prescient few. Mr Gladstone's first Budget was prepared and presented on the eve of the Crimean War, and carried into effect amid all the horrors of that grim campaign.

VI

The Crimean War—Resignation—Ecclesiastical troubles—A free lance—The 'Arrow'—The Divorce Bill—Opposition to Lord Palmerston—Declines to join Tory Government—Lord High Commissioner to the Ionian Islands—Chancellor of the Exchequer in Whig Government—The French Treaty and the Paper Duties—Conflict with the House of Lords—Opinion on the American War

MR BRIGHT WAS ONCE WALKING with one of his sons—then a schoolboy—past the Guards' monument in Waterloo Place. The boy caught sight of the solitary word 'CRIMEA' inscribed on the base, and asked his father what it meant. Mr Bright's answer was as emphatic as the inscription—'A CRIME.' It was indeed a crime, a grave, a disastrous, and a wanton crime, that committed Christian England to a war in defence of the great anti-Christian Power. By what processes Mr Gladstone became and remained involved in such accountability is a subject of interesting but painful and perhaps profitless inquiry.

The history of the war may be briefly told. For nearly forty years Europe had enjoyed the sunshine of unbroken peace. Towards the end of 1852 a little cloud, no bigger than a man's hand, was seen to hover over the Holy Places of Jerusalem. The Greek and Roman Churches contended for the custody of these sacred spots which are associated with the most august events of Christian history, and are therefore in some sense the common heritage of the whole Christian family. The claims of the rival Churches were supported respectively by Russia and France, and to this cause of dispute was soon added a formal claim on the part of the Czar to a Protectorate over all the Greek subjects of the Porte. On July 2 and 3, 1853, the Russians crossed the Pruth, and occupied the Danubian principalities, which by the Treaty of Balta Liman (1849) were to be evacuated by the forces both of the Czar and the Sultan, and not to be entered by either except for the repression of internal disturbance. In this conjuncture England might have taken one or other of two courses, either of which, if plainly announced and persistently followed, would probably have averted war. The alternatives were to inform Turkey that England would render her no assistance, or to warn Russia that, if she went to war, England would fight for Turkey. But here the inherent weakness of the coalition, founded on an attempted amalgamation of really immiscible elements, produced a fatal indecision. Lord Aberdeen wished England to stand aloof; Lord Palmerston and Lord John Russell wished her to support Turkey; and, generally speaking, the Peelite members of the Government were a shade more pacific than the Whigs. Thus halting between two opinions, the country 'drifted into war' with Russia, and the fatal step was formally announced to Parliament on March 27, 1854. It thus fell to the lot of the most pacific of Ministers, the devotee of retrenchment, and the anxious cultivator of all industrial arts, to prepare a War Budget, and to meet as well as he might the exigencies of a conflict which had so cruelly dislocated all the ingenious devices of financial optimism.

No amount of skill in the manipulation of figures, no ingenuity in shifting fiscal burdens, could prevent the addition of forty-one millions to the national debt, or could countervail the appalling mismanagement which was rampant at the seat of war. The paralysis which springs from divided counsels seemed to have affected the whole of our military administration. To the inseparable evils of war—bloodshed and sickness—were added the horrors of a peculiarly cruel winter, and a vast amount of unnecessary privation and hardship, due to divided responsibility and to an inconceivable clumsiness of organization. England lost some twenty-four thousand men, of whom five-sixths died from preventable disease, and the want of proper food, clothing and shelter. Well might Mr Gladstone declare that the state of the army in the Crimea was 'a matter for weeping all day and praying all night.' But the critics of the Government were not disposed to content themselves with tears and prayers. Their sentiments took the more homely and more inconvenient form of what was practically a vote of censure. As soon as Parliament met in January, 1855, Mr Roebuck, the Radical member for Sheffield, gave notice that he would move for a Select Committee 'to enquire into the condition of our army before Sebastopol, and into the conduct of those departments of the Government whose duty it has been to minister to the wants of that army.' On the same day Lord John Russell, without announcing his intention to his colleagues, resigned his office as Lord President of the Council, sooner than attempt the defence of the Government. It is only fair to Lord John to say that he had long been unsuccessfully urging upon his colleagues the need of greater activity and better organization, and that he honestly felt that the conduct which he would be called upon to defend was indefensible. But this fact did not make his sudden resignation, in face of a hostile motion, less embarrassing to his colleagues; and Mr Gladstone, in defending the Government against Mr Roebuck, rebuked in dignified and significant terms the conduct of men who, 'hoping to escape from punishment, ran away from duty.' But the case against Ministers was so overwhelmingly strong that all the resources of dialectical ingenuity were powerless to withstand it; and, on the division on Mr Roebuck's motion, the Government was beaten by the unexpected majority of 157.

Thus perished Lord Aberdeen's Ministry, amid circumstances that justified the remarkable warning with which Mr Disraeli had greeted its birth—'England does not love coalitions.'

Lord Derby essayed to form a Ministry, but the Peelites would not join him, nor would their adhesion have been welcome to his own followers. Lord John Russell, though the Queen applied to him, was obviously impossible; and Lord Palmerston became Prime Minister. The Peelites joined him, and Mr Gladstone resumed office as Chancellor of the Exchequer. A shrewd observer at the time pronounced him 'indispensable. Any other Chancellor of the Exchequer would be torn in bits by him.' This was the first time that he had served under a Whig chief. It was a marked step in the road towards Liberalism. The Government was formed on the understanding that Mr Roebuck's proposed Committee was to be resisted. Lord Palmerston soon saw that further resistance was useless. His Peelite colleagues stuck to their text, and, within three weeks after resuming office, Mr Gladstone, Sir James Graham, and Mr Sidney Herbert resigned. From this time forward, Mr Gladstone had of course no direct or official responsibility for the war, though he defended the policy which had dictated it, and the general lines on which it had been pursued, in more than one impressive and well-argued speech. More than twenty years after the conclusion of peace, he vindicated his share in the unhappy business, in a careful and elaborate essay, in which, without professing an absolute confidence in the wisdom of his action, he sought to prove that, in its inception, the Crimean War was wise and good, and was rendered necessary by the actual state of Europe. 'The design of the Crimean War was, in its groundwork, the vindication of European law against an unprovoked aggression. It sought, therefore, to maintain intact the condition of the menaced party against the aggressor; or, in other words, to defend against Russia the integrity and independence of the Ottoman Empire.' From the doctrine of public duty thus suggested, Englishmen who are jealous of the Christian honour of their country, and who revere Mr Gladstone as the foremost champion of that honour in domestic and foreign relations, may appeal to the authority of one whom even he calls master.

> I have never before heard it held forth (said Mr Burke) that the Turkish Empire has ever been considered as any part of the balance of power in Europe. They despise and condemn all Christian princes as infidels, and only wish to subdue and exterminate them and their people! What have these worse than savages to do

with the Powers of Europe, but to spread war, destruction, and pestilence amongst them? The Ministers and the policy which shall give these people any weight in Europe will deserve all the bans and curses of posterity.

When, in February, 1855, Mr Gladstone resigned, or, as he now tells us was the case, was 'driven' from office, his position was one of peculiar isolation, and his political prospects were involved in profound uncertainty. The degree and nature of this uncertainty are well illustrated by the record, lately given to the world, of a conversation which took place at the time between two experienced lookers-on, Mr Nassau Senior and Sir Frederic Elliot. It is worth recalling, if only to show the innate and incurable fallibility of the political prophet:

'As to the secession,' Elliot said, 'of Herbert and Gladstone, it is a great blow to the future Government and a prodigious accession to the Tories.'

* * * *

'Will Gladstone,' I said, 'oust Disraeli? Will he be able, as soon as he crosses the floor of the House, to assume the command of his old enemies?'

'Not immediately,' said Elliot. 'He will at first take a neutral position. He will protect the Government, but from time to time candidly admit its shortcomings, and gradually, from damaging them by his support, will slide into damaging them by his attacks, until Dizzy is deposed and Herbert, and Gladstone, and Cardwell become the leaders of the Opposition without anybody's knowing how it was done.'

'Dizzy,' I said, 'will scarcely submit to be so blandly absorbed. If the Tories throw him off he will return to his early love, the Radicals.'

'He may try it,' said Elliot, 'but he will fail. They will not accept him. He is purely a rhetorician, and a rhetorician powerful only in attack. He wants knowledge, he wants the habits of patient investigation by which it is to be acquired, he wants sincerity, he wants public spirit, he wants tact, he wants birth, he wants fortune: he wants, in short, nine out of ten of the qualities that fit a man to lead a party. Nothing but the penury of talent among the Tories after the secession of the Peelites gave him importance. If the Peelites rejoin their old associates, he is lost.'*

But, happily for Mr Disraeli, the Peelites did not 'join their old associates.' Released from office, Mr Gladstone assumed the position of an influential private member, belonging to neither party, but related in some degree to both;

---

* 'Behind the Scenes in English Politics,' by the late Nassau W. Senior (*Nineteenth Century*, September 1890).

and, while not immediately available for construction and defence, more than ever dreaded in criticism and attack. 'His sympathies,' he himself said, were 'with Conservatives, his opinions with Liberals': a dangerous dichotomy for both parties involved.

In the August of this year Lord Aberdeen said:

> Gladstone intends to be Prime Minister. He has great qualifications, but some serious defects: the chief, that when he has convinced himself, perhaps by abstract reasoning, of some view, he thinks everyone else ought at once to see it as he does, and can make no allowance for difference of opinion. Gladstone must thoroughly recover his popularity. This unpopularity is merely temporary. He is supreme in the House of Commons. The Queen has quite got over her feeling against him, and likes him much ... I have told Gladstone that when he is Prime Minister, I will have a seat in his Cabinet if he desires it, without an office.

Two interesting conversations with Sir James Graham may here be noticed. On April 3, 1856, Mr Greville writes:

> Yesterday, I met Graham ... He began talking over the state of affairs generally ... He says there is not one man in the House of Commons who has ten followers—neither Gladstone, nor Disraeli, nor Palmerston ... that Gladstone is certainly the ablest man there ... His religious opinions, in which he is zealous and sincere, enter so largely into his political conduct as to form a very serious obstacle to his success, for they are abhorrent to the majority of this Protestant country, and (I was rather surprised to hear him say) Graham thinks approach very nearly to Rome. Gladstone would have nothing to do with any Government unless he were leader in the House of Commons ... Disraeli appears to be endeavouring to approach Gladstone, and *a confederacy between those two and young Stanley* (now Lord Derby) *is by no means an improbability.*

In connexion with Sir James Graham's remarks on Mr Gladstone's religious opinions, the following letter may be read with interest. Archdeacon Denison had been prosecuted for teaching the doctrine of the Real Presence in the Holy Eucharist, and was condemned by Dr Lushington, acting as assessor to Archbishop Sumner. With reference to this judgment Mr Gladstone writes on August 18, 1856:

> Whatever comes of it, two things are pretty plain: the first, that not only with executive authorities, but in the sacred halls of justice, there are now two measures and not one in use—the straight one for those supposed to err in believing overmuch, and the other for those who believe too little. The second, that this is another blow to the dogmatic principle in the Established Church: the principle

on which, as a Church, it rests, and on which, as an establishment, it seems less and less permitted to rest. No hasty judgment is pardonable in these matters, but for the last ten or twelve years undoubtedly the skies have been darkening for a storm.

On the 23rd of August he writes:

The stewards of doctrine should, on the general ground of controversy and disturbance, deliver from their pulpits or as they think fit, to the people the true and substantive doctrine of the Holy Eucharist. This freely done, and without any notice of the Archbishop or Dr Lushington, I should think far better for the time than any declaration ...

It is high time that there should be a careful argument upon the justice and morality of late ecclesiastical proceedings; that the Archbishop should be awakened out of his fool's paradise, and made to understand that, though reverence for his office has up to this time, in a wonderful manner, kept people silent about his proceedings, yet the time has come when a beginning must be made towards describing them without circumlocution in their true colours; and it must likewise be shown how judicial proceedings are governed by extra-judicial considerations, and a system is growing up under which ecclesiastical judges are becoming the virtual legislators of the Church, while its legislature is silent.

On September 27, 1856, Bishop Wilberforce, writing at Netherby, notes Sir James Graham's views of Mr Gladstone thus:

In the highest sense of the word *Liberal*; of the greatest power, very much the first man in the House of Commons. Detested by the aristocracy for his succession-duty—the most truly Conservative measure passed in my recollection. 'Just reading De Tocqueville, and when I read his statement that unequal taxation was the most effective of all the causes of the Revolution, I thought at once of Gladstone and his succession-duty. He must rise to the lead in such a Government as ours, even in spite of all that hatred to him ... Gladstone must rise; he is young, he is by far the ablest man in the House of Commons, and, in it, in the long run, the ablest man must lead.

Mr Gladstone has said of himself and of his Peelite colleagues, during this period of political isolation, that they were like roving icebergs, on which men could not land with safety, but with which ships might come into perilous collision. Their weight was too great not to count, but it counted first this way and then that. 'It is not alleged against them that their conduct was dishonourable, but their public action was attended with much public in convenience.' In the autumn of 1856 he is reported to have said to an intimate friend: 'It would be a great gain if I and Sidney Herbert and Graham could be taken out of the House, and let them shake up the bag and make new combinations. If Lord Derby and Lord Aberdeen understood one another, all would be easy. Palmerston has never been a successful Minister—great love of power, and even stronger a principle of false shame, cares not how much dirt he eats, but it must be gilded dirt. Palmerston is strong in the House of Commons, but he does not understand the House of Commons.' The friend to whom these disclosures were made adds this comment: 'Manifestly Gladstone leans to a Conservative alliance. The Conservative is the best chance for the Church.' And a few months later Lord Malmesbury writes: 'Gladstone and Sidney Herbert appear anxious to join Lord Derby.'

But in whatever direction his leanings lay, it is evident that he was very little disposed to be friendly to the Whig Government. He was a peculiarly acute thorn in the side of the Chancellor of the Exchequer, and criticized the Budgets with unsparing vigour. 'Gladstone seems bent on leading Sir George Lewis a weary life,' wrote Mr Greville. But finance was by no means the only subject which excited the pugnacious ardour of this terrible free-lance. Armed *cap-à-pie* with his panoply of knowledge, dialectic, and eloquence, he ranged over the wide plains of foreign and domestic policy, now threatening the most impassioned resistance to the imposition of heavier duties on the working man's tea and sugar, now championing the cause of religious and voluntary education against Lord John Russell's very moderate endeavours after a national system; one day denouncing the secret enlistment of American soldiers under the English flag, and another repudiating the high-handed behaviour of the English authorities towards the Chinese in the matter of the lorcha *Arrow*.

The debate on the last-named subjects proved fatal to the Government.

Mr Greville writes on March 4: 'A majority of sixteen against Government, more than any of them expected. A magnificent speech of Gladstone. Palmerston's speech is said to have been very dull in the first part, and very bow-wow in the second.' In consequence of the ministerial defeat, Parliament was dissolved on March 21, 1857. The General Election resulted in a majority for Lord Palmerston. Mr Gladstone was returned unopposed for the University of Oxford. On June 3 Mr Greville writes: 'Gladstone hardly ever goes near the House of Commons, and never opens his lips.' But this silence was not destined to last long. In the later part of the session Mr Gladstone's great powers and peculiar knowledge found abundant and congenial employment in strenuous opposition to the infamous Divorce Bill which had come down from the House of Lords. He spoke more than seventy times on the various stages of the Bill, endeavouring first to defeat it on the clear issue of principle, then to postpone it for more mature consideration, and, when beaten in these attempts, to purge it of its most glaringly offensive features. The debates were marked by some passages of arms between him and the Attorney-General, Sir Richard Bethell (afterwards Lord Chancellor Westbury), which were highly characteristic of the two men. The main ground of Mr Gladstone's opposition to the Bill was the highest. Marriage was not only or chiefly a civil contract, but a 'mystery' of the Christian religion. By the law of God it could not be so annulled as to permit of the re-marriage of the parties. Not content with his energetic and multiform resistance to the Bill in Parliament, he fought it in the Press. He contributed to the July number of the *Quarterly Review* an elaborate essay, which was freely quoted in the debate, and in which he argued the case against divorce with immense force and learning. 'Our Lord,' he says, 'has emphatically told us that, at and from the beginning, marriage was perpetual, and was on both sides single.' Again: 'Christian marriage is, according to Holy Scripture, a lifelong compact, which may sometimes be put in abeyance by the separation of a couple, but which can never be rightfully dissolved so as to set them free during their joint lives to unite with other persons.' He dwelt with pathetic force on the injustice between man and woman of the proposed legislation, which would entitle the husband to divorce from an unfaithful wife, but would give no corresponding protection to the woman and predicted the gloomiest consequences to the conjugal morality of the country from the erection of this new and odious tribunal. The general soundness of these views and these anticipations he deliberately vindicated after a lapse of twenty-one years.

But learning, eloquence, moral sentiment, and, above all, arguments from the New Testament and ecclesiastical tradition, were thrown away upon a Government over which Lord Palmerston presided. The Divorce Court was duly established; and it is significant of Mr Gladstone's state of mind at this season that, in the autumn of the year, he said to the friend who has been quoted before: 'I greatly felt being turned out of office. I saw great things to do. I longed to do them. I am losing the best years of my life out of my natural service. Yet I have never ceased to rejoice that I am not in office with Palmerston, when I have seen the tricks, the shufflings, the frauds he daily has recourse to as to his business. I rejoice not to sit on the Treasury Bench with him.'

Ecclesiastical difficulties occupied at this time a great share of Mr Gladstone's attention. The conduct of some of the Bishops in respect of the Divorce Act had been little less than scandalous, and he seems to have been painfully impressed by the weakness of the Church of England in her capacity of *Ecclesia Docens*, and by the need of some competent tribunal to express her authoritative judgment on disputed questions of doctrine and of ecclesiastical procedure. The following letter of Mr Gladstone's may be profitably read in connexion with Sir James Graham's remark on his religious opinions quoted a few pages farther back:

November 2, 1857—It is neither disestablishment, nor even loss of dogmatic truth, which I look upon as the greater danger before us, but it is the loss of those elementary principles of right and wrong on which Christianity itself must be built. The present position of the Church of England is gradually approximating to the Erastian theory that the business of an establishment is to teach all sorts of doctrines and to provide Christian ordinances by way of comfort for all sorts of people, to be used at their own option. It must become, if uncorrected, in lapse of time a thoroughly immoral position. Her case seems as if it were like that of Cranmer—to be disgraced first and then burned. Now, what I feel is that the Constitution of the Church provides the means of bringing controversy to issue; not means that can be brought at all times, but means that are to be effectually, though less determinately, available for preventing the general devastation of doctrine, either by a positive heresy, or by that thesis I have named above, worse than any heresy. Considering that the condition of the Church with respect to doctrine is gradually growing into an offence to the moral sense of mankind, and that the question is, Shall we get, if we can, the means of giving expression to her mind? I confess that I cannot be repelled by fears connected with the state of the episcopal body from saying, Yes. Let me have it if I can. For, regarding the Church as a privileged and endowed body, no less than as one with spiritual prerogatives, I feel these two things: *If the mind of those who rule and of those who compose the Church is deliberately anti-Catholic, I have no right to seek a hiding-place within the pale of her possessions by keeping her in a condition of voicelessness*, in which all are entitled to be there, because none are. That is, viewing her with respect to the enjoyment of her temporal advantages; spiritually, how can her life be saved by stopping her from the exercise of functions essential to her condition? It may be said, she is sick—wait till she is well. My answer is, she is getting more and more sick in regard to her own function of authoritatively declaring the truth; let us see whether her being called upon so to declare it may not be the remedy, or a remedy at least. I feel certain that the want of combined and responsible ecclesiastical action is one of the main evils, and that the regular duty of such action will tend to check the spirit of individualism, and to restore that belief in a Church which we have almost lost. The Bishops will act much *better* from acting in the way proposed, and the very law which commits it to them so to act will in itself not only do much for the ecclesiastical principles of our Constitution, but still more, I believe, for the healthiness of our moral tone. I can bear the reproaches of those who say, 'You believe so and so; you have no business to believe that here: go elsewhere and believe it if you please.' I know that it would be much more just to retort them. But if I felt that I am myself trying to gag the Church of England, or to keep in her mouth the gag that is now there I should not feel so sure that honesty was not compromised in my own measure by me. It is, in a word, the desire that honesty should be maintained at all costs which governs me in the main, and would govern me even if I saw less than I seem to do of conservative and restorative action in the measure itself.

When Parliament met in February, 1858, Lord Palmerston introduced a Bill to amend the law of conspiracy to murder. An attempt made by an Italian refugee—Felice Orsini—on the life of the Emperor Napoleon had created general consternation, and the adherents of the Emperor were loud in declaring that foreign conspirators in London were left unmolested by the authorities while they planned the murderous plots which they carried out in foreign capitals. To meet this reproach, Lord Palmerston proposed to make conspiracy to murder a felony, punishable with five years' penal servitude. This proposal was strenuously opposed from various quarters of the House, and mainly on the ground that the English Government had been actuated by an unduly anxious desire to execute the behests of the Emperor. Mr Gladstone and the Peelites joined the Conservatives and a considerable number of the Liberals in opposing the Bill, and it was defeated by a majority of nineteen. Lord Palmerston resigned. Lord Derby succeeded him, with Mr Disraeli as Chancellor of the Exchequer and Leader of the House of Commons.

Mr Gladstone was now thoroughly out of harmony with Lord Palmerston, and in the April number of the *Quarterly Review* he expressed his strong dissent from the French policy of the late Government, and especially from the 'ill-starred and detested measure' for altering the law of conspiracy. Lord Palmerston, he said, had kept his seat on the top of Fortune's wheel, 'during such a number of its revolutions, as had all but covered what may be termed the utmost space allowed to the activity of human life. But suddenly a difficulty that he himself had created, as if for the purpose, by a contempt of the most ordinary caution and the best-established customs, caught him in his giddy elevation, and precipitated the old favourite of millions into the depths of the Tartarus of politics, almost without a solitary cry of regret to mingle in the crash of his fall, or a word of sympathy to break its force.'

It is said that Lord Derby, when he formed his Administration, had offered Mr Gladstone the post of Secretary of State for the Colonies, and when, a few months later, in consequence of difficulties arising out of the Indian Mutiny, Lord Ellenborough resigned the Presidency of the Board of Control, we have it on high authority that the most strenuous efforts were made to induce Mr Gladstone to fill the vacant place in the Cabinet.

Mr Greville writes on May 23, 1858:

Derby will get Gladstone if possible to take the India Board, and this will be the best thing that can happen. His natural course is to be at the head of a Conservative Government, and he may, if he acts with prudence, be the means of raising that party to something like dignity and authority, and emancipating it from its dependence on the discreditable and insincere support of the Radicals.

Writing in 1862 to Bishop Wilberforce, Lord Beaconsfield said, 'I wish you could have induced Gladstone to have joined Lord Derby's Government when Lord Ellenborough resigned in 1858. It was not my fault that he did not: I almost went on my knees to him.'

This is a truly Disraelish touch: the astute old schemer 'almost on his knees' to his dreaded and detested rival, imploring him to take a prominent place in the Cabinet of which he was himself the ruling spirit. It is a delightful picture, and the reason for the genuflexion is not far to seek. The Leader of the House of Commons, if he is a man of character and intellect, is in fact the Prime Minister. And if Mr Disraeli could have induced Mr Gladstone to become his colleague and submit to his leadership, he would have had the satisfaction of knowing that the one contemporary statesman whose powers and ambition were equal to his own was subordinated, in all probability for ever, to his own imperious will. When a man joins a political party in his fiftieth year, he cannot easily forsake it. Mr Gladstone, if he became a Liberal, would challenge, and probably attain, the supreme place in Parliament. If he returned to the Tories, with Mr Disraeli leading the House, he would be doomed to a position which, however high, was still less than the highest. There was indeed a grotesque idea of sending Mr Disraeli to India as Governor-General. Had the field been thus left clear, it seems probable that Mr Gladstone would have returned to his old associations, becoming Chancellor of the Exchequer in the Tory Government, and Leader of the House of Commons. Events, however, were otherwise ordered, and Mr Disraeli continued to block the way.

Though he saw, and prudently declined, the snare obligingly set for him by a master of parliamentary manoeuvre, Mr Gladstone, unhampered by binding alliance with any political party, was at liberty to give to Lord Derby's Government his valuable support in debate whenever he deemed that they deserved it; but, lest the entertainment should partake of sameness, he appeared not seldom in the character of the candid friend. During the course of the Session, we find Bishop Wilberforce, after a talk with Lord Aberdeen, making the significant entry in his journal 'Gladstone getting more averse to Disraeli.' On October 16, this conversation with Lord Aberdeen is recorded:

'Will Gladstone ever rise to the first place?'

'Yes; I have no doubt he will. But gradually, after an interval. He must turn the hatred of many into affection first; and he *will* turn it if he has the opportunity given him. Gladstone has some faults to overcome. He is too obstinate. If a man could be too honest, I should say he is too honest. He does not enough think of what other men think.' ...

'Whom is he to head?'

'Oh! it is impossible to say! Time must show, and new combinations. I told

John Russell that what I wished to see was, him in the House of Lords at the head of the Government, and Gladstone leading the Commons ... He could *trust* Gladstone in such a post, which he could hardly any other man.'

When a Government exists by sufferance and has to reckon on the periodical criticisms of a candid friend who is also a most formidable debater, prudence dictates to get him, if possible, out of the way; and it was probably with this view that in 1858 Lord Derby asked Mr Gladstone to go out as Lord High Commissioner Extraordinary to the Ionian Isles. The inhabitants of these islands, which had been since 1815 under English protection, desired to unite themselves to Greece. The task of governing them from England had become difficult, and Mr Gladstone was commissioned to examine into grievances and to report to the Government at home. He went out full of sympathy with the people, well acquainted with their history, and keenly alive to all their interests and associations.

On December 3, he addressed the Senate of the Ionian Islands at Corfu, speaking in Italian. He announced that 'the liberties guaranteed by the Treaties of Paris, and by Ionian law, are, in the eyes of her Majesty, sacred. On the other hand, the purpose for which she has sent me is not to enquire into the British Protectorate, but to examine in what way Great Britain may most honourably and amply discharge the obligations which, for purposes European and Ionian rather than British, she has contracted.' He concluded with a characteristic aspiration for the happiness of the Ionian people, to be secured by 'the double union of freedom with public order, and of knowledge with the Christian faith.' The Lord High Commissioner Extraordinary made an official tour of the islands, holding levees, receiving deputations, and delivering harangues. He promised a full enquiry into every grievance, and offered an elaborate system of constitutional government, which Lord Aberdeen called fanciful. The Ionians, however, had one, and only one, object—they wished to be united with Greece. The Legislative Assembly of the Ionian Islands, sitting at Corfu, voted an address to the Queen praying for the annexation of their republic to Greece. The Lord High Commissioner despatched their petition to the Queen, and then, having fulfilled his mission, returned to England.

A story highly characteristic both of Mr Gladstone's severe regard for public economy, and of the late Lord Lytton's taste for display, is told in connexion with this mission. Mr Gladstone had taken the utmost pains to keep down the expenses of the mission, and was congratulating himself on his success, when, just towards the end, the Colonial Secretary, Sir Edward Bulwer Lytton, as he then was, desired that a special steamer might be chartered in order to convey a despatch to the Lord High Commissioner, and the cost of this steamer of course dislocated all Mr Gladstone's economical schemes.

When the Queen opened Parliament on February 3, 1859, she announced in the Speech from the Throne that the attention of the Legislature would be called to the state of the law regulating the representation of the people. On the 28th, Mr Disraeli unfolded the ministerial plan. It was a fanciful performance. The Government, said the Chancellor of the Exchequer, proposed, not to alter the limits of the franchise, but to introduce into boroughs a new kind of franchise founded on personal property, and to give a vote to persons having property to the amount of £10 a year in the Funds, Bank Stock, and East India Stock. Persons having £60 in a Savings Bank would, under the Bill, be electors for the borough in which they resided; as also recipients of pensions in the naval, military, and civil services, amounting to £20 a year. Lodgers, graduates, ministers of religion, solicitors, doctors, and schoolmasters were, under certain conditions, enfranchised, and the Government proposed to recognize the principle of identity of suffrage between the counties and towns. Two members of the Government promptly resigned rather than be parties to these proposals. Lord John Russell moved an amendment condemning interference with the franchise which enabled freeholders in boroughs to vote in counties, and demanding a wider extension of the suffrage in boroughs. Mr Gladstone, though agreeing with Lord John in these particulars, declined to support the amendment, because, if carried, it would upset the Government and bring in a weaker Administration. He did not profess to support the Government, but he desired to see a settlement of the question of reform, and he thought the present opportunity advantageous for such settlement. He pleaded eloquently for the retention of the small boroughs. He voted, therefore, for the second reading of the Bill, but it was lost by a majority of thirty-nine. Lord Derby advised the Queen to dissolve Parliament, and this was done on April 23. Mr Gladstone was returned unopposed for the University of Oxford. The first Session of the new Parliament was opened by the Queen on June 7. An amendment to the Address in reply to the Speech from the Throne was moved, in a maiden speech, by Lord Hartington. It was simply a vote of want of confidence in the Ministers. After three nights' debate, it was carried on June 10 by a majority of thirteen, Mr Gladstone voting with the Government. Lord Derby and his colleagues immediately resigned. The Queen, naturally averse to the 'invidious and unwelcome task' of choosing between Lord Palmerston and Lord John Russell, turned, in her perplexity, to Lord Granville, who led the Liberal party in the House of Lords. He failed to form an Administration, and Lord Palmerston again became Prime Minister. Lord John Russell joined him as Foreign Secretary, and Mr Gladstone as Chancellor of the Exchequer. A spirited opposition to Mr Gladstone's candidature was immediately organized at Oxford. Lord Chandos, afterwards last Duke of Buckingham, came forward as the Conservative candidate. Professor Mansel, afterwards Dean of St Paul's, was chairman of his committee. The traditions of the University forbade the candidates to address the electors by word of mouth, but Mr Mansel issued a manifesto in which this passage occurred:

> By his acceptance of office, Mr Gladstone must now be considered as giving his definite adhesion to the Liberal party, as at present reconstructed, and as approving of the policy of those who overthrew Lord Derby's Government on the late division. By his vote on that division, Mr Gladstone expressed his confidence in the Administration of Lord Derby. By accepting office, he now expresses his confidence in the Administration of Lord Derby's opponent and successor.

Mr Gladstone naturally took a very different view of this rather complicated transaction, and he explained it in a long and elaborate letter to Dr Hawkins, the Provost of Oriel:

> Various differences of opinion (he said), both on foreign and domestic matters, separated me, during great part of the Administration of Lord Palmerston, from a body of men with the majority of whom I had acted, and had acted in perfect harmony, under Lord Aberdeen. I promoted the vote of the House of Commons, in February of last year, which led to the downfall of that Ministry. Such having been the case, I thought it my clear duty to support, as far as I was able, the Government of Lord Derby. Accordingly, on the various occasions during the existence of the late Parliament when they were seriously threatened with danger of embarrassment, I found myself, like many other independent members, lending them such assist as was in my power. And, although I could not concur in the late Reform Bill, and considered the dissolution to be singularly ill-advised, I still was unwilling to found on such disapproval a vote in favour of the motion of Lord Hartington, which appeared to imply a course of previous opposition, and which has been the immediate cause of the change of Ministers. Under these circumstances, it was, I think, manifest that, while I had not the smallest claim on the Victorious party, my duty as towards the late advisers of the Crown had been fully discharged. It is hardly needful to say that, previously to the recent vote, there was no negotiation or understanding with me in regard to office; but when Lord Palmerston had undertaken to form a Cabinet, he acquainted me with his desire that I should join it ...
>
> With respect to reform, I understood, the counsels of Mr Walpole and Mr Henley, and I believe if they had been followed the subject of would in all likelihood have been settled at this date, without either a dissolution of Parliament or a change of Administration. But I have never understood the principles on which that subject has been managed since the schism in the late Government. I also think it undeniable that the fact of the dissolution, together with the return of an adverse and now no longer indulgent majority,

rendered the settlement of this question by the late Ministers impossible. I therefore naturally turn to the hope of its being settled by a Cabinet mainly constituted and led by the men together with whom I was responsible for framing and proposing a Reform Bill in 1854 ...

I understand that misgiving exists with respect to my sitting in a Cabinet of which Mr Gibson is a member, and which Mr Cobden is invited to join. The very same feelings were expressed, as I well recollect, when the late Sir William Molesworth entered the Cabinet of Lord Aberdeen. Sir William Molesworth never, to my knowledge, compromised his political independence; and these apprehensions were, I think, not justified by the subsequent course of events ...

Were I permitted the mode of address usual upon elections, I should, after this preliminary explanation, proceed to submit with confidence to my constituents that, as their representative, I have acted according to the obligations which their choice and favour brought upon me, and that the Ministry which has thought fit to desire my co-operation is entitled in my person, as well as otherwise, to be exempt from condemnation at the first moment of its existence. Its title to this extent is perhaps the more clear, because among its early as well as its very gravest duties will be the proposal of a Reform Bill which, if it be accepted by Parliament, must lead, after no long interval, to a fresh general appeal to the people, and will thus afford a real opportunity of judging whether public men associated in the present Cabinet have or have not forfeited by that act, or by its legitimate consequences, any confidence of which they may previously have been thought worthy.

The contest was brisk and animated, and when the poll closed Mr Gladstone was returned by a majority of 191 over Lord Chandos. He had polled twenty-eight more votes than on taking office in 1853, and his opponent thirty-six less. His separation from his old party was now complete. His hand was fairly set to the plough, and there was no more looking back. He had taken suit and service with the Liberals, and henceforward his growth in the principles of freedom and progress was to be continuous and often rapid.

It is interesting to observe that the brilliant convert from Toryism soon became allied by a bond of peculiar sympathy with the Nestor of the Whigs; and in the most crucial questions which engaged the attention of the Cabinet Lord John Russell and Mr Gladstone agreed with and supported one another. Mr Gladstone worked heartily, alike in the Cabinet and the House, for the Reform Bill on which Lord John Russell had set his affections; and Lord John shared Mr Gladstone's dislike of the immense expenditure on fortifications which Lord Palmerston compelled his colleagues to undertake. With reference to Mr Gladstone's scruples on this subject, Lord Palmerston wrote this amazing letter to the Queen: 'Viscount Palmerston hopes to be able to overcome his objections, but, if that should prove impossible, however great the loss to the Government by the retirement of Mr Gladstone, it would he better to lose Mr Gladstone than to run the risk of losing Portsmouth or Plymouth.'

Not less extraordinary is the mode in which the Prime Minister announced to the Sovereign that his colleague's scruples had been overcome. 'Mr Gladstone told Viscount Palmerston this evening that he wished it to be understood that, though acquiescing in the step now taken about the fortifications, he kept himself free to take such course as he may think fit upon that subject next year to which Viscount Palmerston entirely assented. That course will probably be the same which Mr Gladstone has taken this year—namely, ineffectual opposition and ultimate acquiescence.'

To this period belongs the following grotesque passage from Lord Malmesbury's diary: 'Gladstone, who was always fond of music, is now quite enthusiastic about negro melodies, singing them with the greatest spirit and enjoyment, never leaving out a verse, and evidently preferring such as "Camp Town Races."'

Having been elected Lord Rector of the University of Edinburgh, he was installed in office, on April 16, 1860, and delivered his inaugural address on the Work of Universities. From singing nigger melodies, to discoursing on the possibilities of higher education and preparing financial statements, the transition is certainly abrupt, but all forms of effort seem to have been equally natural to the versatile Chancellor of the Exchequer. The Prince Consort writes: 'Gladstone is now the real Leader of the House of Commons, and works with an energy and vigour altogether incredible.'

The Budget of 1860 was marked by two distinctive features. It asked the sanction of Parliament to the commercial treaty which Mr Cobden, acting in the first instance on his own responsibility, had privately arranged with the Emperor Napoleon, and it proposed the abolition of the duty on paper. By the commercial treaty France undertook to remove all prohibitory duties on British manufactures, and to reduce the duties on our raw materials; while England was to abolish duties on foreign manufactures, and to reduce the duties on foreign wines.

On February 15 Mr Greville writes:

> When I left London a fortnight ago the world was anxiously expecting Gladstone's speech, in which he was to put the commercial Treaty and the Budget before the world. His own confidence and that of most of his colleagues in his success was unbounded, but many inveighed bitterly against the Treaty, and looked forward with great alarm and aversion to the Budget. Clarendon shook his head, Overstone pronounced against the Treaty, the *Times* thundered against it, and there is little doubt that it was unpopular, and becoming more so every day. Then came Gladstone's unlucky illness, which compelled him to put off his *exposé*, and

made it doubtful whether he would not be physically disabled from doing justice to the subject. His doctor says he ought to have taken two months' rest instead of two days. However, at the end of his two days' delay he came forth, and *consensu omnium* achieved one of the greatest triumphs that the House of Commons ever witnessed. Everybody I have heard from admits that it was a magnificent display, not to be surpassed in ability of execution, and that he carried the House of Commons completely with him. I can well believe it, for when I read the report of it next day it carried me along with it likewise.

February 22.—I returned to town on Monday. The same night a battle took place in the House of Commons, in which Gladstone signally defeated Disraeli, and Government got so good a majority that it looks like the harbinger of complete success for their Treaty and their Budget. Everybody agrees nothing could be more brilliant and complete than Gladstone's triumph.

February 26.—On Friday night Gladstone had another great triumph. He made a splendid speech, and maintained a majority of 116, which puts an end to the contest. He is now the great man of the day ... Clarendon, who watches him and has means of knowing his disposition, thinks that he is moving towards a Democratic union with Bright, the effect of which will be increased income-tax, and lowering the Estimates by giving up the defences of the country.

A second feature of the Budget, scarcely less important than the Treaty with France, was the abolition of the duty on paper. That duty was a heavy tax on knowledge. To abolish it would be to make the production of all books easier and cheaper, and particularly to quicken the development of cheap newspapers. Vague alarms were aroused. Obscurantism and reaction did their best to perplex the public mind. All the forces which dread the spread of knowledge among the masses of mankind took up arms against Mr Gladstone's proposal, and made common cause with the manufacturers of paper and the proprietors of expensive newspapers. Manufacturers and proprietors organized themselves in defence of their lucrative monopolies. The ministerial proposal was not enthusiastically supported in the House of Commons: the second reading of the Bill had been carried by fifty-three, the third was carried by nine. In reference to this diminution of support the Queen received from Lord Palmerston a letter even more grossly disloyal to his colleague than those already quoted:

> This may probably encourage the House of Lords to throw out the Bill when it comes to their House, and Viscount Palmerston is bound in duty to say that, if they do so, they will perform a good public service. Circumstances have greatly changed since the measure was agreed to by the Cabinet, and although it would undoubtedly have been difficult for the Government to have given up

the Bill, yet, if Parliament were to reject it, the Government might well submit to so welcome a defeat.

What Lord Palmerston predicted came to pass, and there can be little doubt that he did much to secure the accomplishment of his own prediction. The diminution of the majority in the House of Commons encouraged the House of Lords, always ready and eager for such work, to oppose an effort for popular enlightenment. Lord Monteagle, a renegade Liberal, headed the resistance of the Peers, and he was reinforced by the dashing eloquence of Lord Derby and the argumentative skill of Lord Lyndhurst, whose speech was delivered on his eighty-eighth birthday. Thus emboldened, the Lords threw out the Paper Duty Bill by a majority of 89. It was a momentous vote. The House of Commons, in the exercise of its undoubted privilege, had determined to remit a tax; the House of Lords determined to continue it. This act of the Peers was in effect an act of taxation, and as such was vehemently and indignantly repudiated by all lovers of constitutional freedom. Lord Palmerston, willing to avert a conflict between the Houses, appointed a Committee to enquire into precedents. This was a merely dilatory motion. After two months' enquiry, the Committee presented a guarded and colourless report, on which Lord Palmerston moved some resolutions asserting in very general terms the right of the Commons to impose taxation, and, in effect, apologized for the action of the Lords. This gave Mr Gladstone his opportunity. His ardent temper, ruffled by the rejection of his financial scheme, had not been soothed by Lord Palmerston's sportsmanlike consolation: 'Of course you are mortified and disappointed; but your disappointment is nothing to mine, who had a horse with whom I hoped to win the Derby, and he went amiss at the last moment.' He had been very near resigning, and I now gave vent to his indignation in a speech aimed a directly as the decencies of official life would permit against Lord Palmerston. He declared that the action of the Lords was a gigantic innovation. The House of Commons had the undoubted right of selecting the manner in which the people should be taxed, and they were bound to preserve that precious deposit intact. The resolutions of the Committee were all very well in their way, but he was prepared to go further. He reserved to himself the right to take such action as should give effect to the resolution of the House of Commons.

This speech was pronounced by Lord Russell 'magnificently mad,' and Lord Granville said, on July 7, that 'it was a toss-up whether Gladstone resigned or not, and that, if he did, it would break up the Liberal party.' But everything calmed down, and the action which Mr Gladstone had threatened was taken in the Budget of the following year (1861), and in an adroit and effective form. The chief proposals of that Budget, including the repeal of the duty on paper, instead of being divided, as in previous years, into several Bills, were included in one. By this device the House of Lords was bound to acquiesce in the repeal of the paper-duty, or else to incur the responsibility of rejecting the whole financial scheme for the year. Of course, the Peers and their henchmen grumbled at this device. Lord Robert Cecil, now Lord Salisbury, distinguished himself by the studied rudeness of his attack. He had said that the conduct of the Government was only worthy of a country attorney. He now begged to apologize to the attorneys. They were very humble men, but they would have scorned the course which the Queen's Ministers had pursued. An apostate Whig, by protesting that the Budget was a mortal stab to the Constitution, gave Mr Gladstone the opportunity for an excellent retort:

> I want to know what Constitution it gives a mortal stab to. In my opinion it gives no stab at all; but, as far as it alters, it alters so as to revive and restore the good old Constitution which took its root in Saxon times, which groaned under the Plantagenets, which endured the hard rule of the Tudors, which resisted the Stuarts, and which had now come to maturity under the House of Brunswick. I think that Constitution will be all the better for the operation. As to the Constitution laid down by my right hon. friend, under which there is to be a division of function and office between the House of Commons and the House of Lords—with regard to fixing the income and charge of the country from year to year, both of them being equally responsible for it, which means that neither would be responsible—as far as that Constitution is concerned, I cannot help saying that, in my humble opinion, the sooner it receives a mortal stab the better.

The Bill passed safely through the House of Commons, and though the Duke of Rutland was rash enough to urge the House of Lords to throw it out, Lord Derby was too prudent to sanction such a course, and it passed into law without a division. The Peers had tried conclusions with Mr Gladstone, and had come off second-best.

On August 29, 1861, Mr Gladstone addressed to a member of the Royal Commission on Public Schools a remarkable letter on the merits of classical education. The following passage deserves citation, both as an interesting contribution to an important controversy and as a valuable illustration of the writer's mind:

> The modern European civilization from the Middle Age downwards is the compound of two great factors, the Christian religion for the spirit of man, and the Greek (and, in a secondary degree, the Roman) discipline for his mind and intellect. St Paul is the Apostle of the Gentiles, and is in his own person a symbol of this great wedding. The place, for example, of Aristotle and Plato in Christian education is not arbitrary nor in principle mutable. The materials of what we call

classical training were prepared, and, we have a right to say, were advisedly and providentially prepared, in order that it might become, not a mere adjunct, but (in mathematical phrase) the complement of Christianity in its application to the culture of the human being, as a being formed both for this world and for the world to come.

In April, 1862, Mr Gladstone delivered at Manchester, before the Association of Lancashire and Cheshire Mechanics' Institutes, an eloquent and feeling address on the Prince Consort, who had died in the preceding December, and pointed out the eminent services which he had rendered to the diffusion of useful knowledge and popular cultivation.

To the year 1862 belongs a notable instance of the fallibility which besets even the cleverest men, with the amplest opportunities of knowledge, when they trust themselves to speculate upon the issue of political events. Civil war had broken out in America. A quarrel, originating in a question of constitutional law, had become complicated and infinitely embittered by the introduction of a moral element. Whatever the official pretext, men were really fighting, not to try the claim of each State in the Union to autonomy, but to decide whether slavery, odious alike to God and man, should still be numbered among the institutions of the American republic. The Southern States had begun hostilities. They had formed themselves into a confederacy and elected a president. The English Government issued a proclamation of neutrality, warning all subjects of the Queen against helping either of the belligerents. This was practically a recognition of the South as a separate Power, and the sensibilities of the North were naturally aroused. England had rushed to extend equality of treatment to a friendly State and its rebellious subjects. On October 9, 1862, the Chancellor of the Exchequer, speaking at Newcastle, used words which deepened this unfortunate impression. There could be no doubt, he said, that Jefferson Davis had made a nation of the South. This utterance created an immense sensation at the time, and five years afterwards Mr Gladstone, having, in the interval, been taught by events, made his confession of error in these memorable words:

> I must confess that I was wrong; that I took too much upon myself in expressing such an opinion. Yet the motive was not bad. My sympathies were then—where they had long before been, where they are now—with the whole American people. I probably, like many Europeans, did not understand the nature and working of the American Union. I had imbibed conscientiously, if erroneously, an opinion that twenty or twenty-four millions of the North would be happier and would be stronger (of course assuming that they would hold together) without the South than with it, and also that the negroes would be much nearer to emancipation

under a Southern Government than under the old system of the Union, which had not at that date (August, 1862) been abandoned, and which always appeared to me to place the whole power of the North at the command of the slave-holding interests of the South. As far as regards the special or separate interest of England in the matter, I, differing from many others, had always contended that it was best for our interest that the Union should be kept entire.

VII

Growth in Liberal principles—The General Election of 1865—Defeated at Oxford—Returned for South Lancashire—Death of Lord Palmerston—Leader of the House of Commons—The Reform Bill—The Cave of Adullam—Defeat and resignation

A CALM, WHICH COULD SCARCELY be described as holy, but was certainly profound, had settled down on English politics. Europe and America were disturbed by wars and rumours of wars, but England was at peace. Material prosperity exercised its sedative influence. The revenue advanced by leaps and bounds. Political agitation had died away for lack of workable material. Much of this tranquillity was due to Lord Palmerston. That remarkable man, now on the verge of eighty, had been established by the election of 1859 in a position of undisputed supremacy. His policy abroad had been active and turbulent enough: at home it was easy-going to the point of lethargy. His strength was to sit still. Yielding to the urgent representations of Lord John Russell, he had presented a very mild Reform Bill in 1860. The Bill had proved, as it deserved to be, abortive, and it became generally understood that, as long as Lord Palmerston lived, there was to be no more nonsense of this sort. When the Radical butcher at Tiverton asked him why he and his colleagues did not bring in another Reform Bill, he airily replied, 'Because we are not geese'; and this was all the satisfaction that sincere reformers, and Liberals who were in earnest about their beliefs, could obtain from their venerable leader. No wonder that under these circumstances the relations between Lord Palmerston and his supporters became a little strained, and that thoughtful men, regarding the enormous interests which hung upon the single thread of a life already far prolonged, began to speculate on the forces which his death would loose, and to enquire who was to direct them. The Parliament of 1859-65 is interesting, not for anything which it accomplished, but because it afforded the first indications of tremendous changes which were soon to come. Everyone saw and felt the tempest which was looming, and only wondered when it would break and what it would destroy. At such times of subdued but eager expectation there is peculiar value in the observations of a shrewd onlooker who, free from the distracting bias of party, can regard political events with the penetrating but unimpassioned gaze which a biologist or an astronomer fixes upon the phenomena of nature. Such an onlooker was Bishop Wilberforce.

In 1863 he writes: 'That wretched Pam seems to me to get worse and worse. There is not a particle of veracity or noble feeling that I have ever been able to trace in him. He manages the House of Commons by debauching it, making all parties laugh at one another: the Tories at the Liberals, by his defeating all Liberal measures; the Liberals at the Tories, by their consciousness of getting everything that is to be got in Church and State; and all at one an other, by substituting low ribaldry for argument, bad jokes for principle, and an openly-avowed, vainglorious, imbecile vanity as a panoply to guard himself from the attacks of all thoughtful men. I think if his life lasts long, it must cost us the slight remains of Constitutional Government which exist among us.'

On October 17 in the same year, the Bishop records that Mr Speaker Denison said: 'I now anticipate that Gladstone will be Premier. Neither party has any leader. I hope that Gladstone may get support from the Conservatives who now support Palmerston. Palmerston specially well and young.' A few days later: 'Long talk with Gladstone as to Premiership; he for acting under John Russell.'

On December 10 he writes 'Hayward says that Lord Palmerston is far better this year than last. "Last year I could beat him at billiards, but this year he plays so much better a game that he beat me easily." ... Sir H. Holland, who got back safe, from all his American rambles, has been taken by Palmerston through the river at Broadlands and lies very ill. The Dean of Lincoln (Garnier) is just dead, and another deanery for Palmerston to abuse vacant.' 'Lord Palmerston's wicked appointments meet us here at every turn.'

On July 8, 1864, a vote of want of confidence in the Government was carried in the House of Lords. Just before he went down to vote for it the Bishop wrote to Mr Gladstone: 'Supporting what is counter to you gives me a pang I cannot describe. *Against you*, in the long run, I do not believe it will be. Anything which breaks up, or tends to break up, Palmerston's supremacy must bring you nearer to the post in which I long to see you, and, if I live, shall see you.' On December 7, 1864, he wrote 'Palmerston seems stronger than ever! Gladstone, I think, is certainly gaining power. You hear now almost everyone say he must be the future Premier, and such sayings tend greatly to accomplish themselves.' On February 7, 1865, he writes 'What Gladstone is to head is all uncertain. Walpole still thinks that, having gone a certain way with the Radicals, he will on some Church measure wheel round and break wholly with them ... I do not believe

Pam thinks of retiring; he means, I believe, to dissolve as soon as the Estimates are voted in the summer.' But on July 2: 'Old Palmerston is breaking, and I think it very doubtful if he can meet another Parliament.'

These extracts speak for themselves. Lord Palmerston was in high favour with the easy-going and the well-to-do. An aristocrat by birth and association, he was the ideal politician of the middle classes. But his supporters were confined to no one social section. Everyone who preferred banter to argument, and who found lazy swimming with the stream more congenial than a bold stand for principle, delighted in the octogenarian worldling. They admired and liked a man who mocked at enthusiasm and despised earnestness; who hectored and bullied on the continental stage, and ruthlessly though jocosely burked all efforts for reform at home. No one who was in earnest, whatever his convictions, could make terms with Lord Palmerston. It is easy to guess the amount of sympathy which existed between him and Mr. Gladstone, with whom every opinion was a belief, and every feeling a passion; who, from boyhood to old age, could never take anything lightly; and who regarded a jest on a serious subject as flat blasphemy. Indeed, some hint of Mr Gladstone's sentiments towards his chief may be gleaned from his conversations with Bishop Wilberforce. Lord Palmerston, on his part, was not slow to reciprocate these compliments. Lord Shaftesbury writes: 'Palmerston had but two real enemies, Bright and Gladstone ... Palmerston knew all this, but never mentioned it with asperity. Once he said to me, though he seldom dealt in predictions, "Gladstone will soon have it all his own way; and, whenever he gets my place, we shall have strange doings." He feared his character, his views, and his temperament greatly. He rarely spoke severely of anyone. Bright and Gladstone were the only two of whom he used strong language. He saw clearly, but without any strong sentiment, Gladstone's hostility. He remarked to me one day, when we were discussing some appointments, "Well, Gladstone has never behaved to me, as a colleague, in such a way as to demand from me any consideration." And this he said with the air and tone of a man who perceived the enmity but did not care for it.'

The two men were by temperament incompatible. And the incompatibility which nature had begun, every circumstance of training and life had intensified. The marvel is, not that they had scant sympathy with one another, but that they should have worked together and preserved the outward semblance of harmony so long as (in spite of Mr Gladstone's frequent threats of resignation) they contrived to do.

But the very qualities which made Mr Gladstone uncongenial to Lord Palmerston, and to the whole Palmerstonian school, endeared him to the more advanced section of the Liberal party. He himself once defined a Radical as a Liberal in earnest, and his earnestness made him the idol of the Radicals. His high aspirations, his earnest faith, his constantly widening sympathy with progress and freedom, and his steady recognition of the moral element in politics, won to his side thousands of electors to whom his constitutional lore was an antiquarian curiosity, and his theology an irritating and dangerous delusion. Growth has always been the most marked characteristic of Mr Gladstone's intelligence, and his growth during these quiet years of waiting and preparation was not the less rapid, although it was in some sense out of sight and underground. In two significant instances it was permitted to show itself, and each of these instances contained the germ of great events.

On May 11, 1864, a private member submitted to the House of Commons a Bill for reducing the parliamentary franchise in boroughs from £10 rental to £6. The Bill, of course, was lost, but the debate was rendered memorable by Mr Gladstone's speech. Two years before, in private conversation, he had declared himself strongly in favour of an extension of the franchise. He now supported the proposed reduction. He declared that the burden of proof rested upon those 'who would exclude forty-nine fiftieths of the working classes from the franchise. It is for them to show the unworthiness, the incapacity, and the misconduct of the working class.' 'I say,' he repeated, 'that every man who is not presumably incapacitated by some consideration of personal unfitness or political danger is morally entitled to come within the pale of the Constitution.'

> We are told (he continued) that the working classes don't agitate; but is it desirable that we should wait until they do agitate? In my opinion, agitation by the working classes upon any political subject whatever is a thing not to be waited for, not to be made a condition previous to any parliamentary movement, but, on the contrary, is to be deprecated, and, if possible, prevented by wise and provident measures. An agitation by the working classes is not like an agitation by the classes above them having leisure. The agitation of the classes having leisure is easily conducted. Every hour of their time has not a money value; their wives and children are not dependent on the application of those hours of labour. When a working man finds himself in such a condition that he must abandon that daily labour on which he is strictly dependent for his daily bread, it is only because then, in railway language, the danger-signal is turned on, and because he feels a strong necessity for action, and a distrust of the rulers who have driven him to that necessity. The present state of things, I rejoice to say, does not indicate that distrust; but if we admit that, we must not allege the absence of agitation on the part of the working classes as a reason why the Parliament of England and the public mind of England should be indisposed to entertain the discussion of this question.

Protesting against the 'inarticulate reasoning' of Tories, who, after their manner, expressed their dissent in groans, he went on to say that 'fitness for the franchise, when it is shown to exist, is not repelled on sufficient grounds from the portals of the

Constitution by the allegation that things are well as they are.' Self-command, self-control, respect for order, patience under suffering, confidence in the law, regard for superiors—these were the qualifications of citizenship, and they had been signally displayed by the working men of England in the trying winter of 1862. As to their practical fitness for public work, he cited the success of the co-operative movement which had emanated from Rochdale, and argued that men so eminently qualified to manage their own affairs had intelligence sufficient to guide them in the use of a vote. No wonder that this generous declaration was received with dismay by Tories and reactionary Liberals, nor that an Irish lawyer, who followed Mr Gladstone in the debate, deplored the absence of Lord Palmerston, who, he thought, would have given 'an unanswerable reply to his refractory Chancellor of the Exchequer.'

In March, 1865, Mr Dillwyn, then, as now, the Radical member for Swansea, moved 'that the present position of the Irish Church Establishment is unsatisfactory, and calls for the early attention of her Majesty's Government.' No one who has carefully read the earlier pages of this memoir can be surprised at what then occurred. The Government, of course, could not accept the resolution, but the Chancellor of the Exchequer stated that they were not prepared to deny the abstract truth of the former part of it. They could not assert that the present position of the Establishment was satisfactory. The Irish Church, as she then stood, was in a false position. She ministered only to one-eighth or one-ninth of the whole community. It was much more difficult, however, to decide upon the practical aspect of the question, and no one had ventured to propose the remedy required for the existing condition. Consequently, 'we feel that we ought to decline to follow the hon. gentleman into the lobby and declare that it is the duty of the Government to give their early attention to the subject; because if we gave a vote to that effect we should be committing one of the gravest offences of which a Government could be guilty—namely, giving a deliberate and solemn promise to the country, which promise it would be out of our power to fulfil.' The debate was adjourned, and was not resumed during the Session, but the speech of the Chancellor of the Exchequer caused great excitement. Mr (afterwards Chief Justice) Whiteside promptly denounced it as intended to be fatal to the Established Church of Ireland when an opportunity should arise. Sir Stafford Northcote wrote on March 29:

> Gladstone made a terribly long stride in his downward progress last night, and denounced the Irish Church in a way which shows how, by and by, he will deal not only with it, but with the Church of England too ... was evidently annoyed that his colleagues had decided on opposing Dillwyn's motion. He laid down the doctrines that the tithe was national property, and ought to be dealt with by the State in the manner most advantageous to the people; and that the Church of England was only national because the majority of the people still belonged to her ... It is plain that he must hold that the tithe of Wales, where the Dissenters are in a majority,

does not properly belong to the Church; and by and by we shall find that he will carry the principle a great deal further. It is sad to see what he is coming to.

Mr Gladstone's opponents in the University of Oxford printed his speech, and circulated it, to his prejudice, among his constituents. One of these, Dr Hannah, Warden of Trinity College, Glenalmond, wrote to Mr Gladstone for an explanation, and received the following reply, dated June 8, 1865:

> My reasons are, I think, plain. First, because the question is remote, and apparently out of all bearing on the practical politics of the day, I think it would be for me worse than superfluous to determine upon any scheme, or basis of a scheme, with respect to it. Secondly, because it is difficult; even if I anticipated any likelihood of being called upon to deal with it, I should think it right to take no decision before hand on the mode of dealing with the difficulties. But the first reason is that which chiefly weighs. As far as I know my speech signifies pretty clearly the broad distinction which I make between the abstract and the practical views of the subject, and I think I have stated strongly my sense of the responsibility attaching to the opening of such a question, except in a state of things which gave promise of satisfactorily closing it. For this reason it is that I have been so silent about the matter, and may probably be so again; but I could not, as a Minister and as member for Oxford University, allow it to be debated an indefinite number of times and remain silent. One thing, however, I may add, because I think it a clear landmark. In any measure dealing with the Irish Church, I think (though I scarcely expect ever to be called on to share in such a measure) the Act of Union must be recognized, and must have important consequences, especially with reference to the position of the hierarchy. I am much obliged to you for writing, and I hope you will see and approve my reasons for not wishing to carry my *own mind* further into a question lying at a distance I cannot measure.

In this year Mr Gladstone's term of office as Lord Rector of the University of Edinburgh expired, and he took leave of the University in an admirable and interesting discourse on the place of Ancient Greece in the Providential Order.

The general election was now near at hand. There was no burning question, no cry, nothing to 'go to the country on.' But then, again, on the other hand, there was the less demand for these commodities, because the Government was not seriously threatened. In spite of the murmurs of high-flying Tories and the fierce disappointment of baffled reformers, the mass of the country seemed pretty well satisfied with Lord Palmerston and his Administration. This satisfaction arose, in great part, from the flourishing condition in which the finances of the country had been established by the colleague whom Lord Palmerston so much disliked and dreaded.

The election now impending was charged with great consequences to Mr Gladstone's career. His seat at Oxford was seriously imperilled. The further he had gone from Toryism, and the more nearly he had approached through association with Whiggery (for he never was a Whig himself) to Liberalism, and even Radicalism, the more he had weakened his hold upon the constituency. He had, indeed, a numerous and powerful following of devoted friends, but the average elector of the University viewed him with increasing suspicion. We saw how his attitude towards national education involved him in a contest in 1853. In 1855 Bishop Wilberforce writes: 'A great deal of talk with Gladstone about his seat. He disposed to relinquish it, and on noble grounds—that the University would get a better representative if they had a free choice than if merely brought in by the bigotry party in opposition to him.' In 1860 Mr Gladstone writes: 'Without having to complain, I am entirely sick and weary of the terms upon which I hold the seat.' In 1861 the following correspondence passed between him and two of his chief supporters at Oxford:

The Bishop of Oxford to the Right Hon. W. E. Gladstone.

Cuddesdon Palace, April 8, 1861.

My dear Gladstone,—I have seen to-day the Rector of Exeter, and he asked me to say to you that, though he has sent you the petition against paper-voting to present, he does not wish you to say a word upon it, being more and more persuaded that any opposition to the Bill from you would injure you greatly, and caring more for keeping your seat and throwing out the Bill; so far the Rector. As I know not your mind, nor whether you wish for opinions, I give none on the great question of your seat. Only let me say: 1. That if I can be of any use, you know how freely you may command me; 2. That I can hardly bear the thought of the degradation to us of your ceasing to be our Member.—I am, ever very affectionately yours,

S. OXON.

The Right Hon. W. E. Gladstone to the Bishop of Oxford.

11 Downing Street, July 11, 1861.

On the question of the seat, obliged as I am to write in haste, I cannot do better than send you a copy of a letter which I have just addressed to the Rector of Exeter.

To-morrow Palmer's prospects are to be considered. I think, so far as my personal feelings are concerned, that they may not be good enough to justify my taking the South Lancashire seat.

The Right Hon. W. E. Gladstone to the Rector of Exeter College.

11 Downing Street, July 11, 1861.

My dear Rector of Exeter,—If I have apparently neglected to answer your most kind letters, it has been from great anxiety to advance to a stage, before replying, at which my reply might be worth your having.

I have never forgotten the ties which bind me to my kind and generous supporters in the University, and no prospect elsewhere could induce me to quit them, unless I could think that at a juncture like this they might, with every prospect of success, support a candidate who would fill my place to their full and general satisfaction. Recent events have made it requisite to consider carefully Mr Palmer's position. He writes to his brother by this post on the subject, and we are both alike sensible that no time is to be lost.

I make no great demand on your power of belief when I assure you that it has not been any selfish motive which induced me to open, in the second year of Parliament, or rather to allow to be opened, the idea of my quitting the seat to which I have been elected. It will be very pleasant to me should the balance of public considerations, when we have ascertained it (I trust to-morrow or next day) to the best of our power, admit of my retaining my position. To quit Oxford under any circumstances would be to me a most sad, even if it ever become a prudent, and even a necessary, measure.—Believe me, with great regard, sincerely yours,

W. E. GLADSTONE.

And so matters went on, Mr Gladstone feeling that every year relaxed his hold upon the University, but still shrinking with natural reluctance from the severance of a bond which had brought in its time so much honour and so much happiness. Two important steps in the conflict were these. In 1864 a strong committee induced Mr Gathorne Hardy, now Lord Cranbrook, and then member for Leominster, to consent to contest the seat with Mr Gladstone at the next election; and an Act was passed which, by establishing the system of voting-papers, enabled all the country clergymen and non-resident MA's to swamp the votes of the resident and effective members of the University. The determination of the High Tory party to defeat Mr Gladstone at any cost was widely deplored, not only or chiefly by Liberals, but by all believers in orderly and regulated progress. Radicals rejoiced in the prospect that their favourite politician would soon be unshackled by academic and ecclesiastical obligations: but Bishop Wilberforce, in spite of his hatred of the Whig Government, used his strongest endeavours to save Mr Gladstone's seat, and Lord Palmerston said, with friendly frankness, 'He is a dangerous man. Keep him in Oxford, and he is partially muzzled; but send him elsewhere, and he will run wild.'

Parliament was dissolved on July 6. When the voting at Oxford closed, Mr Gladstone was at the bottom of the poll. On July 18, he issued his valedictory address:

After an arduous connexion of eighteen years, I bid you, respectfully, farewell. My earnest purpose to serve you, my many faults and shortcomings, the incidents of the political relation between the University and myself, established in 1847 so often questioned in vain, and now, at length, finally dissolved, I leave to the judgment of the future. It is one imperative duty, and one alone, which induces me to trouble you with these few parting words—the duty of expressing my profound and lasting gratitude for indulgence as generous, and for support as warm and enthusiastic in itself, and as honourable from the character and distinctions of those who have given it, as has, in my belief, ever been accorded by any constituency to any representative.

In the following correspondence, it is touching to observe the sharp sense of unworthy and ungenerous treatment at the hands of a body whose highest interests he had manfully defended, struggling with the proud humility which shrinks from a public exhibition of its open wounds:

The Bishop of Oxford to the Right Hon. W. E. Gladstone.

Glenthorne, Lynmouth, July 18, 1865.

My dear Gladstone,—I have just received the account of the numbers polled at Oxford up to last night, and I cannot forbear expressing to you my grief and indignation at the result. It is needless for me to say that everything I could with propriety do I did heartily to save our University this great loss and dishonour, as well from a loving honour of you. But the truth is that, except on the footing which Sir R. Peel's last contest destroyed, the University of Oxford is about the worst constituency existing for a man before his age in intellectual development and above it in self-respect. Of course, if half of these men had known what I know of your real devotion to our Church, that would have outweighed their hatred of a Government which gave Waldegrave to Carlisle, and Baring to Durham, and the youngest Bishop on the Bench to York, and supported Westbury in seeking to deny for England the faith of our Lord. But they could not be made to understand the truth, and have inflicted on the University and the Church the gross indignity of rejecting the best, noblest, and truest son of each, in order to punish Shaftesbury and Westbury. You were too great for them.—In all heartiest affection and honour, I am, my dear Gladstone, most truly yours,

S. OXON.

Hawarden, July 21, 1865.

My dear Bishop of Oxford,—Your letter comes amid many and most kind ones, but I am deeply sensible of its overflowing kindness. I do not doubt this to me great event is all for good, and the consolations of cordial support, indulgent judgment and warm affection are given me in abundance—in more than abundance by you.

Do not conceal from yourself that my hands are much weakened: it was only as representing Oxford that a man whose opinions are disliked and suspected could expect or could have a title to be heard. I look upon myself now as a person wholly extraneous on one great class of questions: with respect to legislative and Cabinet matters I am still a unit. But as far as my will, my time, my thoughts are concerned, they are where they ever were.

I have had too much of personal collision with Lord Westbury to be a fair judge in his case, but, in your condemnation of him, as respects attacks upon Christian doctrine, do not forget either what coadjutors he has had, or with what painful or lamentable indifference not only the public, but so many of the clergy, so many of the warmest religionists, looked on.

Do not join with others in praising me because I am not angry, only sorry, and that deeply. For my revenge—which I do not desire, but would baffle if I could—all lies in that little word 'FUTURE' in my address, which I wrote with a consciousness that it is deeply charged with meaning, and that that which shall come will come.

There have been two great deaths, or transmigrations of spirit, in my political existence—one, very slow, the breaking of ties with my original party; the other, very short and sharp, the breaking of the tie with Oxford.

There will probably be a third, and no more.

Again, my dear Bishop, I thank you for bearing with my waywardness, and manifesting, in the day of need, your confidence and attachment.—Ever affectionately yours

W. E. GLADSTONE.

July 24, 1865.

My dear Gladstone,—I thank you very specially for your kind language to me. There is one expression of yours which I wish I were quite sure I understood aright— 'there will probably be a third, and no more.' And now will you let me once more say that your present position seems to me energetically to require you to take (when the occasion comes) the step which Canning took when he claimed the Premiership? I put aside Church considerations, because they are so obvious that they need no statement. But, politically, for yourself—and that is, I believe, the same thing as for our country—this seems to me a paramount necessity: your charge is what Pitt's was—it is to make England wealthy; to diffuse that wealth specially among the working classes; to enlarge and to purify our institutions. In doing this, if you early put yourself at the head of a Government and disclose your views, you may command an immense support from all real patriots on all sides, and you will be true to yourself, to your earliest and to your present noble self. You are not a Radical, and yet you may by political exigencies, if you submit to be second, be led in heading a Radical party until its fully-developed aims assault all that you most value in our country, and it (the Radical party) turns upon you and rends you. You have never had fair play, or you would now have a vast ostensible following. All the opposition you would have to meet would be at first if you took your proper place.

Pardon me for venturing on all this; your loving kindness is answerable for it.—I am, my dear Gladstone, very affectionately yours,

S. OXON.

Osborne, July 28, 1865.

My dear Bishop of Oxford,—The oracular sentence has little bearing on present affairs or prospects, and may stand in its proper darkness. But the hortatory part of your letter, coming, as it does, from you, with such sincerity, such authority, and such affection, I must not pass unnoticed. I think if you had the same means of estimating my position, jointly with my faculties, as I have, you would be of a different opinion. It is my fixed determination never to take any step whatever to raise myself to a higher level in official life; and this not on grounds of Christian self-denial, which would hardly apply, but on the double ground, first, of my total ignorance of my capacity, bodily or mental, to hold such a higher level; and, secondly—perhaps I might say especially—because I am certain that the fact of my seeking it would seal my doom in taking it. This is a reason of a very practical kind: every day brings me fresh evidence of its force and soundness.—Ever affectionately yours,

W. E. GLADSTONE.

Dr Pusey wrote thus to a triumphant Tory:

You are naturally rejoicing over the rejection of Mr Gladstone, which I mourn. Some of those who concurred in that election, or who stood aloof, will, I fear, mourn hereafter with a double sorrow because they were the cause of that rejection. I, of course, speak only for myself, with whatever degree of anticipation may be the privilege of years. Yet, on the very ground that I may very probably not live to see the issue of the momentous future now hanging over the Church, let me, through you, express to those friends from whom I have been separated, who love the Church in itself, and not the accident of Establishment, my conviction that we should do ill to identify the interests of the Church with any political party; that we have questions before us, compared with which that of the Establishment (important as it is in respect to the possession of our parish churches) is as nothing. The grounds alleged against Mr Gladstone bore at the utmost upon the Establishment. The Establishment might perish, and the Church but come forth the purer. If the Church were corrupted, the Establishment would become a curse in proportion to its influence. As that conflict will thicken, Oxford, I think, will learn to regret her rude severance from one so loyal to the Church, to the faith, and to God.

Shaking off the dust of Oxford from his feet, Mr Gladstone now turned his face towards South Lancashire. He appeared there, as he said, 'unmuzzled.' Speaking in the Free Trade Hall at Manchester, he said:

After an anxious struggle of eighteen years, during which the unbounded devotion and indulgence of my friends have maintained me in the arduous position of representative of the University of Oxford, I have been driven from that position. But do not let me come among you under false colours or with false pretences. I have loved the University of Oxford with a deep and passionate love, and as long as I live that attachment will continue. If my affection is of the smallest advantage to that great, that ancient, that noble institution, that advantage—such as it is, and it is most insignificant—Oxford will possess as long as I breathe. But don't mistake the issue which has been raised. The University has at length, after eighteen years of self-denial, been drawn by what I might, perhaps, call the overweening exercise of power, into the vortex of mere party politics. Well, you will readily understand why, as long as I had a hope that the zeal and kindness of my friends might keep me in my place, it was impossible for me to abandon them. Could they have returned me by but a majority of one, painful as it is to a man at my time of life, and feeling the weight of public cares, to be incessantly struggling for his seat, nothing could have induced me to quit that University to which I had so long ago devoted my best care and attachment. But by no act of mine I am free to come among you. And having been thus set free, I need hardly tell you that it is with joy, with thankfulness, and enthusiasm, that I now, at this eleventh hour, a candidate without an address, make my appeal to the heart and the mind of South Lancashire, and ask you to pronounce upon that appeal. As I have said, I am aware of no cause for the votes which have been given in considerable majority against me in the University of Oxford, except the fact that the strongest conviction that the human mind can receive, that an overpowering sense of the public interests, that the practical teachings of experience, to which from my first youth Oxford herself taught me to lay open my mind—all these have shown me the folly—I will say the madness—of refusing to join in the generous sympathies of my countrymen, by adopting what I must call an obstructive policy.

* * * * *

Without entering into details, without unrolling the long record of all the great measures that have been passed—the emancipation of Roman Catholics; the removal of tests from Dissenters; the emancipation of the slaves; the reformation of the Poor Law; the reformation—I had almost said the destruction, but it is the reformation—of the Tariff; the abolition of the Corn Laws; the abolition of the Navigation Laws; the conclusion of the French treaty; the laws which have relieved Dissenters from stigma and almost ignominy, and which in doing so have not weakened, but have strengthened, the Church to which I belong—all these great acts, accomplished with the same, I had almost said sublime, tranquillity of the whole country as that with which your own vast machinery performs its appointed task, as it were in perfect repose—all these things have been done. You have seen the acts. You have seen the fruits. It is natural to enquire who have been the doers. In a very humble measure, but yet according to the degree and capacity of the powers which Providence has bestowed upon me, I have been desirous not to obstruct but to promote and assist this beneficent and blessed process. And if I entered Parliament, as I did enter Parliament, with a warm and anxious desire to maintain the institutions of my country, I can truly say that there is no period of my life during which my conscience is so clear, and renders me so good an answer, as those years in which I have co-operated in the promotion of Liberal measures ... Because they are Liberal, they are the true measures, and indicate the true policy by which the country is made strong and its institutions preserved.

Speaking on the evening of the same day in the Amphitheatre at Liverpool, Mr Gladstone said:

During eighteen years I have been the representative of Oxford. It has been my duty in her name to deal with all those questions bearing upon the relations of Religion and Education to the State, which this critical period has brought to the surface. Long has she borne with me; long, in spite of active opposition, did she resist every effort to displace me. At last she has changed her mind. God grant it may be well with her; but the recollection of her confidence which I had so long enjoyed, and of the many years I have spent in her service, never can depart from me; and if now I appear before you in a different position, I do not appear as another man ... If the future of the University is to be as glorious as her past, the result must be brought about by enlarging her borders, by opening her doors, by invigorating her powers, by endeavouring to rise to the heights of that vocation with which, I believe, it has pleased the Almighty to endow her. I see represented in that ancient institution the most prominent features that relate to the past of England. I come into South Lancashire, and find here around me an assemblage of different phenomena. I find the development of industry. I find the growth of enterprise. I find the progress of social philanthropy. I find the prevalence of toleration. I find an ardent desire for freedom ...

If there be one duty more than another incumbent upon the public men of England, it is to establish and maintain harmony between the past of our glorious history and the future which is still in store for her ... I am if possible more firmly attached to the institutions of my country than I was when, a boy, I wandered among the sand-hills of Seaforth. But experience has brought with it its lessons. I have learned that there is wisdom in a policy of trust, and folly in a policy of mistrust. I have observed the effect which has been produced by Liberal legislation; and if we are told that the feeling of the country is in the best and broadest sense Conservative, honesty compels us to admit that that result has been brought about by Liberal legislation.

At this time South Lancashire returned three members. There were six candidates, of whom Mr Gladstone was returned in the third place, with two Tories above him. He had thus secured his seat, but he held it by a tenure which was alarmingly insecure.

The result of the general election was favourable to the Government, but trouble was impending. It was only the restraining and controlling influence of Lord Palmerston's great authority which kept the discordant elements of the Liberal party in even the outward semblance of harmony. And Lord Palmerston was eighty years old, and in failing health. In the spring of 1365 he had a severe attack of gout, from which he rallied. On July 10, Lord Shaftesbury wrote:

> This is considered a calm. But it is in reality no such thing. It is simply the peg driven through the island of Delos; unloose the peg, and all will be adrift. Palmerston is that peg. Let him be drawn out by defeat, by sickness, or by retirement, and all will be confusion. Gladstone and the Manchester party will ensure that issue.
>
> *July* 11.—In fearful anxiety about Palmerston. He is—the Lord be praised!—better; but he has not recovered, nor will he ever recover at eighty years of age, his former strength. I have long thought that he will not meet another Parliament, or, if he does, it will only be to take his leave. He is gone to Tiverton: his friends declared that such a step, however hazardous, was necessary to sustain the public confidence. How ardently do I pray, day and night, that he may return in safety! He is the only true Englishman left in public life.

The old campaigner got back safe from Tiverton, but he had fought and won his last battle, and the end was at hand. Early in October he caught a chill, from over-exertion and undue exposure, and on October 17 it was announced to the public that he had been ill, but was better. The next day he died.

The fifth Duke of Newcastle, Secretary for War in the Coalition Government, had died in the preceding year, leaving his life-long friend and associate, Mr Gladstone, one of the trustees of his son's estate. In this capacity, the Chancellor of the Exchequer applied himself, with characteristic thoroughness, to the duties pertaining to the management of a rural property, and acquired, in the supervision of the woodlands of Clumber, that practical knowledge of woodcraft which has afforded him such constant interest and recreation. This new charge required frequent visits to Clumber, and it was from there that, on October 18, he addressed the following letter to Lord Russell:

I have received to-night by telegraph the appalling news of Lord Palmerston's decease. None of us, I suppose, were prepared for this event in the sense of having communicated as to what should follow. The Queen must take the first step, but I cannot feel uncertain what it will be. Your former place as her Minister, your powers, experience, services, and renown, do not leave room for doubt that you will be sent for. Your hands will be entirely free. You are pledged probably to no one, certainly not to me. But any Government now to be formed cannot be wholly a continuation: it must be in some degree a new commencement. I am sore with conflicts about the public expenditure, which I feel that other men would either have escaped or have conducted more gently and less fretfully. I am most willing to retire. On the other hand, I am bound by conviction, even more than by credit, to the principle of progressive reduction in our military and naval establishments, and in the charges for them, under the favouring circumstances which we appear to enjoy. This is, I think, the moment to say thus much on a subject-matter which greatly appertains to my department. On the general field of politics, having known your course in Cabinet for eight and a half years, I am quite willing to take my chance under your banner in the exact capacity I now fill, and I adopt the step, perhaps a little unusual, of saying so, because it may be convenient to you at a juncture when time is precious, while it can hardly, I trust, after what I have said above, be hurtful.

Mr Gladstone's expectations were well founded. On October 19, the Queen wrote that she could 'turn to no other than Lord Russell, an old and tried friend of hers, to undertake the arduous duties of Prime Minister, and to carry on the Government.' Mr Gladstone resumed office, as Chancellor of the Exchequer, but not 'in the exact capacity' which he had filled before; for he now became for the first time Leader of the House of Commons.

During the winter he found time to compose an elaborate and appreciative review of the famous, but then anonymous book, in which Professor Seeley attempted to survey the Life and Work of our Lord. In this essay, in which, to quote Dr Liddon, 'genius and orthodoxy have done their best for the Christian honour of "Ecce Homo,"' Mr Gladstone drew an analogy between the original function of the Synoptic Gospels in the first propagation of the faith, and what he conceived to be the scope and effect of Professor Seeley's work.

The formation of the new Government filled timid men with uneasy misgivings. It was obvious that in an Administration presided over by a delicate old man in the House of Lords, the ardent and vigorous Leader of the House of Commons would be virtually Prime Minister. Had any difference of opinion arisen between Lord Russell and his distinguished lieutenant, the position of the elder statesman would, no doubt, have been difficult. But on the immediate business of the Government they were absolutely of one mind. Lord Russell was from first to last a parliamentary reformer. The Reform Act of 1832 had been the main achievement of his life; but he still had the cause at heart, and no long period ever passed without some attempt on his part to give further effect to his favourite policy of measured and moderate reform. In 1849 he unsuccessfully tried to persuade his colleagues in the Cabinet that the time was ripe for a further extension of the suffrage. In 1852 he brought in a Reform Bill, but was turned out of office before it proceeded further; in 1854 he brought in a second Bill, which the outbreak of the Crimean War compelled him to withdraw; and in 1860 he brought in and withdrew a third. After these repeated failures and disappointments, he gladly embraced the opportunity of completing in old age the work to which his youth and early manhood had been dedicated; and it is curious to note his sanguine expectation that the measure which, in concert with Mr Gladstone, he now prepared, might settle the question of parliamentary reform 'for a considerable time—say, to the end of the century or longer.' The subjoined extract from Sir Stafford Northcote's diary belongs to this period. It is difficult to read it without a suspicion that the astute Mr Disraeli was practising on the simplicity of the most candid politician in his party:

> *February* 3, 1866.—Long talk with Dis. this afternoon. He says he communicated with Lord D.(erby) after the election, putting before him the scattering of our friends and the necessity of reconstruction; that he told him he thought reconstruction could not be carried through without a change of leader in one or the other House, and that he was himself willing to give up the lead in the Commons in order to facilitate it; that Lord D. rejected that idea, and did not seem to appreciate the alternative; that they had had various communications by letter and by word of mouth; and that they had discussed the question of possible arrangements with the Duke of Cleveland, Lord Clarendon, the Duke of Somerset, and others. Lord D. considered that if Dis. gave up the lead of the Commons, there was nobody for it but WEG, 'who is quite prepared to take the high Conservative line': 'but we should never get on together—he would always be quarrelling with me, and I should be thinking he wanted to trip me up.'

The new Parliament was opened on February 6, 1866, the Queen appearing at the ceremony for the first time since her widowhood.

In the Speech from the Throne, it was announced that the attention of Parliament would be directed to 'such improvements in the laws which regulate the right of voting in the election of members of the House of Commons as may tend to strengthen our free institutions, and conduce to the public welfare.'

Mr Gladstone's first appearance as Leader of the House of Commons was awaited with curiosity, hopeful or anxious according to the prepossessions of the onlooker. His friends were anxious lest his passionate earnestness, his intense volition, his insensibility to moral perspective and proportion, should lead him into fanatical and dangerous excesses. His enemies hoped and believed that he would make himself ridiculous and ruin his cause. Dispassionate outsiders were simply amused by the perplexity of moderate and timid Liberals, who, just returned to Parliament as supporters of Lord Palmerston's easy-going rule, suddenly found themselves chained to the chariot-wheels of his incalculable successor. On March 12 Bishop Wilberforce, always observant and discriminating, writes: 'Gladstone has risen entirely to his position, and done all his most sanguine friends hoped for as leader … There is a general feeling of the insecurity of the Ministry, and the Reform Bill to be launched to-night is thought a bad rock.'

The following quotation from Mr Forster's diary pertains to this period: 'I went with Gibson to Gladstone at ten, and talked hard with him till about twelve. He was very free and cordial, and let me talk as much as anyone but he does as much as Johnny does little. I went over the reform question with him, up and down, and I think he really took in what I said.' Lord Houghton writes: 'I sat by Gladstone at the Delameres'. He was very much excited, not only about politics, but cattle-plague, china, and everything else. It is indeed a contrast to Palmerston's Ha! ha! and *laissez-faire*.'

The Chancellor of the Exchequer introduced the Reform Bill in a speech marked by all his singular skill in exposition, and rising in its peroration to a high pitch of eloquence. The provisions of the Bill were briefly these:

> It was first proposed to create an occupation franchise in counties, including houses at £14 rental, and reaching up to £50, the present occupation franchise. It was calculated that this would add 171,000 persons to the electoral list. Next it was proposed to introduce into counties the provision which copyholders and leaseholders within parliamentary boroughs now possessed for the purpose of county votes. The third proposition was a savings-bank franchise, which would operate in counties and towns, but which would have a more important operation in the former. All adult males who had deposited £50 in a savings-bank for two years would be entitled to be registered for the place in which they resided. This privilege would add from 10,000 to 15,000 electors to the constituencies of England and Wales. In towns it was proposed to place compound householders on the same footing as ratepayers. It was intended to abolish the rate-paying clauses of the Reform Act, which would admit about 25,000 voters above the line of £10. It was also proposed to introduce a lodger franchise, both for those persons holding part of a house with separate and independent access, and for those who held part of a house as inmates of the family of another person. Then there was the £10 clear annual value of apartments, without reference to furniture. It was further proposed to abolish the necessity, in the case of registered voters, for residence at the time of voting. Lastly, following the precedent of the Government of Lord Derby, they would introduce a clause disabling from

voting persons who were employed in the Government yards. The total number of new voters, of all classes, would be 400,000.

The Bill was not well received. The Conservative party was united and eager against it; the Liberals were divided. They had not been elected to support a Reform Bill, and they were angry at a proposal which, apart from its intrinsic purpose, would, if carried, involve another general election at an early date. Those who supported the Bill were not more than lukewarm, and a compact and powerful section of Liberals organized themselves against the Government. Mr Bright gave these gentry a nickname which has passed into the permanent language of politics when he said that their leader had retired into his political cave of Adullam, to which he invited everyone who was in distress and everyone who was discontented.

But, in spite of sarcasm and eloquence, the blandishments of Whips, and the pressure of constituencies, the Cave gained fresh recruits, and the opposition to the Government became more bitter and intense. It found utterance in a series of speeches on the perils of democracy, by Mr Robert Lowe, now Lord Sherbrooke, which in polished beauty of diction, force of argument, and aptness of illustrative quotation, are entitled to rank with the most famous orations ever delivered in Parliament.

In the early morning of April 28 Mr Gladstone rose in a crowded and excited House to wind up the debate on the second reading. When a man has spoken so much and so well, it is a hazardous attempt to single out the best of his speeches. But this may safely be said—that, if Mr Gladstone ever spoke as well as on this occasion, he never spoke better. Mr Disraeli had been foolish enough to remind his rival of that speech in the Oxford Union against the Reform Bill of 1832, of which mention has been made in an earlier chapter. Mr Gladstone now retorted on him with crushing effect:

> The right hon. gentleman, secure in the recollection of his own consistency, has taunted me with the errors of my boyhood. When he addressed the hon. member for Westminster, he showed his magnanimity by declaring that he would not take the philosopher to task for what he wrote twenty-five years ago; but when he caught one who, thirty-six years ago, just emerged from boyhood, and still an undergraduate at Oxford, had expressed an opinion adverse to the Reform Bill of 1832, of which he had so long and bitterly repented, then the right hon. gentleman could not resist the temptation. He, a parliamentary leader of twenty years' standing, is so ignorant of the House of Commons that he positively thought he got a parliamentary advantage by exhibiting me as an opponent of the Reform Bill of 1832. As the right hon. gentleman has exhibited me, let me exhibit myself. It is true, I deeply regret it, but I was bred under the shadow of the great name of

Canning: every influence connected with that name governed the politics of my childhood and of my youth; with Canning I rejoiced in the removal of religious disabilities, and in the character which he gave to our policy abroad; with Canning I rejoiced in the opening which he made towards the establishment of free commercial interchanges between nations; with Canning, and under the shadow of that great name, and under the shadow of that yet more venerable name of Burke, I grant, my youthful mind and imagination were impressed just the same as the mature mind of the right hon. gentleman is now impressed. I had conceived that fear and alarm of the first Reform Bill in the days of my undergraduate career at Oxford, which the right hon. gentleman now feels; and the only difference between us is this—I thank him for bringing it out—that, having those views, I moved the Oxford Union Debating Society to express them clearly, plainly, forcibly, in downright English, and that the right hon. gentleman is still obliged to skulk under the cover of the amendment of the noble lord. I envy him not one particle of the polemical advantage which he has gained by his discreet reference to the proceedings of the Oxford Union Debating Society in the year of grace 1831. My position, sir, in regard to the Liberal party is in all points the opposite of Earl Russell's ... I have none of the claims he possesses. I came among you an outcast from those with whom I associated, driven from them, I admit, by no arbitrary act, but by the slow and resistless forces of conviction. I came among you, to make use of the legal phraseology, *in formâ pauperis*. I had nothing to offer you but faithful and honourable service. You received me, as Dido received the ship wrecked *Æneas*—

Ejectum littore, egentem
Excepi,

and I only trust you may not hereafter at any time have to complete the sentence in regard to me—

Et regni demens in parte locavi.

You received me with kindness, indulgence, generosity, and I may even say with some measure of confidence. And the relation between us has assumed such a form that you can never be my debtors, but that I must for ever be in your debt. It is not from me, under such circumstances, that any word will proceed that can savour of the character which the right hon. gentleman imputes to the conduct of the Government with respect to the present Bill.

The Chancellor of the Exchequer thus concluded his impassioned speech:

Sir, we are assailed; this Bill is in a state of crisis and of peril, and the Government along with it. We stand or fall with it, as has been declared by my noble friend Lord Russell. We stand with it now; we may fall with it a short time hence. If we do so fall, we, or others in our places, shall rise with it hereafter. I shall not attempt to measure with precision the forces that are to be arrayed against us in the coming issue. Perhaps the great division of to-night is not the last that must take place in the struggle. At some point of the contest you may possibly succeed. You may drive us from our seats. You may bury the Bill that we have introduced, but we will write upon its grave stone for an epitaph this line, with certain confidence in its fulfilment—

Exoriare aliquis nostris ex ossibus ultor.

You cannot fight against the future. Time is on our side. The great social forces which move onwards in their might and majesty, and which the tumult of our debates does not for a moment impede or disturb—those great social forces are against you: they are marshalled on our side; and the banner which we now carry in this fight, though perhaps at some moment it may droop over our sinking heads, yet it soon again will float in the eye of Heaven, and it will be borne by the firm hands of the united people of the three kingdoms, perhaps not to an easy, but to a certain, and to a not far distant, victory.

An extraordinary instance of Mr Gladstone's power of dismissing even the most absorbing cares the moment that active business is over, is related in connexion with this debate. In the course of his speech he had referred to certain opponents of reform as 'depraved and crooked little men.' A friend who recognized the allusion to the 517th line of the 'Acharnians,' asked him in the lobby, while the momentous division was proceeding, whether he thought 'crooked' an apt translation of παρακεκομμένα—a word that describes imperfect coin on which the die has fallen askew. The next morning the critic received a letter from Mr Gladstone, written after the division and before he went to bed, explaining that 'misbegotten' would have been in his view nearer the meaning, but that, for purposes of debate, 'crooked' was a better, because a less offensive, word.

The division was taken amid breathless excitement, and its result was announced in a tumult of reactionary delight. The second reading was carried, but only by a majority of five. The authority of the Government was rudely shaken, and resignation was rumoured. On June 6 Bishop Wilberforce wrote: 'Gladstone is, I believe, determined if possible to force through the Reform Bill. Many of his colleagues would defer it.' But Lord Russell and Mr Gladstone agreed to some conciliatory concessions, and went on with the Bill. The concessions, however, proved useless, and difficulties increased. On June 18 Lord Dunkellin carried a motion against the Government, substituting rating for rental as the basis of the franchise in boroughs. It was the anniversary of Waterloo, and the coincidence was thus happily commemorated by Mr (now Sir George) Trevelyan, who, then as how an eager reformer, had first entered Parliament at the preceding election:

> Just one-and-fifty years had gone since on the Belgian plain,
> Amidst the scorched and trampled rye, Napoleon turned his rein,
> And once again in panic fled a gallant host and proud,
> And once again a chief of might 'neath Fortune's malice bowed.
> So vast and serried an array, so brave and fair to view,
> Ne'er mustered yet around the flag of mingled buff and blue—
> So potent in the show of strength, in seeming zeal so bold—
> Since Grey went forth in '32 to storm corruption's hold.
> But in the pageant all is bright, and, till the shock we feel,
> We learn not what is burnished tin, and what is tempered steel,
>
> When comes the push of charging ranks, when spear and buckler clash,
> Then snaps the shaft of treacherous fir, then holds the trusty ash.
> And well the fatal truth we knew when sounds of lawless fight
> In baleful concert down the line came pealing from our right,
> Which, in the hour of sorest need, upon our centre fell,
> Where march the good old houses still that love the people well.
> As to and fro our battle swayed in terror, doubt, and shame,
> Like wolves among the trembling flock the Tory vanguard came,
> And scattered us as startled girls to tree and archway go,
> Whene'er the pattering hailstorm sweeps along the crowded Row.
> A moment yet with shivered blade, torn scarf, and pennon reft,
> Imperial Gladstone turned to bay amidst our farthest left,
> Where, shoulder tight to shoulder set, fought on in sullen pride,
> The Veterans staunch who drink the streams of Tyne, and Wear, and Clyde;
> Who've borne the toil, and heat, and blows of many a hopeless fray;
> Who serve uncheered by rank and fame, unbought by place or pay.
> At length, deserted and outmatched, by fruitless efforts spent,
> From that disastrous field of strife our steps we homeward bent—
> Ere long to ride in triumph back, escorted near and far
> By eager millions surging on behind our hero's car;
> While blue and yellow streamers deck each Tory convert's brow,
> And both the Carltons swell the shout: 'We're all reformers now.'

The Ministry immediately resigned. The Queen was very unwilling to accept their resignation. She pointed out the perils of a change of Government at a moment when war between Prussia and Austria seemed imminent; and the apathy of the south of England about reform, which Lord Russell had assigned as a reason against dissolution, seemed to her Majesty equally valid against resignation. The Ministers, however, felt that they had lost the confidence of the House of Commons, and they persevered in their purpose. On June 26 their resignation was announced to Parliament. It was received with great excitement out of doors. The apathy about reform which Lord Russell had noticed seemed, as far as London was concerned, to have disappeared. On June 27 some ten thousand people assembled in Trafalgar Square, and passed vehement resolutions in favour of reform. The reformers then marched to Carlton House Terrace, singing litanies and hymns in honour or Mr Gladstone. He was away from home, but Mrs Gladstone and her family came out on to the balcony to acknowledge the popular tribute. Indeed, Mr Gladstone now for the first time became a popular hero. At the great meetings in favour of Reform, which were held in the large towns of the North and the Midlands, his name was received with tumultuous acclamation. Everywhere he was hailed as the true leader of the Liberal party.

On July 13, Lord Houghton writes to a friend on the Continent: 'The change of ministry has passed over very quietly. It was a real collapse, and inevitable by human skill. Gladstone showed a real fervour of conviction, which has won him the attachment of 300 men, and the horror of the rest of the House of Commons. He will be all the better for a year or two's opposition.'

In November, 1866, Mr Gladstone, accompanied by his family, paid a visit to Rome, and had an audience of Pio Nono. In reference to this interview it became necessary, two years later, for Mr Gladstone formally to deny 'that when at Rome I made arrangements with the Pope to destroy the Church Establishment in Ireland, with some other like matters, being myself a Roman Catholic at heart.'

VIII

The Tory Reform Bill—Liberal mutiny—Triumphant Opposition—Proposes to disestablish the Irish Church—The General Election of 1868—Defeated in South-west Lancashire—Returned for Greenwich—Liberal majority—Prime Minster—Disestablishment of the Irish Church.

IN ANNOUNCING HIS ACCEPTANCE OF office in the summer of 1866, Lord Derby said that he reserved to himself entire liberty to deal with the question of parliamentary reform whenever suitable occasion should arise. The strong and enthusiastic agitation in favour of reform which proceeded during the recess, and was signalized by some of Mr Bright's most powerful speeches, determined the course of the Government. Parliament met on the 5th of February, 1867, and the Speech from the Throne announced that attention would again be called to the representation of the people. On the 11th of the same month, Mr Disraeli went down to the House of Commons, and, calmly premising that he and his colleagues had come to the conclusion that reform was no longer a question which should decide the fate of Ministries, went on to explain the principles on which the Government intended to proceed.

It was his purpose, he said, to submit resolutions, and on the 25th February he gave the details.

> He proposed to reduce the occupation franchise in boroughs to a £6 rating; in counties to £20; the franchise was also to be extended to any person having £50 in the Funds, or £30 in a savings-bank for a year. Payment of £20 of direct taxes would also be a title to the franchise, as would a university degree. Votes would further be given to clergymen, ministers of religion generally, members of the learned professions, and certificated school masters. It was proposed to disfranchise Yarmouth, Lancaster, Reigate, and Totnes, and to take one member each from twenty-three boroughs with less than 7,000 inhabitants. The House would have thirty seats

to dispose of, and it was proposed to allot fourteen of them to new boroughs in the Northern and Midland districts, fifteen to counties and one to the London University. The second division of the Tower Hamlets would return two members, and several new county divisions named would have two additional members each. The scheme would add 212,000 voters to the borough, and 206,500 to the county, constituencies.

Mr. Gladstone pointed out the inconvenience of proceeding by resolution; his view was supported by the great bulk of the Opposition, and the Government, with amiable willingness to oblige everybody, undertook to introduce a Bill.

Lord Shaftesbury's observations on this conjuncture may be read with interest:

March 4, 1867.—It seems to me monstrous that a body of men who resisted Mr Gladstone's Bill as an extreme measure with such great pertinacity, should accept the power he retired from, and six months afterwards introduce a Bill many degrees nearer than his to universal suffrage, and establishing, beyond all contradiction, the principle they so fiercely combated, of giving a predominant interest to any class.

March 9.—Here are two tigers over a carcase; and each one tries to drive the other away from the tit-bits. 'What was a conflict last year,' says Lowe, 'is a race now' ... Derby told his friends that if they passed his Bill they would be in office for many years. Thus it is; all alike—all equally carnivorous ... '*Voilà ce que nous sommes,*' as the *chiffonier* said over the dead cur.

Even at this moment of supreme interest in the political world, Mr Gladstone still kept a careful eye on the policy and fortunes of the Church. The Bishops, in a sudden fit of puritan panic, proposed to introduce a Bill into the House of Lords for the purpose of stopping ritualistic practices. On March 8, Mr Gladstone chanced to meet Archbishop Longley and heard this project from his lips. 'From me,' he says, 'this communication had the worst reception I could possibly give it, without departing from my great personal respect and deference to the Archbishop ... I think it idle to suppose a Bill such as this can pass the House of Commons without raising many and large questions. I am afraid it would throw me into a very anti-episcopal position. In any case I must reserve to myself perfect freedom.' Mr Gladstone's energetic intervention frightened the Bishops; they dropped their project with all convenient speed, and offered to take instead a Royal Commission, which should enquire into all the rubrics governing the celebration of Divine worship. It sat, examined, and reported innocuously at a later date; and thus, as Bishop Wilberforce gushingly said, Mr Gladstone was enabled to stay this counsel of fear which threatened destruction.

The Reform Bill was introduced on March 18, 1867.

Its principles were that in boroughs the electors should be all who paid rates, or twenty shillings in direct taxes; the franchise would also be extended to certain classes qualified by education, or by the possession of a stated amount in the Funds, or in savings-banks—rated house-holders to have a second vote. The redistribution of seats would be on the lines already specified. To guard against the power of mere numbers, it was proposed to establish a system of checks, based on residence, rating, and dual voting. Mr Gladstone strongly condemned these securities as illusions or frauds, which would be abandoned whenever it suited the Ministry; and he also predicted that the franchise would have to be conferred on lodgers.

The introduction of the Bill led to the resignation of Lord Cranborne (now Lord Salisbury), Lord Carnarvon, and General Peel, and those who wish to know the sentiments with which Lord Salisbury regarded the political morality of his respected predecessor in the Premiership are referred to his speeches on the various stages of the Bill, and to an article on 'The Conservative Surrender' in the *Quarterly Review* for July, 1867. The Bill was read a second time without a division. In committee the fight waxed fast and furious, and was marked by some brisk encounters between the Leader of the House and Mr Gladstone. At the conclusion of one of these passages of arms, Mr Disraeli gravely congratulated himself on having such a substantial piece of furniture as the table of the House between him and his energetic opponent. In May 1867, Lord Houghton writes thus: 'I met Gladstone at breakfast. He seems quite awed with the diabolical cleverness of Dizzy, who, he says, is gradually driving all ideas of political honour out of the House, and accustoming it to the most revolting cynicism.' At the same time Mr Gladstone's relations with his own party were not wholly harmonious, and the refusal of some fifty of his supporters to follow him in the tactics with which he proposed to meet the Bill in committee led to his temporary and partial withdrawal from the functions of leadership. In committee the Bill underwent such extensive alterations at the hands of the Liberals and Radicals that, when it was read a third time, Lord Cranborne expressed his astonishment at hearing the Bill described as a Conservative triumph. It was right that its real parentage should be established. The Bill, he said, had been modified at the dictation of Mr Gladstone, who demanded, first, the lodger franchise; secondly, the abolition of distinctions between compounders and non-compounders; thirdly, a provision to prevent traffic in votes; fourthly, the omission of the taxing franchise; fifthly, the omission of the dual vote; sixthly, the enlargement of the distribution of seats, which had been enlarged by fifty per cent; seventhly, the reduction of the county franchise; eighthly, the omission of voting-papers; ninthly and tenthly, the omission of the educational and savings-banks franchises. All these points had been conceded. If the adoption of the principles of Mr Bright could be described as a triumph, then indeed the Conservative party, in the whole history of its previous annals, had won no triumph so signal as this. 'I desire to protest, in the most earnest language I am capable of using, against the political morality on which the man of this year have been based. If you borrow your political ethics from the ethics of the political adventurer, you may depend upon it the whole of your representative institutions will crumble beneath your feet.'

When the Bill reached the House of Lords, the Duke of Buccleuch, a potentate little given to epigram, declared that the only word in it which remained unaltered was the first word, 'whereas.' This was really a heightened and effective way of stating the plain truth that a Tory Government, acting under Liberal pressure, had given England a democratic reform. Household suffrage in towns was now the foundation on which the English Constitution reposed. Lord Derby admitted that it was a 'leap in the dark.' Mr Disraeli vaunted that he had 'educated his party' to the point of accepting it. But both alike took comfort in the fact that they had 'dished the Whigs.' This was undeniably true, and the section of the Whigs who had coalesced with 'the Tories to defeat Lord Russell's very moderate measure of the previous year now gnashed their teeth in amazed and impotent disgust. It was amusing to witness their grimaces; and the spectacle contained some profitable lessons for those who endeavour by a political combination to defeat the popular will.

For the moment Mr Disraeli's triumph was complete. On August 18, 1867, Bishop Wilberforce wrote 'No one even guesses at the political future. Whether a fresh election will strengthen the Conservatives or not seems altogether doubtful. The most wonderful thing is the rise of Disraeli. It is not the mere assertion of talent, as you hear so many say. It seems to me quite beside that. He has been able to teach the House of Commons almost to ignore Gladstone, and at present lords it over him, and, I am told, says that he *will hold him down for twenty years.*'

On August 24 Mr Maurice wrote thus to his son:

I am glad you have seen Gladstone, and have been able to judge a little of what his face indicates. It is a very expressive one; hard-worked as you say, and not perhaps specially happy; more indicative of struggle than of victory, though, not without promise of that. I admire him for his patient attention to details, and for the pains which he takes to secure himself from being absorbed in them, by entering into large and generous studies. He has preserved the type which I can remember that he bore at the University thirty-six years ago, though it has undergone curious developments.

On October 23 Bishop Wilberforce writes, after meeting Lord Clarendon in a country-house; 'Clarendon spoke to me with the utmost bitterness of Lord

Derby. Had studied him ever since he (Clarendon) was in the House of Lords ... He had only agreed to this (the Reform Bill) as he would of old have backed a horse at Newmarket. Hated Disraeli, but believed in him as he would have done in an unprincipled trainer he wins—that is all. He knows the garlic given, &c. He says to those without, "All fair, gentlemen."'

At Christmas, 1867, the venerable Lord Russell, who had now reached his seventy-sixth year, announced his final retirement from active politics and from the Leadership of the Liberal party in the House of Lords. In a touching and graceful letter, dated December 26, Mr Gladstone assured the gallant old Whig of his 'warm attachment and regard. Every incident that moves me farther from your side is painful to me ... So long as you have been ready to lead, I have been ready and glad to follow ... I am relieved to think that the conclusion you seem to have reached involves no visible severance; and I trust the remainder of my own political life, which I neither expect nor desire to be very long, may be passed in efforts which may have your countenance and approval.'

On February 25th, 1868, it was announced in both Houses of Parliament that Lord Derby, owing to failing health, had resigned the Premiership, and that the Queen had entrusted Mr Disraeli with the task of forming an Administration. It was a striking climax to an extraordinary career. Everyone was interested; most people were amused; some disgusted. Lord Shaftesbury thus comments on the event: 'Disraeli Prime Minister! He is a Hebrew; this is a good thing. He is a man sprung from an inferior station; another good thing in these days, as showing the liberality of our institutions. "But he is a leper," without principle, without feeling, without regard to anything, human or divine, beyond his own personal ambition. He has dragged, and he will long continue to drag, everything that is good, safe, venerable, and solid through the dust and dirt of his own objects.'

Lord Chelmsford (whom, by the way, Mr Disraeli had abruptly dismissed from the Chancellorship) observed, 'The old Government was the Derby; this the Hoax.' The *Pall Mall Gazette*, commenting on this event, wrote:

> One of the most grievous and constant puzzles of King David was the prosperity of the wicked and the scornful; and the same tremendous moral enigma has come down to our own days. In this respect the earth is in its older times what it was in its youth. Even so recently as last week the riddle once more presented itself in its most impressive shape. Like the Psalmist, the Liberal leader may well protest that verily he has cleansed his heart in vain and washed his hands in innocency; all day long he has been plagued by Whig lords, and chastened every morning by Radical manufacturers; as blamelessly as any curate he has written about '*Ecce Homo*,' and he has never made a speech, even in the smallest country town, without calling out with David, 'How foolish am I, and how ignorant!' For all this what does he see? The scorner who shot out the lip and shook the head at him across the table

of the House of Commons last Session has now more than heart could wish; his eyes—speaking in an Oriental manner—stand out with fatness, he speaketh loftily, and pride compasseth him about as with a chain. It is all very well to say that the candle of the wicked is put out in the long run; that they are as stubble before the wind, and as chaff that the storm carries away. So we were told in other times of tribulation. This was the sort of consolation that used to be offered in the jaunty days of Lord Palmerston. People used then to soothe the earnest Liberal by the same kind of argument, 'Only wait,' it was said, 'until he has retired, and all will be well with us.' But no sooner has the storm carried away wicked Whig chaff than the heavens are forthwith darkened by new clouds of Tory chaff.

But the new Prime Minister, though in office, was not in power. He was nominally the leader of a House which contained a large majority of his political opponents. The settlement of the question of reform had healed the schism in the Liberal Party, and they now could defeat the Government whenever they chose to mass their forces. Early in the Session Mr Gladstone brought in a Bill abolishing compulsory Church rates, and this passed into law. On March 16, he took part in the debate on the motion of an Irish member, that the House resolve itself into a Committee to consider the state of Ireland. Towards the close of the debate he said that Ireland had a controversy with us and a long account against us. He enumerated six main points in which we owed her a debt of justice. One of these was the Established Church. Religious equality, he said, must be conceded. Referring to his speech on Mr Dillwyn's motion in 1865, he affirmed 'The opinion I held then and hold now—namely, that in order to the settlement of this question of the Irish Church, that Church, as a State Church, must cease to exist.' The change must come; it was our wisdom and our duty to make ready for it.

> If we are prudent men, I hope we shall endeavour, as far as in us lies, to make some provision for a contingent, a doubtful and probably a dangerous future. If we be chivalrous men, I trust we shall endeavour to wipe away all those stains which the civilized world has for ages seen, or seemed to see, on the shield of England in her treatment of Ireland. If we be compassionate men, I hope we shall now, once for all, listen to the tale of woe which comes from her, and the reality of which, if not its justice, is testified by the continuous migration of her people—that we shall endeavour to
>
> > Raze out the written troubles from her brain,
> > Pluck from her memory the rooted sorrow.
>
> But, above all, if we be just men, we shall go forward in the name of truth and

right, bearing this in mind—that when the case is proved, and the hour is come, justice delayed is justice denied.

And so at last the great secret was out. Mr Gladstone had made up his mind to disestablish the Irish Church. Those who remember his attitude towards Maynooth, and his letter on the spiritual efficiency of the Irish Establishment, will know that it was no sudden resolve. His letter to Dr Hannah in 1865 only meant that he did not see how soon the occasion might arise for giving effect to an opinion which had long been forming in his mind. The occasion was now at hand.

On March 23, Mr Gladstone gave notice of the following resolutions:

1. That, in the opinion of this House, it is necessary that the Established Church of Ireland should cease to exist as an establishment, due regard being had to all personal interests and to all individual rights of property. 2. That, subject to the foregoing considerations, it is expedient to prevent the creation of new personal interests by the exercise of any public patronage and to confine the operations of the Ecclesiastical Commissioners of Ireland to objects of immediate necessity, or involving individual rights, pending the final decision of Parliament. 3. That an humble address be presented to her Majesty, humbly to pray that, with a view to the purposes aforesaid, her Majesty will be graciously pleased to place at the disposal of Parliament her interest in the temporalities, in archbishoprics, bishoprics, and other ecclesiastical dignities and benefices in Ireland and in the custody thereof.

Lord Stanley (now Lord Derby) gave notice, on behalf of the Government, of an extremely mild amendment, admitting the necessity for modifications in the temporalities of the Church of Ireland, but recommending that proposals tending to disestablishment and disendowment should be left to the decision of the new Parliament.

On March 25, Bishop Wilberforce wrote: 'I am very sorry Gladstone has moved the attack on the Irish Church ... It is altogether a bad business, and I am afraid Gladstone has been drawn into it from the unconscious influence of his restlessness at being out of office. I have no doubt that his hatred to the low tone of the Irish branch has had a great deal to do with it.' On the same day the Bishop thus reports Mr Gladstone's opinion on current politics: 'The operations of last year had destroyed the whole power of Conservative resistance.'

On March 30 Mr Gladstone moved his resolutions, in a speech of which the following was the eloquent peroration:

There are many who think that to lay hands upon the national Church Establishment of a country is a profane and unhallowed act. I respect that feeling. I sympathize with it. I sympathize with it while I think it my duty to overcome and repress it. But if it be an error, it is an error entitled to respect. There is something in the idea of a national establishment of religion, of a solemn appropriation of a part of the Commonwealth for conferring upon all who are ready to receive it what we know to be an inestimable benefit; of saving that portion of the inheritance from private selfishness, in order to extract from it, if we can, pure and unmixed advantages of the highest order for the population at large; there is something in this so attractive that it is an image that must always command the homage of the many. It is somewhat like the kingly ghost in 'Hamlet,' of which one of the characters of Shakespeare says:

> We do it wrong, being so majestical,
> To offer it the show of violence;
> For it is, as the air, invulnerable,
> And our vain blows malicious mockery.

But sir, this is to view a religious establishment upon one side only—upon what I may call the ethereal side. It has likewise a side of earth; and here I cannot do better than quote some lines written by the present Archbishop of Dublin, at a time when his genius was devoted to the muses. He said, in speaking of mankind:

> We who did our lineage high
> Draw from beyond the starry sky,
> Are yet upon the other side
> To earth and to its dust allied.

And so the Church Establishment, regarded in its theory and in its aim, is beautiful and attractive. Yet what is it but an appropriation of public property, an appropriation of the fruits of labour and of skill to certain purposes, and unless these purposes are fulfilled, that appropriation cannot be justified. Therefore, sir, I cannot but feel that we must set aside fears which thrust themselves upon the imagination, and act upon the sober dictates of our judgment. I think it has been shown that the cause for action is strong—not for precipitate action, not for action beyond our powers, but for such action as the opportunities of the times and the condition of parliament, if there be a ready will, will amply and easily admit of. If I am asked as to my expectations of the issue of this struggle, I begin by frankly avowing that I, for one, would not have entered into it unless I believed that the final hour was about to sound—

> *Venit summa dies et ineluctabile fatum.*

And I hope that the noble lord will forgive me if I say that before Friday last I thought that the thread of the remaining life of the Irish Established Church was short, but that since Friday last, when, at half-past four o'clock in the afternoon, the noble lord stood at that table, I have regarded it as being shorter still. The issue is not in our hands. What we had and have to do is to consider well and deeply before we take the first step in an engagement such as this; but having entered into the controversy, there and then to acquit ourselves like men, and to use every effort to remove what still remains of the scandals and calamities in the relations which exist between England and Ireland, and to make our best efforts at least to fill up with the cement of human concord the noble fabric of the British Empire.

After an animated debate, marked by much fine speaking on behalf of the resolutions and very little against them, Lord Stanley's amendment was lost by sixty-one votes. When it came to the discussion of the resolutions in Committee, the first was carried by a majority of sixty-five against the Government. Ministerial explanations followed. Mr Disraeli described, in his most pompous vein, his audiences of the Queen, and made an injudiciously free use of the Royal name. Divested of vulgar verbiage his statement amounted to this—that, in spite of adverse votes, the Ministers intended to hold on till the autumn, and then to appeal to the new electorate created by the Reform Act of the previous year. Referring to these Ministerial statements, Lord Malmesbury wrote thus on May 6: 'Gladstone made a bitter attack on the Government, saying that the above-mentioned speeches required further explanation as to what passed between Disraeli and the Queen. Disraeli said the permission her Majesty gave him to dissolve only applied to the Irish Church question, and, if other difficulties arose, of course he must again refer to her. Nothing can exceed the anger of Gladstone at Disraeli's elevation. He wanted to stop the supplies on Monday, the 4th, but found his party would not go with him.'

Lord Houghton writes thus on May 2: 'Gladstone is the great triumph; but as he owns that he has to drive a four-in-hand, consisting of English Liberals, English Dissenters, Scotch Presbyterians, and Irish Catholics, he requires all his courage to look the difficulties in the face, and trust to surmount them.'

As soon as the resolutions were carried, Mr Gladstone brought in a Bill to prevent for a time any fresh appointments in the Church of Ireland, and this, though carried in the House of Commons, was defeated in the Lords.

This practically ended the struggles of the Session, and Parliament was prorogued on July 31.

On August 20, Lord Shaftesbury wrote: 'The Government is a compound of timidity and recklessness. Dizzy is seeking everywhere for support. He is all things to all men, and nothing to anyone. He cannot make up his mind to be Evangelical, Neologian, or Ritualistic; he is waiting for the highest bidder.'

Mr Gladstone promptly opened his electoral campaign. In the redistribution of seats consequent on the Reform Bill, South Lancashire had been divided into two electoral districts. Mr Gladstone determined to contest the South Western division, and he addressed himself to the task with extraordinary vigour. He spoke in rapid succession at St Helen's, Warrington, Liverpool, Newton Bridge, Wigan, and Ormskirk, dilating with all his fiery eloquence on the monstrous foolishness of a religious establishment which ministered only to a handful of the people. The campaign was conducted with increasing vigour throughout the autumn. A single and simple issue was placed before the country—was the Irish Church to be, or not to be, disestablished? Parliament was dissolved on November 11. The returns soon showed an overwhelming victory for the Liberal cause. Mr Gladstone's seat in Lancashire, where Protestant feeling runs high, was considered insecure, and he had therefore been doubly nominated. In Lancashire he was defeated, Mr (now Lord) Cross being at the head of the poll; but he was returned for Greenwich by a substantial majority. He chose this moment to publish a 'Chapter of Autobiography,' which he had written in the previous September, and in which he traced in detail the history of his opinions with respect to the Irish Church.

On November 20, Bishop Wilberforce wrote to his friend Dr Trench, Archbishop of Dublin: 'The returns to the House of Commons leave no doubt of the answer of the country to Gladstone's appeal. In a few weeks he will be in office at the head of a majority of something like a hundred, elected on the distinct issue of Gladstone and the Irish Church.'

On December 2, Mr Disraeli announced that he and his colleagues, by a commendable innovation on existing practice, had resigned their offices without waiting for a formal vote of the new Parliament. On the following day Mr Gladstone was summoned to Windsor, and was commanded by the Queen to form an Administration. He had now reached the highest summit of political ambition. All the industry and self-denial of a laborious life, all the anxieties and burdens and battles of a five-and-thirty years' parliamentary struggle, were crowned by their supreme and adequate reward.

On December 9 the new Ministers received the Seals, Mr Bright taking office for the first time as President of the Board of Trade. On the 10th, the new Parliament was opened by Royal Commission. On the 10th, Mr and Mrs Gladstone paid a visit to Lord and Lady Salisbury at Hatfield, where the ubiquitous Bishop Wilberforce (whom Mr Disraeli had just passed over for the sees of Canterbury and London) had an opportunity of observing his old and honoured friend in the first flush of his new dignity. Here are his comments: 'Gladstone, as ever, great, earnest, and honest; as unlike the tricky Disraeli as possible.'

> I have very much enjoyed meeting Gladstone. He is so delightfully true and the same; just as full of interest, in every good thing of every kind, and so exactly the opposite of the Mystery Man ... When people talk of Gladstone going mad, they

do not take into account the wonderful elasticity of his mind and the variety of his interests. Now, this morning (I am writing in the train on my way to London) after breakfast, he and Salisbury, and I and Cardwell, had a walk round this beautiful park, and he was just as much interested in the size of the oaks, their probable age, &c., as if no care of State ever pressed upon him. This is his safeguard, joined to entire rectitude of purpose and clearness of view. He is now writing opposite to me in the railway carriage on his way to Windsor Castle.

* * * *

I enjoyed meeting Gladstone again very much. In presence he always impresses me, as I know he does you, with the sense of his perfect honesty and noble principles. I never saw him pleasanter, calmer, or more ready to enter freely into everything ... He remarked to me on the great power of charming and pleasant host-ing possessed by Salisbury. All that he did say on public affairs was what we could wish, barring the one subject of the Irish Church. I think that he will hold his own. I do not believe in the excitement and temper, &c., which people talk about. He is far more in earnest than most people, and therefore they revenge themselves by saying that he loses his temper.

On December 30, the Bishop wrote thus to Dr Trench, Archbishop of Dublin:

You say that the time for offering any terms of compromise is not come: that it will be well to let Gladstone taste the various difficulties which beset the carrying-out of his measure, and then, when he has experienced their weight, to offer him terms. Now, this would be fine if you were dealing with a minority, guided by a master of selfish cunning and unprincipled trickery. Doubtless it would be the wise way to meet a mere Mystery Man like Disraeli, who was trading upon the principles and ultimate existence of an honourable minority, and had no real principle, but was ready to catch at any cry to gain a respite from defeat, and was ready, in order to avoid a difficulty he could not meet, to sacrifice any man, party, purpose, principle, or Church—it would doubtless be best to let HIM entangle himself in his own web, and then make his sacrifice of everything for which he had professed to act the price of his extrication from his trouble. But your case is altogether different. You have in Gladstone a man of the highest and noblest principle, who has shown unmistakably that he is ready to sacrifice every personal aim for what he has set before himself as a high object. He is supported, not by a minority conscious of being a minority, but by a great and confident majority. The decision of the constituencies seems to me incapable of misapprehension or reversal. Has there ever yet been any measure, however opposed, which the English people have been unable for its 'difficulty' to carry through, when they have determined to do so? Look at negro slavery, protection, parliamentary reform, and a hundred other questions. They have resolved to carry your disestablishment, and they know that they can and will carry it. Now, what is gained by opposing and chafing such a body? You may frighten away a fox by an outcry; but you only wake up the strength and fury of the lion ... I therefore once more implore you to consider whether the time is not come for you to say, 'The nation has decided against one Establishment, and we bow to its decision. The question of what part of our income is to he left to us, and on what tenure and conditions it is to be held, remains confessedly open. We are ready to enter on it, and if what we must deem still our just rights are provided for, and we are honourably and wisely started on our new career, we shall do our best to aid in the settlement of a very difficult matter.' ... I should have great hopes, knowing the nobleness of him with whom as chief you have to deal, of a tolerably satisfactory result following *immediate* action on your parts in this direction.

But this sagacious and statesmanlike counsel was disregarded. The Irish Bishops ranged themselves in bitter but futile hostility to the Bill. A frantic outbreak of Protestant violence began in Ireland and spread to England. The bulk of the Tory party, and a large proportion (though by no means the whole or the best part) of the English clergy joined the din. Noble lords and right reverend prelates vied with one another in rhetorical extravagances. The Orangemen, as usual, distinguished themselves by the indecency of their language and the brutality of their idle threats; and some calmer spirits, who dreaded attacks on property and the unsettlement of institutions, were seriously perturbed. Bishop Wilberforce notes this conversation at Windsor Castle: 'The Queen very affable. "So sorry Mr Gladstone started this about the Irish Church, and he is a great friend of yours."' On February 16, Parliament was opened by Commission. In the Speech from the Throne it was announced that 'the ecclesiastical arrangements of Ireland' would be brought under the consideration of Parliament at a very early date. On the same evening Bishop Wilberforce notes: 'Gladstone's first speech as Prime Minister. Calm, moderate, and kindly. Disraeli constrained *suo more.*'

On March 1, 1869, Mr Gladstone introduced this momentous Bill. His speech lasted three hours, but contained, even his enemies being judges, not one superfluous word. It was proposed that on January 1, 1871, the Irish Church should cease to exist as an establishment and should become a Free Church. The Irish Bishops were to lose their seats in Parliament. A Synod, or governing body, was to be elected from the clergy and laity of the Irish Church, and was made a corporation capable of holding property and performing other public acts. The union between the English and Irish Churches was to be dissolved, the ecclesiastical courts abolished, and the ecclesiastical law retained only as the rule of the Church till altered by the governing body. All vested interests were to receive ample—if, indeed, it was not excessive—compensation. When they were disposed of, out of the property of the disestablished Church, there would remain a surplus estimated at some nine millions, and this was to be devoted to the relief of unavoidable calamity and suffering.

> I do not know in what country so great a change, so great a transition, has been proposed for the ministers of a religious communion who have enjoyed for many ages the preferred position of an Established Church, I can well understand that to many in the Irish Establishment such a change appears to be nothing less than ruin and destruction; from the height on which they now stand the future is to them an abyss, and their fears recall the words used in *King Lear*, when Edgar endeavours to persuade Glo'ster that he has fallen over the cliffs of Dover, and says:
>
> > Ten masts at each make not the altitude
> > Which thou hast perpendicularly fallen:
> > Thy life's a miracle!
>
> And yet but a little while after the old man is relieved from his delusion, and finds he has not fallen at all. So I trust that when, instead of the fictitious and adventitious aid on which we have too long taught the Irish Establishment to lean, it should come to place its trust in its own resources, in its own great mission, in all that it can draw from the energy of its ministers and its members, and the high hopes and promises of the Gospel that it teaches, it will find that it has entered upon a new era of existence—an era bright with hope and potent for good. At any rate, I think the day has certainly come when an end is finally to be put to that union, not between the Church and religious association, but between the Establishment and the State, which was commenced under circumstances little auspicious, and has endured to be a source of unhappiness to Ireland and of discredit and scandal to England. There is more to say. This measure is in every sense a great measure—great in its principles, great in the multitude of its dry, technical, but interesting detail, and great as a testing measure; for it will show for one and all of us of what metal we are made. Upon us all it brings a great responsibility—great and foremost upon those who occupy this bench. We are especially chargeable—nay, deeply guilty—if we have either dishonestly, as some think, or even prematurely or unwisely challenged so gigantic an issue. I know well the punishments that follow rashness in public affairs, and that ought to fall upon those men, those Phaetons of politics, who, with hands unequal to the task, attempt to guide the chariot of the sun. But the responsibility, though heavy, does not exclusively press upon us; it presses upon every man who has to take part in

the discussion and decision upon this Bill. Every man approaches the discussion under the most solemn obligations to raise the level of his vision and expand its scope in proportion with the greatness of the matter in hand. The working of our constitutional government itself is upon its trial, for I do not believe there ever was a time when the wheels of legislative machinery were set in motion, under conditions of peace and order and constitutional regularity, to deal with a question greater or more profound. And more especially, sir, is the credit and fame of this great assembly involved; this assembly which has inherited through many ages the accumulated honours of brilliant triumphs, of peaceful but courageous legislation, is now called upon to address itself to a task which would, indeed, have demanded all the best energies of the very best among your fathers and your ancestors. I believe it will prove to be worthy of the task. Should it fail, even the fame of the House of Commons will suffer disparagement; should it succeed, even that fame, I venture to say, will receive no small, no insensible addition. I must not ask gentlemen opposite to concur in this view, emboldened as I am by the kindness they have shown me in listening with patience to a statement which could not have been other than tedious; but I pray them to hear with me for a moment while, for myself and my colleagues, I say we are sanguine of the issue. We believe, and for my part I am deeply convinced, that when the final consummation shall arrive, and when the words are spoken that shall give the force of law to the work embodied in this measure—the work of peace and justice—those words will be echoed upon every shore where the name of Ireland or the name of Great Britain has been heard, and the answer to them will come back in the approving verdict of civilized mankind.

The Bill was supported by Mr Bright in a speech of infinite beauty and pathos, and his solemn peroration is one of the finest of his recorded utterances. Mr Lowe attacked the Irish Church with characteristic bitterness and the Solicitor-General, Sir John Coleridge (now Lord Chief Justice of England), justified its destruction in an oration so eloquent and so persuasive that it might almost have reconciled an Irish Bishop to his own extinction. Mr Disraeli opposed the Bill in a speech which, as was said at the time, was, like a columbine's skirt, all flimsiness and spangles, and Mr Gathorne Hardy (now Lord Cranbrook), who really thought the proposal of the Government wicked, thundered against it with impressive vehemence. Sir Roundell Palmer (now Lord Selborne), who refused to join a Government which contemplated disendowment, drew refined distinctions, and contrived to appear for and against the Bill at the same time. But none of these rhetorical exercises mattered much. The Irish Establishment was doomed. The second reading was carried by a majority of 118. The Bill passed practically unaltered through Committee. Even the Lords were too prudent to resist the Government, though urged thereto by the inflammatory rhetoric of the present Archbishop of York, who in the previous winter had declared that the Church had everything to lose and nothing to gain by prolonging a hopeless contest. Lord Salisbury, and some other Tories who were also High Churchmen, voted for the Bill, which passed the second reading; but in Committee a variety of enfeebling amendments were carried against the Government. For a moment there seemed some risk of serious conflict between the two Houses. There were rumours that Mr Gladstone, if beaten, would resign. But Mr Bright, in a letter to Birmingham, gave the Lords an emphatic warning of what might happen if they persevered in a course of arrogant obstinacy, and, like prudent men and true Britons, they hastily betook themselves to the safe haven of compromise. The Bill, not altered in a single important feature, received the Royal Assent on July 26, 1869.

IX

*The Irish Land Act—The abolition of Purchase—The 'Alabama' claims—
Disaffection at Greenwich—Waning popularity—Dissolution—Defeat—
Resignation—Retirement from leadership—Theological controversy*

'I HAVE NOT ANY MISGIVINGS about Gladstone personally. But, as leader of the party to which the folly of the Conservatives and the selfish treachery of Disraeli bit by bit allied him, he cannot do what he would, and, with all his vast powers, there is a want of sharp-sighted clearness as to others. But God rules. I do not see how we are, after Disraeli's Reform Bill, long to avoid fundamental changes both in Church and State.' The friend who, writing on August 3, 1869, thus expressed his uneasy sense of impending change, soon found his expectations verified by results.

These were golden days for the Liberal party. They were united, enthusiastic, victorious, full of energy, confidence, and hope. Great works of necessary reform, too long delayed, lay before them, and they were led by a band of men as distinguished as had ever filled the chief places of the State. At their head was a statesman who, by his rare combination of high principle, passionate earnestness, and practical skill, was beyond any other qualified to inspire, to attract, and to lead. He had now carried to a successful issue his first great act of constructive legislation—for the erection of the Irish Church into a voluntary body with self-governing powers was at least as much a constructive as a destructive act—and his impetuous spirit was already seeking fresh worlds to conquer.

The Session of 1870 was devoted to two great measures which ran concurrently through Parliament. The one was the Irish Land Bill, the other the English Education Bill. In his electioneering campaign Mr Gladstone had declared that Ireland was shadowed and blighted by an upas-tree, and that this tree had three main branches—the Established Church, the system of land tenure, and the system of public education. One of these he hewed down in 1869; to the second he addressed himself in 1870. He introduced his Land Bill on February 15. A custom had long existed in Ulster which recognized a certain property or partnership of the tenant in the land which he cultivated. He could not be evicted as long as he paid his rent, and he was entitled to sell the goodwill of his farm for what it would fetch in the market. This was familiarly called 'tenant right.' When agrarian reformers had urged its extension as a method of allaying Irish discontent, Lord Palmerston had said that 'tenant-right was landlord's wrong,' and this imbecile jest had been meekly accepted as closing the controversy. But Mr Gladstone now proposed to make this tenant-right a legal institution, and where it did not exist he threw upon the landlord the burden of proving that he had a right to evict. This reversed the existing condition, in which, except in Ulster, the Irish tenantry were tenants at will. A legal machinery was created by which the circumstances of any tenant whose landlord sought to evict him might be enquired into, and justice secured him. In brief; the object of the Bill was to protect the tenant against eviction as long as he paid his rent, and to secure to him the value of any improvements which his own industry had made. Mr Gladstone regarded the Bill as pertaining 'not so much to the well-being as to the being of civilized society for the existence of Society can hardly be such as to deserve that name until the conditions of peace and order, and of mutual goodwill and confidence, shall have been more firmly established in Ireland.'

The Bill passed, with much protest indeed, but with no serious challenge, into law, and received the Royal Assent on August 1.

Simultaneously, the Government, by the hand of Mr Forster, established for the first time a national and compulsory system of elementary education. We need not stay to trace the progress of this measure, because Mr Gladstone's personal relations with it were slight. But it is important to note that the concessions made during its course to the convictions of Tories and Churchmen, in the matter of religious education, stirred the bitter and abiding wrath of the political Dissenters.

On May 26 Lord Shaftesbury, whose strong feelings misled him as to the views of the Nonconformists, wrote in his diary: 'Deputation to Gladstone about education. The unanimity of the Churchmen and Dissenters—that is, the vast majority of them—is striking and consolatory. Gladstone could now settle the question by a single word. But he will not. He would rather, it is manifest, exclude the Bible altogether than have it admitted and taught without the intervention and agency of catechisms and formularies.'

The following letter of Mr Gladstone's is interesting and instructive:

June 17, 1870.—My dear Shaftesbury,—I was not at liberty on Wednesday to speak to you otherwise than in very general terms on the intentions of the Government respecting the Education Bill. We have now taken our stand ; and I write to say how ready I shall be to communicate with you freely in regard to the prospects and provisions of the measure. I can the better make this tender because *the plan we have adopted is by no means, in all its main particulars, the most agreeable to my individual predilections.* But I have given it a deliberate assent, as a measure due to the desires and convictions of the country, and as one rendering much honour and scope to religion, without giving fair ground of objection to those who are so fearful that the State should become entangled in theological controversy. Energetic objection will, I have some fear, be taken in some quarters to our proposals; but I believe they will be generally satisfactory to men of moderation. Pray understand that the willingness I have expressed is not meant to convey any request, but only to be turned to account if you find it useful.—Believe me, sincerely yours,

W. E. GLADSTONE.

The 'energetic objection' which Mr Gladstone foresaw was duly taken, and drew him into a sharp passage of arms with that stern champion of parliamentary nonconformity, the late Mr Edward Miall. Mr Gladstone told him frankly that he was too exacting—that he looked too much to the section of the community which he adorned, and too little to the interests of the people at large. 'We,' concluded Mr Gladstone, 'are the Government of the Queen, and those who have assumed the high responsibility of administering the affairs of this Empire must endeavour to forget the parts in the whole, and must, in the great measures they introduce into the House, propose to themselves no meaner or narrower object than the welfare of the Empire at large.' The answer of the Nonconformists to this proud vaunt—an emphatic and an unpleasant answer—was given in the general election of 1874, and helped to make 'the Government of the Queen,' a term of very different import.

On June 27, 1870, Lord Clarendon died, and Lord Granville succeeded him as Foreign Secretary. He entered on his duties at the Foreign Office July 5, and was informed by the experienced Under-Secretary that he had never known so profound a lull in foreign affairs. Ten days later France and Germany were at war. Into the history of that memorable campaign there is, happily, no need for us to enter. Mr Gladstone and his colleagues were true to the sacred principle of non-intervention, and held firmly to their purpose of neutrality, in spite of political pressure, furious partisanship, and diplomatic allurements. On July 27, Mr Gladstone wrote to a friend: 'It is not for me to distribute praise and blame; but I think the war as a whole, and the state of things out of which it has grown, deserve a severer condemnation than any which the nineteenth century has exhibited since the peace of 1815.' On September 28, Bishop Wilberforce writes: 'Sat some time with Gladstone. Full as ever of intellect and interest on all subjects. France and Prussia: hoping that for the present great sacrifice of life over.'

In October Mr Gladstone published in the *Edinburgh Review* an article on 'Germany, France, and England,' in which he distributed blame with great impartiality between both belligerent Powers. The fact is interesting because he has since told us that this (which contains the famous phrase 'the streak of silver sea') was the only article ever written by him which was meant, for the time, to be, in substance as well as in form, anonymous. Its authorship was disclosed by the *Daily News* on November 3.

Turning for a moment from foreign to ecclesiastical affairs, we note that in the summer of 1870, Dean Stanley invited the company of divines appointed to revise the English translation of the Bible to open their proceedings by receiving the Holy Communion in King Henry VII's Chapel; and a Unitarian minister who was a member of the company was admitted to communion with the rest. The incident created great searchings of heart among orthodox Churchmen, and Mr Gladstone's views of it are worth recording. 'Talked of "Westminster Scandal"—the "right name." Of little import when merely Stanley's eccentricity; but the Bishops' speeches, especially Bishop of Salisbury's. "How difficult with temper of House of Commons to maintain Church, if such the internal voice! No organic change will be made whilst I am in power. But that may be a short time."'

On December 16, Mr Gladstone, yielding to pertinacious pressure, announced the release of the Fenian prisoners, on the condition that they should not remain in or return to England. In his second Administration he tasted the fruits of this clemency.

In the Session of 1871 the ardour of reform was still unabated. Mr Gladstone repealed the ridiculous Ecclesiastical Titles Bill which, twenty years before, Lord Russell had passed in a moment of Protestant panic. He abolished religious tests in the universities. He carried through the House of Commons, in spite of some rudimentary forms of that obstruction which has since been developed into a fine art, a Bill to establish secret voting. This was thrown out by the Lords, but became law a year later.

It is highly characteristic of the Premier's versatile intelligence, and of his power of rapidly turning his mind from one theme to another, that, at the very hottest moment of the battle for the ballot, Bishop Wilberforce notes, on June 22 'Breakfast Gladstone, who unusually bright; *Italy*, &c., &c.'

Emboldened by their success in the matter of the ballot, the Lords plucked up courage to throw out a Bill to abolish the purchase of commissions in the army, which formed part of Mr Cardwell's general system of military reorganization.

This performance of the Peers was the signal for a decisive and even startling act on the part of Mr Gladstone. Having failed to attain his object by the consent of Parliament, he dispensed with that consent, and effected his purpose by his single-handed act. Purchase in the army, he found, existed only by royal sanction. He advised the Queen to issue a Royal Warrant declaring that, on and after November 1 following, all regulations authorizing the purchase of commissions should be cancelled. Purchase in the army was thus abolished by the single will of the Prime Minister, acting through the royal prerogative. This high-handed act of executive authority was received with general disapproval. The Tories and the Peers, of course, were beside themselves with baffled rage; but even devout Gladstonians were dismayed. Sturdy Radicals were unsparing in their condemnation; and the venerable Lord Russell, though he approved of the reform, gravely denounced the conduct of a Minister who invoked the royal prerogative to override the will of one of the Houses of Parliament.

But Mr Gladstone's friends and admirers had a more agreeable subject for contemplation in his dealings with America. His passionate love of peace and his sense of its value as the greatest of human blessings were nobly illustrated in the transactions of this year. The United States had a just quarrel with us. Five privateers which, during the Civil War, had done a vast deal of damage to the navy and commerce of the Union, were built in English dockyards. The most famous of them was the *Alabama.* She captured seventy Northern vessels. She was manned by an English crew. Some of her gunners belonged to the Naval Reserve and received English pay. She left port under the British flag. What made all this infinitely worse was that, while the *Alabama* was building, the American Minister warned the English Government of the use to which she was to be put; and the English Government, hide-bound in official pedantry, and paralyzed by infirmity of purpose, let the *Alabama* get out to sea and begin her two years' cruise of piracy and devastation. This deplorable incident, and others like it, gave rise to a diplomatic correspondence which dragged on for years. At first the English Government declined to admit any responsibility for the losses inflicted by the English-built cruiser. Then Lord Stanley (now Lord Derby), more prudent than his Whig predecessors, began to talk of arbitration. Then Lord Clarendon, advancing from talk into action, agreed to a pettifogging convention, which the Senate of the United States refused to ratify. Then, warned by this failure and by some ominous words addressed by the American President to Congress, England agreed to send a Commission to Washington, to confer with an American Commission on all matters in dispute between the two countries. Mr Gladstone wisely included in the Commission a prominent Conservative statesman, Sir Stafford Northcote. The Commissions of the two countries soon agreed to the Treaty of Washington; England unreservedly expressed regret for the escape of the *Alabama* from the British port, and a board of arbitration was arranged. How that board sat at Geneva, and decided against England, we all remember. The incident is only recalled because, on the one hand, it did much to undermine Mr Gladstone's popularity with the bellicose portion of the British public; and because, on the other, it cemented his hold on the confidence and regard of those who concur in the sentiments which he expressed in the House of Commons on June 16, 1880, when the late Mr Henry Richard moved a resolution, requiring the Government to urge a 'simultaneous reduction of armaments' on all the Powers of Europe:

There is a third way, however, in which I think it is in the power of the Government to qualify itself for becoming a missionary for those beneficial purposes which are contemplated by my hon. friend—that is, by showing their disposition, when they are themselves engaged in controversy, to adopt these amicable and pacific means of escape from their disputes, rather than to resort to war. Need I assure my hon. friend and my right hon. friend behind me (Mr Baxter) that the dispositions which led us to become parties to the arbitration on the *Alabama* case are still with us the same as ever; that we are not discouraged; that we are not damped in the exercise of these feelings by the fact that we were amerced, and severely amerced, by the sentence of the international tribunal; and that, although we may think the sentence was harsh in its extent and unjust in its basis, we regard the fine imposed on this country as dust in the balance compared with the moral value of the example set when these two great nations of England and America, which are among the most fiery and the most jealous in the world with regard to anything that touches national honour, went in peace and concord before a judicial tribunal to dispose of these painful differences, rather than resort to the arbitrament of the sword.

The remainder of the year 1871 was signalized by some public appearances of Mr Gladstone which were in various ways remarkable. In the autumn he was in attendance on the Queen at Balmoral, and thence conducted an amusing correspondence with that eccentric bulwark of the Protestant religion, the late Mr Whalley, MP, who asked with all due solemnity if he was a member of the Church of Rome. Later he received the freedom of the city of Aberdeen, and speaking on this occasion he referred to the newly-invented cry of Home Rule. He spoke of the political delusions to which the Irish people were periodically subject, the lengths to which England had gone in meeting their complaints, the removal of all their grievances except that which related to higher education. Any inequalities which still existed between England and Ireland were in favour of Ireland. And as to Home Rule, if Ireland was entitled to it, Scotland was better entitled, and even more so Wales. 'Can any sensible man, can any rational man, suppose that at this time of day, in this condition of the world, we are going to disintegrate the great capital institutions of this country for the purpose of making ourselves ridiculous in the sight of all mankind, and crippling any power we possess for bestowing benefits, through legislation, on the country to which we belong?'

It was now apparent that the Prime Minister's popularity was on the wane. His seat was threatened. He had shown scant interest in the local affairs of Greenwich (which was perhaps not surprising), and his policy of retrenchment had deprived the borough of a great part of its trade. The air was heavy with murmurs and threats, and with characteristic courage Mr Gladstone resolved to meet the murmurers on their own ground, and boldly challenge the judgment of his constituents. On a cold afternoon at the end of October he stood bare-headed on Blackheath, and, facing an audience of 20,000 persons, defended the whole policy of his Administration in a speech as long, as methodical, as argumentative, and in parts as eloquent, as if he had been speaking at his ease under the friendly and commodious shelter of the House of Commons. The scene was thus described by an eyewitness. 'There was something deeply dramatic in the intense silence which fell upon the vast crowd when the renewed burst of cheering, with which he was greeted, had subsided. But the first word he spoke was the signal of a fearful tempest of din. From all around the skirts of the crowd rose a something between a groan and a howl. So fierce was it that for a little space it might laugh to scorn the burst of cheering that strove to overmaster it. The battle raged between the two sounds, and looking straight upon the excited crowd stood Mr Gladstone, calm, resolute, patient. It was fine to note the manly British impulse of fair-play that gained him a hearing when the first ebullition had exhausted itself, and the revulsion that followed so quickly and spontaneously on the realization of the suggestion that it was mean to hoot a man down without giving him a chance to speak for himself. After that Mr Gladstone may be said to have had it all his own way. Of course at intervals there were repetitions of the interruptions. When he first broached the dockyard question there was long, loud, and fervent groaning; when he named Ireland a cry rose of "God save Ireland!" from the serried files of Hibernians that had rendezvoused on the left flank. But long before he had finished he had so enthralled his audience that impatient disgust was expressed at the handful who still continued their abortive efforts at interruption. When at length the two hours' oration was over, and the question was put—that substantially was, whether Mr Gladstone had cleared away from the judgment of his constituency the fog of prejudice and ill-feeling that unquestionably encircled him and his Ministry—the affirmative reply was given in bursts of all but unanimous cheering, than which none more earnest ever greeted a political leader.'

We see the versatility which these pages have so often illustrated, and the constant interest in the concerns of the Church which underlay all this political activity, when we turn from this turbulent and triumphant scene to an entry in Bishop Wilberforce's journal. This was the period when an abortive attempt was made by such Churchmen as Archbishop Tait and Dean Stanley to abolish the use of the Athanasian Creed in Divine service. On October 25 the Bishop writes: 'Interview with WEG. Most friendly. Full talk as to Athanasian Creed. Cabinet not willing to stir needless difficulties ... Noble as ever.'

To this same autumn belong the incidents familiarly known as the 'Ewelme Scandal' and the 'Colliery Explosion'—two cases in which Mr Gladstone, while observing the letter of an Act of Parliament, violated, or seemed to violate, its spirit, in order to qualify highly-deserving gentlemen for posts to which he wished to appoint them. The incidents are only worth recalling now because they unquestionably helped to undermine Mr Gladstone's authority. Both these appointments were angrily challenged in the House of Commons as soon as Parliament met in 1872. The Prime Minister defended them with energy and skill, and logically his defence was unassailable. But these were cases where a plain man—and Parliament is full of plain men—feels, though he cannot prove, that there has been a departure from ordinary straightforwardness and plain dealing. Though he is powerless to demonstrate the wrongfulness of the act, he cherishes a kind of sulky grudge against the nimble-witted opponent whose logic and ethics he cannot assail, but who yet seems to have paltered in a double sense with unmistakable obligations. Perhaps it is not fanciful to trace in these appointments, and the defence of them, the influence exercised by the discipline of Oxford on a mind naturally prone to what the vulgar call hair-splitting and the learned casuistry. 'Let us distinguish, said the philosopher,' and at Oxford men are taught to distinguish with scrupulous care between propositions closely similar but not identical. But in the House of Commons they are satisfied with the roughest and broadest divisions between right and wrong; they see no shades of colour between black and white. Members of Parliament were even brutally indifferent to Mr Gladstone's distinctions between 'judicial status' and 'judicial experience' as qualification for Sir Robert Collier's elevation. They could not be induced to appreciate the difference between membership of the University of Oxford and membership of the Convocation of Oxford in the matter of the Rectory of Ewelme.

On May 4, 1872, Bishop Wilberforce, describing the opening of the Royal Academy, writes 'Nothing high above, but much careful and good painting. At the dinner much the same of the speaking ... Gladstone best, but never kindling into fire.'

'*September 3; Hawarden.*—To early church with WEG, as lovable as ever ... Talk with Gladstone on Athanasian Creed; for no violence; would keep all possible; suspects it as only a preliminary of attack on Prayer-Book.'

In December 1872, Mr Gladstone addressed the students of Liverpool College on some modern aspects of Free Thought in Religion, dealing in particular with the teaching of Strauss. The late Mr H. A. Bright (author of *A Year in a Lancashire Garden*) writes thus on Christmas Eve:

> Saturday I heard Mr Gladstone at the Liverpool College. It was on all accounts a most interesting meeting. Tories and Liberals, Churchmen and Dissenters, all were there, and all delighted. Some because an orthodox Churchman was speaking, some because the Liberal chief was before them in the flesh. He read from a

MS; but this was hardly noticeable, his voice was so finely modulated, his action so easy and impressive. Butler very happily quoted when it was over,

> The guests were spell-bound in the dusky hall.

In the year 1873 came the long-deferred and ineffectual attack upon the third branch of the upas-tree. Mr Gladstone attempted to settle the difficult question of higher education in Ireland, and to adjust and reconcile the discordant demands of Romanism and Protestantism for a university which, in its idea and methods, should not conflict with the convictions of either faith.

Mr Gladstone's scheme was admitted to be ingenious, plausible, and honestly intended to promote intellectual culture while safeguarding the rights of conscience. Unhappily, it satisfied no one. The Roman Catholics wanted more; the English Dissenters thought they ought to have less. The Irish Protestants resisted the abolition of their old university; the Roman Bishops denounced the new body which was to replace the old. Mr Disraeli made fun of the Bill; stalwart Liberals condemned it; the Irish members voted against it. The following extract from Mr Forster's diary describes the close of the debate on the second reading:

'*March* 11, 1873.—Gladstone rose with the House dead against him and his Bill, and made a wonderful speech—easy, almost playful, with passages of great power and eloquence, but with a graceful play which enabled him to plant deep his daggers of satire in Horsman, Fitzmaurice, and Co.'

The Bill was thrown out by three votes. Mr Forster continues:

'*March* 13.—Cabinet again at twelve. Decided to resign… Gladstone made us quite a touching little speech. He began playfully. This was the last of some 150 Cabinets or so, and he wished to say to his colleagues with what "profound gratitude"—And here he completely broke down and could say nothing, except that he could not enter on the details … Tears came to my eyes, and we were all touched.'

The Queen, of course, sent for Mr Disraeli, but he refused to take office in a minority of the House of Commons, and Mr Gladstone was compelled to resume. But he and his colleagues were now, in Disraelitish phrase, extinct volcanoes. All their authority, all their power, was gone. It was the beginning, and something more than the beginning of the end.

The summer was marked by an event which, though not strictly personal to Mr Gladstone, is highly germane to this memoir of his career. On July 19 his life-long friend, counsellor, and supporter, Samuel Wilberforce, Bishop of Oxford and subsequently of Winchester, was killed by a fall from his horse near the famous woods of Wotton, in Surrey. Readers of these pages will know his keen appreciation of Mr Gladstone's character and gifts; his shrewd perception of his friend's motives and impulses, and of the diverse influences which swayed him. His journals afford, in the writer's opinion, the best material yet available for a right judgment on the great career which we are considering. The Bishop was four years older than Mr Gladstone. They had become acquainted with one another in very early life. Acquaintance soon ripened into friendship. The one became a Bishop about the time that the other became a Cabinet Minister. This friendship was sealed by common interests and purposes in the sphere of religion and the Church; increased in tenacity and tenderness as years went on, and remained inviolate to the end. It is no secret that had Mr Gladstone become Prime Minister a month earlier than he did in 1868, Bishop Wilberforce, and not Bishop Tait, would have been Archbishop of Canterbury. An eye witness, describing the scene at Sir Thomas Farrer's house, where the Bishop's body lay, says: 'Among those who came that Monday morning were Mr Gladstone and Lord Granville, and well the writer of these lines remembers the scene in that room; the peaceful body of the Bishop, the lines of care and trouble smoothed out of the face, the beautiful smile of satisfaction, and, kneeling reverentially by that body, Mr Gladstone, whose sobs attested how deeply his feelings were moved by the sudden loss of his long-tried friend.'

The end of Mr. Gladstone's first Administration was now nigh at hand. The Cabinet was beset from within and from without. Within, Mr Gladstone had indeed one or two colleagues who were his personal friends, but, as a rule, he kept his friendships and his official relations quite distinct. He did not realize the force of the saying that men who have only worked together have only half lived together; and though, in official intercourse, he was facile and accessible enough, he did not feel bound, merely because a man was his colleague, to cultivate relations of intimacy with him when business was over. A member of his first Cabinet remarked that he had never been invited into the chief's house, except as a unit in an assembly of the Liberal party. Men just outside office, with their faces steadily set towards it, chafed at the difficulty of attaching themselves to the machine of Government, and, finding that assiduous service was of no avail, betook themselves, in some instances successfully, to guerrilla warfare. It has been truly said that Mr Gladstone understands MAN but not men; and meek followers in the House of Commons, who had sacrificed money, time, toil, health, and sometimes conscience, to the support of the Government, turned, like the crushed worm, when they found that Mr Gladstone sternly ignored their presence in the Lobby, or, if forced to speak to them, called them by inappropriate names. And, if these tragedies occurred in the ranks of earnest Liberalism, it is not difficult to guess the feelings with which sham Liberals and Tories regarded him. The sham Liberals had found the pace forced to break-neck speed during four years of breathless reform. The Tories had seen one after another of their dearest monopolies and most sacred tyrannies knocked on the head by this terrible emancipator. His strenuousness of reforming purpose and strength of will were concealed by no lightness of touch, no give-and-take, no playfulness, no fun. He had little of that saving gift of humour which smoothes the practical working of life as much as it adds to its enjoyment. The Liberal chief was gravely, terribly, incessantly in earnest; and unbroken earnestness, though admirable, exhausts, and in the long run alienates. Out of doors, everyone was against him. That noble and numerous class of patriots who are brave with other men's lives and lavish of other men's money, resented his recourse to arbitration, his avoidance of war, his rigorous abstinence from foreign intervention. The clergy, by a curious perversity of fat; were arrayed in increasing numbers against the one Minister of the century who was pre-eminently a Christian and a Churchman. They found an organized contingent of strange allies in the brewers, distillers, and licensed victuallers, whose craft had been menaced, though scarcely injured, by the Liberal Government.

Over and above all these elements of danger, Mr Gladstone was singularly unfortunate in some of his colleagues, of whom it is no libel to say that they succeeded in identifying the name of Liberalism with all that is meanest in policy and most offensive in demeanour. They imposed vexatious taxes; they haggled about the amount of water in the sailors' grog and the price of the window-curtains in a public office; they were assailed by insurrections of half-starved children whose wretched bread their legislation would have destroyed; they were nightly ridiculed on the stage before delighted audiences till they ran to the Lord Chamberlain for protection against the scoffers. Odious to the public, they quarrelled among themselves. They fought for fatter offices, and grudged if they were not satisfied. There were resignations and rumours of resignation. Mr Gladstone took the Chancellorship of the Exchequer, and, as some authorities contended, vacated his seat by doing so. Election after election went wrong. The chorus of the newspapers was unanimous against the Government. Mr Disraeli, always supreme in criticism, made the most of these excellent opportunities. He poured bitter and biting ridicule on his discomfited opponents, and pointed out with triumphant malice the signs of impending catastrophe. That catastrophe was not long delayed. On January 23, 1874, Mr Gladstone, confined to his house by a cold, executed a *coup d'état*. He announced the dissolution of Parliament. His decree was made known to the electors of Greenwich and to the world in an address of extraordinary length. In this address, he declared that his authority had now 'sunk below the point necessary for the due defence and prosecution of the public interests,' and he promised that, if it were renewed by the country, he would repeal the income-tax.

It is needless to describe the public excitement and confusion which attended the general election thus unexpectedly decreed. Mr Gladstone, recovering from his cold, threw himself into his candidature at Greenwich with incredible energy. Writing on February 4, Lord Shaftesbury said: 'It is a new thing, and a very serious thing, to see the Prime Minister "on the stump." Surely there is little due to dignity of position. But to see him running from Greenwich to Blackheath, to Woolwich, to New Cross, to every place where a barrel can be set up, is more like Punch than the Premier.' Using a more flattering comparison, the *Times* observed: 'The Prime Minister descends upon Greenwich amid a shower of gold, and must needs prove as irresistible as the Father of the Gods.'

Alas! this was too sanguine a forecast. Greenwich, which returned two members, placed Mr Gladstone second on the poll, below a local distiller. But even in the second place the Liberal chief was more fortunate than most of his followers, who were blown out of their seats like chaff before the wind. When the election was over the Tories had a majority of forty-six. Following the example of his predecessor in 1868, Mr Gladstone immediately resigned.

Before the new Parliament had met for the rather humdrum business which lay before it, Mr Gladstone burst upon the world with a new surprise. A surprise it certainly was, and yet he had often foreshadowed it. For many years past he had held, in public and in private, language which pointed to an early retirement from public life. He had followed, he said, nearly all his political contemporaries to the grave. He had entered public life in his twenty-third year, and had earned his title to retire at an age when most men are only beginning their career. He was 'strong against going on in politics to the end.' In 1861 he wrote: 'Events are not wholly unwelcome which remind me that my own public life is now in its thirtieth year, and ought not to last very many years longer.' In 1867 he told Lord Russell that he neither expected nor desired that his political life would be very long. On May 6, 1873, Bishop Wilberforce wrote: 'Gladstone much talking how little real good work any Premier had done after sixty: Peel; Palmerston, his work all really done before; Duke of Wellington added nothing to his reputation after. I told him Dr Clark thought it would be physically worse for him to retire. "Dr Clark does not know how completely I should employ myself," &c. *May* 10.—Gladstone again talking of sixty as full age of Premier.'

The author of these sentiments was now sixty-four. His life had been a continuous experience of exhausting labour. Even his iron constitution was beginning to show signs of wear and tear. His private affairs, necessarily neglected under the pressure of office, required his personal attention. There was no great question of public interest before the world. The country which he had served so zealously had expressed its desire for a breathing-time. He was weary and perhaps mortified, and the opportunity seemed to have arrived for change of occupation: idleness would not have been rest. Accordingly, on March 12, he addressed the following letter to Lord Granville:

> I have issued a circular to members of Parliament of the Liberal party on the occasion of the opening of parliamentary business. But I feel it to be necessary that, while discharging this duty; I should explain what a circular could not convey

with regard to my individual position at the present time. I need not apologize for addressing these explanations to you. Independently of other reasons for so troubling you, it is enough to observe that you have very long represented the Liberal party, and have also acted on behalf of the late Government, from its commencement to its close, in the House of Lords.

For a variety of reasons personal to myself, I could not contemplate any unlimited extension of active political service; and I am anxious that it should be clearly understood by those friends with whom I have acted in the direction of affairs, that at my age I must reserve my entire freedom to divest myself of all the responsibilities of leadership at no distant time. The need of rest will prevent me from giving more than occasional attendance in the House of Commons during the present Session.

I should be desirous, shortly before the commencement of the Session of 1875, to consider whether there would be advantage in my placing my services for a time at the disposal of the Liberal party, or whether I should then claim exemption from the duties I have hitherto discharged. If, however, there should be reasonable ground for believing that, instead of the course which I have sketched, it would be preferable, in the view of the party generally, for me to assume at once the place of an independent member, I should willingly adopt the latter alternative. But I shall retain all that desire I have hitherto felt for the welfare of the party, and if the gentlemen composing it should think fit either to choose a leader or make provision *ad interim*, with a view to the convenience of the present year, the person designated would, of course, command from me any assistance which he might find occasion to seek, and which it might be in my power to render.

The retirement of Mr Gladstone from active leadership naturally filled his party with dismay. According to the general law of human life, they only realized their blessings when they had lost them. They had grumbled at their chief, and mutinied against him, and helped to depose him. But, now that this commanding genius was suddenly withdrawn from their councils, they found that they had nothing to put in its place. Their indignation waxed fast and furious, and was not the less keen because they had to some extent brought their trouble on themselves. They complained with an almost ludicrous pathos that Mr Gladstone had led them into the wilderness of Opposition and left them there to perish. They were as sheep without a shepherd, and the ravening wolves of Toryism seemed to have it all their own way. But while they were still murmuring at their former leader and making moan over his desertion, he suddenly revisited the glimpses of the parliamentary moon; and it is not too much to say that, if his disappearance had created consternation, his reappearance created much more. Archbishop Tait had brought in a 'Public Worship Regulation Bill,' of which the object, abruptly stated, was to 'put down ritualism.' The Government took the Bill up and afforded facilities for its consideration; and

Mr Gladstone, suddenly returning from the country, offered it a most strenuous and an almost single-handed opposition. The grounds of his resistance may best be judged by the following resolutions of which he gave notice:

1. That in proceeding to consider the provisions of the Bill for the Regulation of Public Worship, this House cannot do otherwise than take into view the lapse of more than two centuries since the enactment of the present Rubrics of the Common Prayer Book of the Church of England; the multitude of particulars embraced in the conduct of Divine service under their provisions; the doubts occasionally attaching to their interpretation, and the number of points they are thought to leave undecided; the diversities of local custom, which under these circumstances, have long prevailed; and the unreasonableness of proscribing all varieties of opinion and usage among the many thousands of congregations of the Church distributed throughout the land.
2. That this House is therefore reluctant to place in the hands of every single bishop, on the motion of one or of three persons, howsoever defined, greatly increased facilities towards procuring an absolute ruling of many points hitherto left open and reasonably allowing of diversity, and thereby towards the establishment of an inflexible rule of uniformity throughout the land, to the prejudice, in matters indifferent, of the liberty now practically existing.
3. That the House willingly acknowledges the great and exemplary devotion of the clergy in general to their sacred calling, but is not on that account the less disposed to guard against the indiscretion, or thirst for power, or other faults of individuals.
4. That the House is therefore willing to lend its best assistance to any measure recommended by adequate authority, with a view to provide more effectual securities against any neglect of or departure from strict law which may give evidence of a design to alter, without the consent of the nation, the spirit or substance of the established religion.
5. That, in the opinion of the House, it is also to be desired that the members of the Church, having a legitimate interest in her services, should receive ample protection against precipitate and arbitrary changes of established customs by the sole will of the clergyman and against the wishes locally prevalent among them; and that such protection does not appear to be afforded by the provisions of the Bill now before the House.
6. That the House attaches a high value to the concurrence of her Majesty's Government with the ecclesiastical authorities in the initiative of legislation affecting the Established Church.

A shrewd observer of Parliamentary life once said, 'Whenever the House of Commons is unanimous, it is wrong.' The truth of this saying was illustrated in the debate on the Public Worship Regulation Bill. The House was so clearly and strongly in favour of the Bill, which has been a dead letter and a laughing stock ever since it has been law, that it was read a second time without a division, and Mr Gladstone withdrew his resolutions in deference to a unanimous sentiment. He reserved his force of opposition for Committee, where the most entertaining passages of arms took place between him and Sir William Harcourt, who had been Solicitor-General during the last two months of his Administration. Sir William had espoused the Bill with extraordinary ardour, and when the House of Lords dealt rather cavalierly with some amendments of the Commons, he implored Mr Disraeli to take up the cudgels, and expressed his confidence in him in these glowing terms: 'We have a leader of this House who is proud of the House of Commons and of whom the House of Commons is proud. Well may the Prime Minister be proud of the House of Commons, for it was the scene of his early triumphs, and it is still the arena of his later and well-earned glory ... We may well leave the vindication of the reputation of this famous assembly to one who will well know how to defend its credit and its dignity against the ill-advised railing of a rash and rancorous tongue.'

A provision had been introduced into the Bill which would have overthrown the bishop's right of veto on proceedings to be instituted in the new Court, and would have invested the archbishop with power to institute suits, or allow them to be instituted, in a diocese not his own. This provision Mr Gladstone vehemently opposed, on the ground that it was contrary to the whole tradition and structure of the Church, and that it was fundamentally inconsistent with the custom of Christendom as regards the relations between Metropolitans and their suffragans. In support of this view he quoted at large from the canonist Van Espen. Sir William Harcourt poured scorn on these citations; was proud to say he had never heard of Van Espen; pooh-poohed all canonists and casuists; adopted Mr Bright's famous phrase about ecclesiastical rubbish; took the broad and manly ground of common sense, common law, and the Constitution; and accused Mr Gladstone of having come back to wreck the Bill at the eleventh hour. Five days afterwards Sir William resumed his discourse. He had got up the case in the meantime, and met Mr Gladstone on his own ground. He argued the question of canon law. He cited Ayliffe's *Parergon Juris Canonici Anglicani*, and Burn's *Ecclesiastical Law*, and sought to show that the power claimed for the Metropolitan was as sound canonically as constitutionally. This unexpected display of erudition gave Mr Gladstone an opportunity, which he was not slow to use.

He rebuked 'the hon. and learned gentleman' for having given one of the most conspicuous and most objectionable examples he had ever known of the vicious practice of discussing speeches delivered in the Lords. And then, referring to Sir William's canonical exercitations, he said:

I confess, fairly, I greatly admire the manner in which he has used his time since Friday night. On Friday night, as he says, he was taken by surprise. The lawyer was taken by surprise, and so was the professor of law in the University of Cambridge; the lawyer was taken by surprise, and, in consequence, he had nothing to deliver to the House except a series of propositions on which I will not comment. I greatly respect the order and the spirit of the order of the House which renders it irregular, as, in my opinion, it is highly inconvenient, especially when there is no practical issue, to revive the details and particulars of a former debate. Finding that he has delivered to the House most extraordinary propositions of law and history that will not bear a moment's examination, my hon. and learned friend has had the opportunity of spending four or five days in better informing himself upon the subject, and he is in a position to come down to this House, and for an hour and a half to display and develop the erudition he has thus rapidly and cleverly acquired. Human nature could not possibly resist such a temptation, and my hon. and learned friend has succumbed to it on this occasion.

Thus ended this rather unequal duel, and the incident is only worth recording because it showed the distracted and shattered Gladstonians that their chief, though temporarily withdrawn from active service, was as vivacious and as energetic as ever, as formidable in debate, and as unquestionably supreme in his party whenever he chose to assert his supremacy.

Mr Gladstone was now the delight and glory of the Ritualists. The committee organized to defend the ritualistic church of St Alban's, Holborn, against the paternal attentions of the Bishop of London made a formal and public acknowledgment of 'their gratitude for his noble and unsupported defence of the rights of the Church of England, as exhibited more particularly on the occasion of the recent debate on the Public Worship Regulation Bill.' Cultivated and earnest Churchmen everywhere were attracted to his standard, and turned in righteous disgust from the perpetrator of clumsy witticisms about 'Mass in masquerade.' In towns where, as at Oxford and Brighton, the Church is powerful, the effect of these desertions was unmistakably felt at the general election of 1880.

Theological controversy has always exercised an irresistible fascination over Mr Gladstone's mind. We have seen, at every stage of his career, his inclination to turn aside from the most exacting and exciting business of State or party to argue nice questions of dogmatic theology, or to discuss the position and prospects of the Church. The passage of the Public Worship Regulation Act drew Mr Gladstone, by an irresistible attraction, back into these familiar fields; and he uttered his views in an article on 'Ritual and Ritualism,' contributed to the *Contemporary Review* for October, 1874. In this paper he maintained with great earnestness and great sobriety the lawfulness and expediency of moderate ritual in the services of the Church of England. He claimed for ritual apostolic authorization in St Paul's words, 'Let all things be done decently and in order,' or, as Mr Gladstone more exactly renders the Greek, 'in right, graceful, or becoming figure, and by fore-ordered arrangement.'

Immersed in ecclesiastical study, which was destined soon to develop into acrimonious controversy, Mr Gladstone resolved to shake himself free from the burden of political leadership. On January 13, 1875, he said, in a letter to Lord Granville:

> The time has, I think, arrived when I ought to revert to the subject of the letter which I addressed to you on March 12. Before determining whether I should offer to assume a charge which might extend over a length of time, I have reviewed, with all the care in my power, a number of considerations both public and private, of which a portion, and these not by any means insignificant, were not in existence at the date of that letter. The result has been that I see no public advantage in my continuing to act as the leader of the Liberal party; and that, at the age of sixty-five, and after forty-two years of a laborious public life, I think myself entitled to retire on the present opportunity. This retirement is dictated to me by my personal views as to the best method of spending the closing years of my life. I need hardly say that my conduct in Parliament will continue to be governed by the principles on which I have heretofore acted; and, whatever arrangements may be made for the treatment of general business, and for the advantage or convenience of the Liberal party, they will have my cordial support. I should, perhaps, add that I am at present, and mean for a short time to be, engaged on a special matter, which occupies me closely.

It is worth while to notice, as an amusing instance of fallibility in high places, that the *Times* took this retirement as quite serious and final:

'It may be assumed as certain that there will be occasions when his mind will revert to Westminster, and a sense of duty to the nation may bring him back at recurrent intervals to the scene of so many triumphs. Yet we cannot but believe that a resolution which can be traced back through many Sessions, and has stood twelve months' trial, will grow rather than diminish in strength, and that we must not again expect Mr Gladstone's habitual presence in the House of Commons.'

The 'special matter' with which Mr Gladstone was busied proved to be theological investigation. In July, 1875, he replied to the various and inconsistent criticisms of his article on Ritualism in a second article, called 'Is the Church of England worth Preserving?' The drift of this paper was thus summarized by the author:

> I. The Church of this great nation is worth preserving, and for that end much may well be borne. II. In the existing state of minds and of circumstances, preserved it cannot be, if we now shift its balance of doctrinal expression, be it by any

alteration of the Prayer Book (either way) in contested points, or be it by treating rubrical interpretations of the matters heretofore most sharply contested on the basis of doctrinal significance. III. The more we trust to moral forces, and the less to penal proceedings (which are to a considerable extent exclusive one of the other), the better for the establishment, and even for the Church. IV. If litigation is to be continued, and to remain, within the bounds of safety, it is highly requisite that it should be confined to the repression of such proceedings as really imply unfaithfulness to the national religion. V. In order that judicial decisions on ceremonial may habitually enjoy the large measure of authority, finality, and respect, which attaches in general to the sentences of our courts, it is requisite that they should have uniform regard to the rules and results of full historical investigation, and should, if possible, allow to stand over for the future matters insufficiently cleared, rather than decide them upon partial and fragmentary evidence.

To vindicate the claims of the Church of England, and to enforce the policy which seemed most conducive to her well-being and efficiency, was the purpose of these remarkable papers, which were widely circulated and republished under the title of 'The Church of England and Ritualism.' But in dealing with his main proposition Mr Gladstone had made a startling and an unfortunate digression. Ridiculing the notion that a handful of ritualistic clergy could, if they would, Romanize the Church of England, he said:

'At no time since the sanguinary reign of Mary has such a scheme been possible. But, if it had been possible in the seventeenth or eighteenth centuries, it would still have become impossible in the nineteenth; when Rome has substituted for the proud boast of *semper eadem* a policy of violence and change in faith; when she has refurbished and paraded anew every rusty tool she was fondly thought to have disused; when no one can become her convert without renouncing his moral and mental freedom and placing his civil loyalty and duty at the mercy of another; and when she has equally repudiated modern thought and ancient history. I cannot persuade myself to feel alarm as to the final issue of her crusades in England, and this although I do not undervalue her great powers of mischief.'

This passage created a sudden storm of honest indignation. Every Roman Catholic in the Queen's dominions felt aggrieved. There was a flavour of No Popery about the words which offended the palate of Liberal politicians. Contradictions and protests were heard on every side, and the statement that a Roman Catholic had of necessity placed his civil loyalty and duty at the mercy of another was the subject of peculiarly angry comment.

Mr Gladstone replied to his assailants by publishing a pamphlet called 'The Vatican Decrees in their Bearing on Civil Allegiance,' and in this he reaffirmed, amplified, and maintained his propositions with fullness, force, and precision. A hundred and twenty thousand copies of the pamphlet were sold in a few weeks, and the Press teemed with replies. To the protests, criticisms, and rebukes which were lavished on him the indefatigable controversialist made a rejoinder in an essay called 'Vaticanism,' in which he summed up the controversy by maintaining that although in practice Roman Catholics might be as loyal as their fellow-citizens, still in theory the modern claim of Papal infallibility was always liable to clash with the requirements of civil allegiance.

X

The Eastern Question—The Midlothian campaign— The General Election of 1880—Liberal triumph—Prime Minister a second time—Ireland and Egypt—Defeat and resignation—The General Election of 1885—Home Rule—Prime Minister a third time—The Home Rule Bill defeated—The General Election of 1886—Resignation—Leadership of Opposition—Golden wedding—Life at Hawarden.

THE SMOKE AND DIN OF this theological battle had scarcely cleared away when the great protagonist of Anglicanism was suddenly and imperiously summoned to a fresh campaign. An insurrection had broken out in Bulgaria, and the Turkish Government despatched a large force to repress it. This was soon done, and repression was followed by a hideous orgy of massacre and outrage. A rumour of these horrors reached England, and public indignation spontaneously awoke. Mr Disraeli with a strange frankness of cynical brutality, sneered at the rumour as coffee-house babble, and made odious jokes about the oriental way of executing malefactors. But Christian England was not to be pacified with these Asiatic pleasantries, and the country rose in passionate indignation against what were known as 'the Bulgarian atrocities.' Lord Hartington was now the titular leader of the Liberal party, and his sympathies were entirely on the right side. But he is a man of slow-moving mind and calm, if not lethargic, temperament. He would probably have done what was right and proper in his place in Parliament: submitted a resolution, asked for a return, or moved an amendment to the Address. But the national temper, and the feeling of the Liberal party in particular, demanded prompter action and more emphatic speech. The Liberals' extremity was Mr Gladstone's opportunity. He rushed from his library at Hawarden, forgot alike ancient Greece and modern Rome, and flung himself into the agitation against Turkey with a zeal which in his prime he had never excelled, if, indeed, he had equalled it. He made the most impassioned speeches, often in the open air; he published pamphlets which rushed into incredible circulations; he poured letter after letter into the newspapers; he darkened the sky with controversial post-cards; and, as soon as Parliament met, he was ready with all his unequalled resources of eloquence, argumentation, and inconvenient enquiry, to drive home his great indictment against the Turkish Government and its friends and champions in the House of Commons. Lord Hartington, whose homely mind moved more slowly and uttered itself more cautiously, soon found himself pushed aside from his position of titular leadership. Though there was a section of the Whigs who doggedly supported Turkey, it soon became evident that, both in the House and in the country, the fervour, the faith, the militant and victorious element in the Liberal party were sworn to Mr Gladstone's standard. It was just two years since he had resigned the leadership of the party, and he was again its dominating and inspiring influence.

The reason of all this passion is not difficult to discover. Mr Gladstone is a humane man: the Turkish tyranny is founded on cruelty. He is a worshipper of freedom: the Turk is a slave owner. He is a lover of peace: the Turk is nothing if not a soldier. He is a disciple of progress: the Turkish empire is a synonym for retrogression. But above and beyond and before all else, Mr Gladstone is a Christian and in the Turk he saw the great anti-Christian Power standing where it ought not, in the fairest provinces of Christendom, and stained with the record of odious cruelty practised through long centuries on its defenceless subjects who were worshippers of JESUS CHRIST.

It is unnecessary at this time of day to trace in detail the history of a great controversy so fresh in every memory that can reach back for fifteen years. For the purpose of this narrative it is enough to say that Mr Gladstone's resolute and splendid hostility to Lord Beaconsfield's whole system of foreign policy restored him to his paramount place among English politicians. For four years—from 1876 to 1880—he sustained the high and holy strife, with an enthusiasm, a versatility, a courage, and a resourcefulness, which raised the enthusiasm of his followers to the highest pitch, and filled his guilty and baffled antagonists with a rage which went near to frenzy. It is not too much to say that, by frustrating Lord Beaconsfield's design of going to war on behalf of Turkey, he saved England from the indelible disgrace of a second and more gratuitous Crimea. But it was not only in Eastern Europe that his saving influence was felt. In Africa, and India, and wherever British arms were exercised and British honour was involved, he was the resolute and unsparing enemy of that odious system of bluster and swagger and might against right, on which Lord Beaconsfield and his colleagues bestowed the tawdry nickname of Imperialism. The County of Edinburgh, or Mid Lothian, which he contested against the dominant influence of the Duke of Buccleuch, was the scene of his most astonishing exertions. In his own phrase, he devoted himself to 'counterworking the purpose of Lord

Beaconsfield.' As the general election approached one and only one question was submitted to the electors—'Do you approve or condemn Lord Beaconsfield's system of foreign policy?'

The answer was given at Easter, 1880, when Lord Beaconsfield and his colleagues received the most emphatic condemnation which had ever been bestowed on an English Government, and the Liberals were returned in an overwhelming majority over Tories and Home Rulers combined.

One of the most accomplished and most spiritually-minded men of his time—the late Dean Church—wrote thus to a friend:

> You were always sanguine that the country had 'found out' Lord Beaconsfield. But here in London people had not found him out, and wherever you went you heard people, not merely Tories and Jingoes, but lofty, intellectual people, who would have been inclined to challenge you if you had doubted their Liberalism, repeating the same hollow cry of trust in the Government, and dislike and distrust of Gladstone. If you have not seen it, I don't think you can form a notion of the intensity of that dislike ... Of all the evil symptoms about, this incapacity to perceive Gladstone's real nobleness, and to keep in check the antipathies created by his popular enthusiasm and his serious religiousness, is one of the worst. It is a bad thing to have a great man before a nation, and a great minority in it should not be able to recognize him. I don't wonder at your remembering the Song of Miriam.

Mr Gladstone was now member for Mid Lothian, having retired from Greenwich at the dissolution, He was also the unquestioned chief, the idol, and the pride of the victorious army of Liberalism. But he was not the titular leader of the Liberal party. When Lord Beaconsfield resigned—which he had the grace to do without meeting Parliament—the Queen, in strict conformity with constitutional usage, sent for Lord Hartington as nominal leader of the Liberal party in the House of Commons. He could do nothing, and her Majesty applied to Lord Granville. The two statesmen went together to Windsor on April 23. They both assured the Queen that the victory was Mr Gladstone's; that the Liberal party would be satisfied with no other leader; and that he was the inevitable Prime Minister. They returned to London in the afternoon, and called on Mr Gladstone in Harley Street. He was expecting them and the message which they brought, and he went down to Windsor without a moment's delay. That evening he kissed hands, and returned to London as Prime Minister for the second time. Truly his enemies had been made his footstool.

The history of Mr Gladstone's second Administration must be very briefly told. Before he came into office the Eastern question was closed, and, chiefly through his influence, it had been closed in a sense compatible with humanity and religion. His Administration did good and useful work at home, but its best performances were not sensational. It was seriously, and at length fatally, embarrassed by two controversies which sprang up with little warning, and found the Liberal party and its leaders totally unprepared to deal with them. The first of these controversies related to Ireland.

Here it was Mr Gladstone's singular misfortune to make enemies of both sides a once. He alienated considerable masses of English opinion by his attempts to reform the tenure of land in Ireland and he provoked the Irish people by his attempts to establish social order and to repress crime. At the general election of 1880 Irish questions were completely in the background: the demand for Home Rule was not taken seriously: the country was politically tranquil, and the distress due to the failure of the crops had been alleviated by the combined action of Englishmen irrespective of party. During the summer of 1880 it was found that the Irish landlords were evicting wholesale the tenants whom famine had impoverished. A well-meant but hastily-drawn Bill to provide compensation for these evicted tenants passed the Commons, but was shipwrecked in the Lords and the natural consequence of its rejection was seen in the ghastly record of outrage and murder which stained the following winter. The Session of 1881 was divided between a Coercion Bill which only irritated while it failed to terrify, and a Land Bill which, in itself a magnificent performance, was yet so mangled by the Lords that the best part of 1882 was taken up in mending it. The Irish showed no gratitude for boons which they did not ask, and, demanding self-government, would make no terms with any English Administration which refused it. Political disaffection was, or seemed to be, associated with odious crimes.

In the spring of 1882 the Government resolved on a change of tactics. They determined to release Mr Parnell and some of his followers, who had been arrested without trial under the Coercion Act of the previous year. The Chief Secretary, Mr Forster, dissented from the policy of his colleagues, and resigned office. His resignation was announced on May 2. On the evening of that day Mr Gladstone said to a friend, 'The state of Ireland is very greatly improved.' Ardent Liberals on both sides of the Channel shared this sanguine faith but they were doomed to a cruel disappointment. On May 6 the Queen performed the public ceremony of dedicating Epping Forest to the use of the people for ever. It was a brilliant and an animating scene. The late Mr W. H. O'Sullivan, member of Parliament for the county of Limerick, was standing by the writer of this book in the space reserved for the House of Commons. He was accounted a man of extreme opinions, but he was a blithe and genial creature, and on this occasion he actually overflowed with friendly fervour. 'This is a fine sight,' he exclaimed, 'but please God we shall yet see something like it in Ireland. *We have entered at last upon the right path. You will hear no more of the Irish difficulty.*' Within an hour of the time at which he spoke, the newly-appointed Chief Secretary for Ireland—the gallant and high-minded Lord Frederick Cavendish—and his Under-Secretary, Mr Burke, were stabbed to death in the Phoenix Park at Dublin, and the 'Irish difficulty' entered on the acutest phase which it has ever known.

This murder—not morally more reprehensible than many which had preceded it, but more startling and sensational—aroused a furious indignation in England, and, the Coercion Act of the previous year having proved a dismal failure, it was succeeded by a Crimes Act of the utmost rigour. This Act, courageously administered by Lord Spencer and Sir George Trevelyan, abolished exceptional crime in Ireland, but completed the breach between the English Government and the Irish party in Parliament.

Another controversy which proved disastrous to Liberalism arose from he occupation of Egypt in 1882. The bombardment of Alexandria and the subsequent expedition were profoundly distasteful to the great bulk of Liberals. Mr Bright resigned office rather than be a party to them. They were but little congenial to Mr Gladstone's own mind and temper. But a policy undertaken by his Administration bore the stamp of his own authority; and the great majority of Liberals accepted with reluctance, but without resistance, a line of action which wore an unpleasantly close resemblance to the antics of Lord Beaconsfield. Nothing but absolute confidence in Mr Gladstone's political rectitude and tried love of peace could have secured even this qualified and negative sanction from his party; and, at each succeeding step in the dismal progress, shamefaced Liberals found themselves dogged by the inexorable Nemesis which waits on the abandonment, even for a moment, of political principles once deliberately and conscientiously adopted. The beginning of the Liberal downfall may be traced to the shame and annoyance which followed a too ready acceptance of the Egyptian policy. That shame and that annoyance relaxed the efforts of countless Liberals who in 1880 had been enthusiastic for Mr Gladstone and his cause, but, in 1885, felt that they could no longer support a course repugnant alike to reason and to conscience. The heroic career and striking personality of General Gordon had fascinated the public imagination; and the circumstances of his untimely death awoke an outburst of indignation against those who were, or seemed to be, responsible for it. When the popularity of a Government out of doors declines, signs of disaffection are never wanting in the House of Commons. When parliamentary discipline can no longer be enforced by the threat, expressed or implied, of a penal dissolution, mutiny is imminent. The Tories, encouraged by the by-elections and reinforced by the Irish vote, were in a militant and unscrupulous mood. The Liberals, ashamed of the endless self-contradictions of the Egyptian policy, and the aimless loss of life which they were asked to sanction, were more and more unwilling to oppose the votes of censure which the Tories incessantly proposed. A noble majority steadily declined. The Cabinet was rent by intestine contentions. The Whiggish majority of the Ministers were in favour of renewing the Irish Crimes Act. A Radical minority dissented from this course, and wished to conciliate Ireland by establishing Provincial Self-Government. While the dispute was at its hottest, on June 8, 1885, the Government were beaten on the Budget. In reference to this event, Lord Shaftesbury writes: 'Have just seen the defeat of Government on the Budget by Conservatives and Parnellites combined; an act of folly amounting to wickedness. God is not in all their thoughts, nor the country either. All seek their own, and their own is party spirit, momentary triumph, political hatred, and the indulgence of low, personal, and unpatriotic passion.'

It was generally believed in the House of Commons, and not least firmly on the Liberal side, that the Government courted this defeat, as a way of escape from their manifold perplexities. Certainly no strenuous efforts were made to avert it.

Mr Gladstone, disgusted with the course of policy into which he had insensibly drifted, and weary of dissensions among his colleagues, resigned office. The Queen offered him the dignity of an earldom, which, happily for his party, he declined. After some rather complicated negotiations, he was succeeded by Lord Salisbury.

The general election took place in the following November. In the boroughs the Liberals lost heavily. The clergy, the publicans, and the Parnellites were found arrayed in scandalous alliance against the Liberal cause. Tory enthusiasm took advantage of Liberal lukewarmness, and the result was disastrous to the Liberal party. But in the counties the good cause triumphed. The agricultural labourer proved, as a general rule, loyal to those who had just secured for him the rights of citizenship. That peculiar doctrine of agricultural politics which has become famous under the nickname of 'Three Acres and a Cow,' was beyond doubt attractive to the voter and advantageous to its authors. In the bulk of English counties the Irish voter is unknown, and the Established Church is politically weakest just where she has relied most exclusively upon her traditional authority. In brief, the counties went far to redeem the losses in the boroughs; but not quite far enough. When the election was over, the Liberal party was just short of the numerical strength which was requisite to defeat a combination of Tories and Parnellites. Lord Salisbury, therefore, retained office, but the life of his Administration hung by a thread.

Though not in office, the Liberals held an extremely satisfactory position. They were strong in numbers, in enthusiasm, and, for the time at least, in union. They had at their head Mr Gladstone's unique personality and commanding authority. In Mr Chamberlain they had a champion of great ability and industry, and of a popularity just at its zenith. Their opponents were notoriously distracted by internecine jealousies, and dependent for their continuance in office on the precarious support of the Parnellites. In a word, the Liberals were an exceptionally strong Opposition, and the difficulties which lay before the Government promised abundant opportunities for harassing and successful attack.

Thus all might still have gone well, and very well, for the Liberal party, when suddenly the fates decreed a fresh exemplification of the mischief which arises from hurrying an unprepared party into a novel and perplexing course.

On November 24, 1884, Lord Shaftesbury, moved by the spirit of prophecy, wrote 'In a year or so we shall have Home Rule disposed of (at all hazards), to save us from daily and hourly bores.' On December 17, 1885, the world was astonished by the appearance of an anonymous paragraph, stating that, if Mr Gladstone returned to office, he was prepared to deal in a liberal spirit with the demand for Home Rule. The genesis of that paragraph has never been clearly ascertained, but it was surrounded by an atmosphere of vulgar mystery, little suited to the importance of the new policy or the personal dignity of an illustrious statesman. Its appearance was the signal for a storm of questions, contradictions, explanations, enthusiasms, and jeremiads. But amidst all the hurly-burly Mr Gladstone held his peace. He would neither confirm nor deny. The public must wait and see. The subject was one which could only be handled by a responsible Ministry. The bewilderment and confusion of the Liberal party were absolute. No one knew what was coaling next; who was on what side; or whither his party—or, indeed, himself—was tending. One point only was clear: if Mr Gladstone meant what he appeared to mean, the Parnellites would support him, and the Tories must leave office. The Government seemed to accept the situation when Parliament met, they executed, for form's sake, some confused manoeuvres in which Mr W. H. Smith was a prominent figure, and then they rode for a fall on a resolution in favour of municipal allotments.

There was a moment of uncertainty, during which it seemed possible that the Tory Government might try to defy parliamentary opinion and retain office until defeated on a distinct vote of non-confidence. But wiser counsels prevailed, and, late at night on January 29, 1886, Sir Henry Ponsonby arrived at Mr Gladstone's house with a message from the Queen. On the 1st of February Mr Gladstone kissed hands at Osborne, and was, for the third time, Prime Minister of England.

'When Gladstone runs down a steep place, his immense majority, like the pigs in Scripture, but hoping for a better issue, will go with him, roaring in grunts of exultation.' This was Lord Shaftesbury's prediction in the preceding year; but it was based on an assumption which proved erroneous. It took for granted the unalterable docility of the Liberal party.

The moment that the Queen empowered Mr Gladstone to form an Administration, it became apparent that docility had given place to a spirit of a different kind. Of those who had been, in the previous June, his colleagues in the Cabinet, Lord Hartington, Lord Selborne, Lord Derby, Lord Northbrook and Lord Carlingford declared themselves against what they understood to be his policy, and they gained formidable allies in Sir Henry James and Mr Courtney. It may be questioned whether such losses were adequately balanced even by the high character and literary genius of Mr Morley, or the forensic skill and learning of Lord Herschell. What followed may be briefly told. In April Mr Gladstone brought in his Bill for the government of Ireland, and his Bill for buying out the Irish landlords. Meanwhile the ranks of the seceders were reinforced by Mr Chamberlain, the enterprising and able exponent of the new Radicalism, and he was accompanied by Mr (now Sir George) Trevelyan, the very flower of political honour and chivalry, who combined the most dignified traditions, social and literary, of the Whig party with a fervent and stable Radicalism which the vicissitudes of twenty years had constantly tried and never found wanting.

Each of these secessions had its special weight, but the most important resistance which the new policy encountered was that of Mr Bright. His high reputation as a man whose politics were part of his religion, and who had never turned aside by a hair's breadth from the narrow path of civil duty as he understood it, gave him a weight of moral influence such as no contemporary politician could command.

It is unnecessary to multiply instances. In every constituency a large number of leading Liberals declared themselves against Mr Gladstone's Irish Bills; and this necessarily produced its effect on the minds of the Liberal rank-and-file. It was no sufficient compensation for these defections that the Liberals gained, in certain districts, the support of that very broken reed, the Irish vote, which was destined to pierce the hand of so many a confiding candidate who leant upon it.

Meanwhile the two sections of the dissentient party in Parliament were consolidating themselves. The Whigs under Lord Hartington coalesced with the Radicals under Mr Chamberlain, and both together made a working alliance with the Tories. This alliance was admirably organized in London and in the constituencies. Speeches of immense force were made against the Bills in all the chief towns. The whole Metropolitan Press, with the exception of one morning and one evening paper, daily and weekly denounced the Bills with skill and vigour. A remorseless criticism in Parliament detected in both measures an abundance of faults which could not be denied even by those who believed their general principles to be sound. Mr Gladstone's best friends urged him either to accept such modifications as should disarm his critics, or to withdraw his Bills and substitute for them a resolution affirming the principle of Irish autonomy.

But his official counsellors and the self-styled experts of Liberal organization assured him that the Home Rule Bill would pass the second reading in the House of Commons, and that, even if by some mischance it were defeated by two or three votes, his Irish policy was popular in the country, and he had everything to hope from an early appeal to the constituencies. As the day of the momentous division drew near, hopes of a majority for the Bill faded into fears of a defeat; but still the optimists of party were persuaded that the majority against the Bill would not amount to ten votes. The Liberal Cabinet arrived at a desperate resolution. If they were beaten by this small majority they would not resign. Some faithful adherent should move a vote of confidence on general grounds. This would be supported by many who could not vote for the Home Rule Bill. The settlement of the Irish question would be deferred to a later Session, the Liberals would still be in office, and all would be well. But alas for the vanity of human hopes and the knock-kneed calculations of parliamentary managers! On the early morning of June 8 the Bill was thrown out by thirty. Mr Gladstone immediately advised the Queen to dissolve Parliament. Her Majesty naturally demurred to a second dissolution within seven months, and begged Mr Gladstone to reconsider the advice. He replied that he was sure that a general election would cause less inconvenience to the country than a year of embittered and fanatical agitation for and against Home Rule. The Queen yielded, and Parliament was dissolved on June 26.

The dissolution was a tactical blunder, but Mr Gladstone's appeal to the country was skilfully worded. He freely admitted that the Bills were dead. He asked the country simply to sanction a principle, and that a very plain and, in itself, a most reasonable one. He invited the constituencies to say Aye or No to the question, 'Whether you will, or will not, have regard to the prayer of Ireland for the management by herself of the affairs specifically and exclusively her own?'

This dissociation of the bare principle of self-government from the practical perplexities with which the Bills had abounded enabled many Liberals who dissented from the Land Bill altogether, and from many parts of the Home Rule Bill, to give their support, either as voters or as candidates, to Mr Gladstone in his attack upon seats held by Tories. But with the majority of electors the contrary view prevailed. And this is not surprising. Up to December, 1885, English politicians who were favourable to Home Rule, or, indeed, had seriously considered it, might be counted on the fingers of one hand. With denunciations of Mr Parnell's aims and methods Liberals were indeed abundantly familiar; but sympathy with the demand for Home Rule was extremely rare, and Mr Gladstone's views of it were known only to a privileged few.

Suddenly the electorate was called to approve what it had hitherto been taught to condemn. Under the imperious influence of genius and eloquence, men found themselves hurried into new and astonishing courses. The prepossessions, opinions, and prejudices of a lifetime cannot be unlearnt in a moment. It is an excellent characteristic of the English voter that he looks before he leaps; and, if the object which he is asked to clear is very unfamiliar, he will look twice or thrice before the plunge is made. In reference to Home Rule, sufficient time vas not allowed for this process of enquiry and familiarization. The sanction of the voters was asked, at a moment's notice, for a vast and unexpected change; and this sanction they refused to give. There is no reason to believe that the refusal was final. A proposition inherently vicious must be condemned at once and for ever; but a proposition which is objectionable chiefly because it is novel, may be held over for further consideration. Democracy signifies its disapproval in the same guarded form which formerly conveyed the refusal of the Royal Assent: *L'Etat* (as formerly *Le Roi*) *s'avisera.*

But meanwhile Liberal desertions were many, and abstentions more. When the election closed, it showed a majority of considerably more than a hundred against Mr Gladstone's policy. The resignation of Ministers followed in due course, and, after a brief interval in which it had seemed possible, and many had sincerely hoped, that Lord Hartington would become Prime Minister, the Tories re-entered office with Lord Salisbury at their head.

With the opening of the new Parliament Mr Gladstone, now seventy-six years old, entered on an extraordinary course of physical and intellectual efforts, with voice and pen, in Parliament and on the platform, on behalf of the cause, defeated but not abandoned, of self-government for Ireland. The exuberance of bodily and mental activity, the fertility of argumentative resource, and the copiousness of rhetoric which he threw into the enterprise, would have been remarkable at any stage of his public life; continued into his eighty-second year they are little less than miraculous.

One touch of domestic interest may not unfitly close this narrative. On July 25, 1889, Mr Gladstone celebrated the fiftieth anniversary of his marriage with the gracious and gentle lady who, through all vicissitudes, has been the guiding star of his fortunes and the good angel of his house. The day was 'auspicated,' as Burke says, 'with the old warning of the Church, *Sursum corda*' for, in harmony with the spirit of the fifty years which it completed, it began with attendance at the Holy Communion. It was gladdened by the loving presence of family and friends, and the innumerable benedictions of well-wishers at a distance. It was characteristic that even at a moment so heavily charged with memories and emotions, Mr Gladstone found time to attend the House of Commons and deliver an animated speech in support of the Royal Grants. From the countless letters of congratulation and good wishes which were received on that memorable day, the following is taken as one of the most graceful and most touching:

> Archbishop's House, Westminster, S.W., July 23, 1889.
>
> My dear Mrs Gladstone,—The last time we met, you said, 'I do not forget old days.' And truly I can say so too.
>
> Therefore, in the midst of all who will be congratulating you on the fiftieth anniversary of your home-life, I cannot be silent. I have watched you both out on the sea of public tumults from my quiet shores. You know how nearly I have agreed in William's political career, especially in his Irish policy of the last twenty years. And I have seen also your works of charity for the people, in which, as you

know, I heartily share with you. There are few who keep such a jubilee as yours and how few of our old friends and companions now survive! We have had a long climb up those eighty steps—for even you are not far behind—and I hope we shall not 'break the pitcher at the fountain.' I wonder at your activity and endurance of weather. May every blessing be with you both to the end!—Believe me, always yours affectionately,

HENRY E. CARD. MANNING.

In connexion with this domestic incident the following account of Mr Gladstone's daily life at Hawarden may perhaps be read with interest. It was written by an inhabitant of the parish, and may be regarded as accurate.

'Quiet living at Hawarden is Mr Gladstone's supreme pleasure. Of late years peace and quiet have been some what endangered by the growing system of excursions, bent on pleasure and politics. The local politician looks upon politics as relaxation and change from the routine of his profession or trade. He is somewhat slow to understand that speeches, crowds, and cheers are sometimes out of place. Hawarden Park has had to be closed to large parties after Bank Holiday in August. Without this regulation it would be impossible to secure even a moderate amount of privacy to Mr Gladstone. And even now an occasional large party arrives at Hawarden Station from Lancashire in ignorance of the restriction. To avoid spoiling their day's pleasure they are admitted to the park, and Mr Gladstone has then to choose between staying within doors, or encountering the well-meant but inconvenient enthusiasm of the excursionists. So large during the summer months of this year became the number of visitors on Sundays, so considerable was the consequent inconvenience to the parishioners, that Mr Gladstone had to cease reading the lessons in church. Although the general behaviour of those who annually visit Hawarden is excellent, yet the natural consequence is the gradual disappearance of ferns and plants which can be easily uprooted and removed. Some unmannerly person even cut out Mr Gladstone's name from his Bible in church. But these are small drawbacks, having regard to the evident enjoyment derived by excursionists from the use of the park and grounds.

'For some months past Mr Gladstone has been busily engaged with the preliminary steps of a scheme he has long had in his mind. The number of his books began to be too great for the available space in Hawarden Castle. They overflowed into every room. The Glynne library occupied two large rooms. From the first, Mr Gladstone had minutely to study the best system of storing books, and his views on the subject have recently been given in the *Nineteenth Century*. By systematic and ingenious economy of space, the bulk of 20,000 volumes was housed in two rooms. But still the number grew, and large packages unopened began to encumber the rooms. Several thousands of these have now been removed to a commodious iron building fitted as a library. Mr Gladstone is known to have a large ulterior scheme for founding a library, and the present erection is a half-way house. Both in the old and new library the position of every book was determined by Mr Gladstone himself, and he rarely has any difficulty in laying his hand upon the book that may be required. The collection is strong in contemporary and general literature, strongest, perhaps, in theology and the classics, while works on Homer, Dante, and Shakespeare abound. There are three writing tables in the room. At one Mrs Gladstone sits. Of the other two, one is used by Mr Gladstone for his correspondence, the other is devoted to his literary work. Stored in the deep recesses of the bookshelves are stacks of walking-sticks, axes, and many other miscellaneous presents which have been received at various times. About the room are busts and engravings of old friends and colleagues, Sidney Herbert, the Duke of Newcastle, Canning, and Tennyson among others. The "Temple of Peace," as the study is called, is always available for those staying in the house who wish for quiet reading.

'In equally good order are Mr Gladstone's papers. The accumulated correspondence, official papers, and memoranda of fifty years of public life occupy a considerable space. For years they were stowed in wooden cupboards in different rooms, and had the old woodwork of the house caught fire, documents of the greatest historical interest would probably have been destroyed. Fortunately they have all been methodically arranged in the fireproof octagon, of which Mr Gladstone is extremely proud.

'The daily routine of Mr Gladstone's life at Hawarden is well known. The early walk to church before breakfast; the morning devoted chiefly to literary work and the severer kinds of business and study half an hour or an hour for reading or writing after luncheon; the afternoon walk or visit, or tree cutting; correspondence and reading after a cup of tea until dinner-time. As a rule Mr Gladstone reads after dinner until about 11.15. He greatly enjoys an occasional game at backgammon. Of chess, as a game, he has the very highest opinion, but he finds it too long and exciting. Whist he enjoys, but he seldom takes a hand. Music he delights in, and as all the members of his family are musical, and two or three are performers above the average, his wishes in this direction can be readily met.

'During the later years Mr Gladstone's family have discouraged him from cutting down trees. Few forms of exercise are more violent and trying to the heart, and at Mr Gladstone's age the risk must be considerable. Still he has occasionally wielded the axe this summer with much of his old power and with extraordinary energy and keenness. Tree cutting has its dangers, but in his thirty years' experience of it Mr Gladstone has been fortunate in escaping them. The only serious inconvenience he ever suffered was from a chip which caused a slight abrasion of the eyeball. Once an accident almost occurred. Mr Henry Gladstone had climbed a large lime tree which Mr Gladstone had begun to cut, when, without any warning and owing to unexpected rot in its centre, the tree fell. At the moment Mr Henry was high up, and on the underneath side. To the onlookers' relief he managed to get round the trunk as the tree was falling, and escaped with a shaking. The bough on which he had stood was smashed. Mr Gladstone never cuts down a tree for the sake of the exercise. A doubtful tree is tried judicially. Sometimes its fate hangs in the balance for years. The opinion of the family is consulted, and frequently that of visitors. Mr Ruskin sealed the fate of an oak; Sir J. Millais decided that the removal of an elm would be a clear improvement. The trees at Hawarden are treated as the precious gifts of Nature with which no human hand should deal rashly. And when Mr Gladstone does set to work he evidently bears in mind the correct view of Homer:

Μήτι τοι δρυτόμος μέγ αμείων ηε βίηφι

Whatever may be the occupation of the moment, Mr Gladstone's life at Hawarden is a period of contented and perfect enjoyment. It is full of interest and peace. Ever ready to take his part in local matters, whether it is the promotion of an intermediate school or a new water supply, the building of a gymnasium or the furthering of fruit and flower cultivation, he delights in the quiet and familiar scenes far removed from the worries and storms of public life. He lives among his own people, and for his own enjoyment asks for nothing more. The public life of a leading statesman offers the boldest and stateliest outline to the public view. It may be that the most striking and memorable chapters in a future biography of Mr Gladstone will contain the story of his private affairs and domestic life.'

[Reproduced by the kind permission of the proprietors, from the *Daily Graphic*, October 25, 1890.]

XI

Analysis of Character—Religiousness—Attitude towards Nonconformity—Love of power—Political courage—Conservative instincts—Love of beauty—Literary tastes—Mastery of finance—Business-like aptitude—Temper—Courtesy—Attractiveness in private life.

WHOEVER ATTEMPTS TO WRITE A study of Mr Gladstone's character undertakes to handle a rather complicated theme. He has to analyze a nature agitated and perplexed by a dozen cross-currents of conflicting tendency, and to assign their true causes to psychological phenomena which are peculiarly liable to misinterpretation.

Mr Gladstone has for the last half-century loomed so large in the public view as the politician, the Minister, and latterly the demagogue, that other and deeper aspects of his character have been overlooked and obscured. Thus it will probably seem to savour of paradox to affirm, as the writer is prepared to do, that the paramount factor of Mr Gladstone's nature is his religiousness. The religion in which Mr Gladstone lives and moves and has his being is an intensely vivid and energetic principle, passionate on its emotional side, definite in its theory, imperious in its demands, practical, visible, and tangible in its effects. It runs like a silver strand through the complex and variegated web of his long and chequered life. We saw at the beginning of this book that he wished to take Holy Orders instead of entering Parliament. Had the decision gone differently, the most interesting of all the 'Lives of the Archbishops of Canterbury' would still be unwritten. But the mere choice of a profession could make no difference to the ground-tone of Mr Gladstone's thought. While a politician he was still essentially, and above all, a Christian—some would say, an ecclesiastic. Through all the changes and chances of a political career, as a Tory as a Home Ruler, in office and in opposition, sitting as a duke's nominee for a pocket-borough, and enthroned as the idol of an adoring democracy, Mr Gladstone

Plays, in the many games of life, that one
Where what he most doth value must be won.

In his own personal habits, known to all men, of systematic devotion; in his rigorous reservation of the Sunday for sacred uses; in his written and spoken utterances; in his favourite studies; in his administration of public affairs; in the grounds on which he has based his opposition to policies of which he has disapproved—he has steadily and constantly asserted for the claims of religion a paramount place in public consideration, and has reproved the stale sciolism which thinks, or affects to think, that Christianity, as a spring of human action, is an exhausted force.

It is this religiousness of Mr Gladstone's character which has incurred the bitter wrath of those large sections of society whose lax theories and corresponding practice his example has constantly rebuked; which has won for him the affectionate reverence of great masses of his countrymen who have never seen his face; and which accounts for the singular loyalty to his person and policy of those Nonconformist bodies from whom, on the score of merely theological opinion, he is so widely separated. Mr Gladstone's present attitude towards Nonconformity and Nonconformists, so strikingly different from that which marked his earlier days, is due, no doubt, in part, to the necessities of his political position, but due much more to his growing conviction that English Nonconformity means a robust and consistent application of the principles of the Kingdom of God to the business of public life. This was well illustrated by what occurred at the Memorial Hall in Farringdon Street on May 8, 1888, when Mr Gladstone received an address in support of his Irish policy, signed by 3,730 Nonconformist ministers. To this address, which was read by the Rev. J. Guinness Rogers, Mr Gladstone replied:

> I accept with gratitude as well as pleasure the address which has been presented to me, and I rejoice again to meet you within walls which, although no great number of years have passed since their erection, have already become historic, and which are associated in my mind and in the minds of many with honourable struggles, sometimes under circumstances of depression, sometimes under circumstances of promise, but always leading us forward, whatever may have been the phenomena of the moment, along the path of truth and justice. I am very thankful to those who have signed this address for the courageous manner in which they have not scrupled to associate their political action and intention with the principles and motives of their holy religion.

The best theologian in England (as Dr Döllinger called Mr Gladstone) cannot help being aware that the theory of nonconformity, both in respect of its historic basis and of its relation to scientific Theology, leaves much to be desired; but not the less clearly does he recognize the fact that on those supreme occasions of public controversy when the path of politics crosses the path of morality, the Nonconformist bodies of England have pronounced unhesitatingly for justice and mercy, while our authorized teachers of religion have too often been silent or have spoken on the wrong side.

This keen sense of the religious bearing of political questions has determined Mr Gladstone's action in not a few crises of his parliamentary life. It was the exacting rigour of a religious theory that drove him out of the Cabinet in 1845. It was his belief that marriage is a sacred and indissoluble union which dictated his pertinacious opposition to the Divorce Bill in 1857. Ten years later, he felt that the Irish Establishment could no longer be maintained, because it could plead neither practical utility nor 'the seal and signature of ecclesiastical descent.' In the Eastern question he discerned that all the various interests which dread and loathe Christianity were making common cause on behalf of the Power which has for centuries persecuted the worshippers of Christ in Eastern Europe, and that the godless cynicism which scoffed at the red horrors of Bulgaria was not so much an unchristian as an anti-Christian sentiment. In more recent days, it is very probable that among the forces which have drawn him into his passionate advocacy of Irish Nationalism has been the fact that the cause of Home Rule is to a great extent the cause of that august and authoritative Communion to which the Celtic race is so profoundly attached, and which, at least in some of its aspects, Mr Gladstone himself has always regarded with a friendly eye.

When he handles the religious aspects of a political question, Mr Gladstone's eloquence rises to its highest flight, as in his speech on the second reading of the Affirmation Bill in 1883. Under the system then existing (which admitted Jews to Parliament but excluded Atheists), to deny the existence of God was a fatal bar, but to deny the Christian Creed was no bar at all. This, Mr Gladstone contended, was a formal disparagement of Christianity, which was thereby relegated to a place of secondary importance. Those who heard it will not easily forget the solemn splendour of the passage in which this argument was enforced.

The administration of government has always been, in Mr Gladstone's hands, a religious act. Even in the trivial concerns of ordinary life the sense of responsibility to an invisible Judge for the deeds done in the body presses on him with overwhelming weight. He is haunted by responsibility for time, and talents, and opportunities, and influence, and power; responsibility for reading, and writing, and speaking, and eating, and drinking; and to this the task of government superadds responsibility for the material and moral interests of the people entrusted to his charge; responsibility, above all else, for much that vitally affects the well-being, the efficiency, and the spiritual repute of that great religious institution with which the commonwealth of England is so closely intertwined. In the Bidding Prayer at Oxford the congregation is exhorted to pray for those in authority that they 'may labour to promote the glory of GOD and the present and future welfare of mankind; remembering always that solemn account which they must one day give before the judgment-seat of CHRIST.' Those who have been behind the scenes when Mr Gladstone was preparing to make some important appointment in the Church, and have witnessed the anxious and solemn care with which he approaches the task, have seen that high ideal of duty translated into practice.

If we assign the first place in Mr Gladstone's character to his religiousness, we must certainly allow the second to his love of power. And it is neither a sarcasm nor a jest (though it sounds like both) to say that this second characteristic is in some measure related to the first. From his youth up Mr Gladstone has been conscious of high aims and great abilities. He has earnestly desired to serve his day and generation, and he has known that he has unusual capacity for giving effect to this desire. In order that those powers and that capacity may have free scope, it has been necessary that their possessor should be in a position of authority, of leadership, of command. And thus it comes about that ambition has been part of his religion; for ambition means with him nothing else than the resolute determination to possess that official control over the machine of State which will enable him to fulfil his predestined part in the providential order, and to do, on the largest scale, and with the amplest opportunities, what he conceives to be his duty to God and man. This is Mr Gladstone's love of power. It has nothing in common with the vulgar eagerness for place and pay and social standing which governs the lesser luminaries of the political heaven but, in itself an inborn and resistless impulse, it has become identified with his deliberate theory of the public good, and it is confirmed by the unbroken habit of a lifetime. As a Tory, as a Peelite, as a Liberal, and as a Home Ruler, Mr Gladstone has passed the greater part of his life amid the excitements, the interests, and the responsibilities of office; and, when not in office, he has found in the active guidance of a militant Opposition ample scope for the exercise of his astonishing gifts, and a scarcely diminished importance in the public eye.

It is almost unnecessary to observe that Mr Gladstone's love of power is supported by a splendid fearlessness. In proposing in Parliament the national memorial to Lord Beaconsfield he referred in tones of genuine admiration to his dead rival's political courage; and that great quality has been illustrated at least as signally in his own career. No dangers have been too threatening for him to face, no obstacles too formidable, no tasks too laborious, no heights too inaccessible. His courage has, indeed, its inconvenient side. He begins to build his towers without counting the cost, and in going to war forgets to calculate the relative strength of ten and twenty thousand. The natural consequence is frequent failure; but failure only strengthens Mr Gladstone's resolve and stimulates his endeavour. Often defeated, he never despairs; and though his friends have more than once written *Requiescat* on what they believed to be his political tomb, he persists in substituting *Resurgam*.

The love of power and the courage which supports it are allied in Mr Gladstone with a marked imperiousness. Of this quality there is no trace in his manner, which is courteous, conciliatory, and even deferential; nor in his speech, which breathes an almost exaggerated humility. But the imperiousness shows itself in the more effectual form of action in his sudden resolves, his invincible insistence, his recklessness of consequences to himself and his friends, his habitual assumption that the civilized world and all its units must agree with him, his indignant astonishment at the bare thought of dissent or resistance, his incapacity to believe that an overruling providence will permit him to be frustrated or defeated.

It is this last peculiarity of Mr Gladstone's temper which has exposed him to the severest shocks of adverse fate. His friends and relations, his colleagues and supporters, and official guides, know so well this imperious optimism, and shrink so naturally from the consequences of disturbing it, that they insensibly fall into the habit of assuring him that everything is going as he wishes, and that human daring and political perversity will not, in the long run, venture to withstand his wise and righteous will. It is the inconvenient property of those who systematically speak smooth things sometimes to prophesy deceits; and again and again, as in 1874 and 1886, Mr Gladstone's complaisant counsellors have prepared for him a rude awakening from sweet dreams of majorities and office to the grim reality of defeat and Opposition.

Mr Gladstone's love of power is one of the many features of his character which have been widely misconstrued. His political opponents cannot or will not believe that it is only a synonym for disinterested devotion to the public good. Another point in which the general estimate of him is curiously erroneous is his feeling about change. It has fallen to his lot to propose so many and such momentous alterations in our political system that all his enemies, and some of his friends, have come to regard him as a man to whom change for its own sake is agreeable. Never was a greater error. Mr Gladstone is essentially and fundamentally a Conservative. This temper of his mind powerfully affects his feelings about great authors of all types and times. He is a cavalier all over in his devotion to Sir Walter Scott. He reveres St Thomas Aquinas as a chief exponent of the great principle of Authority. His sentiments towards Edmund Burke may be given in his own words, addressed to the writer of this book in 1884.

> I turn from these troublesome reflections to say how glad (not surprised) I am that Burke has a place in your admiration, and on most subjects, as I conjecture, in your confidence. Yet I remember a young Tory's saying at Oxford he could not wish to be more Tory than Burke. He was perhaps the maker of the Revolutionary War; and our going into that war perhaps made the Reign of Terror; and, without

any 'perhaps,' almost unmade the liberties, the Constitution, even the material interests and prosperity of our country. Yet I venerate and almost worship him, though I can conceive its being argued that all he did for freedom, justice, religion, purity of government in other respects and other quarters, was less than the mischief which flowed out from the Reflections.

I would he were now alive.

His natural bias is to respect institutions as they are and nothing short of plain proof that their effect is injurious will induce him to set about reforming them. And even when he is impelled by strong conviction to undertake the most fundamental and far-reaching alterations of our polity, the innate conservatism of his mind makes him try to persuade himself that the revolution which he contemplates is in truth a restoration. Thus, his favourite argument for Home Rule is that it is merely a return to the system of government which commended itself to the wisdom of our fathers, and which their presumptuous children heedlessly set aside; and he seeks to allay the alarms of his Radical followers by dwelling on the encouraging prospect that an Irish Parliament would probably contain a large majority of Conservatives.

The Church, regarded as a divinely-constituted society, has had no more passionate defender than the author of 'Church principles considered in their Results' and 'The State in its Relations with the Church.' His old-world devotion to the Throne has often and severely tried the patience of his Radical followers, as when, amid the plaudits of his foes and the moans of his friends, he championed the Royal Grants in 1889. His sentiment of loyalty is exceedingly strong, and was beautifully expressed in the letter which he addressed to the eldest son of the Prince of Wales, on the attainment of his majority:

Hawarden Castle, January 7, 1885.

Sir,—As the oldest among the confidential servants of her Majesty, I cannot allow the anniversary to pass without a notice which will to-morrow bring your Royal Highness to full age, and thus mark an important epoch in your life. The hopes and intentions of those whose lives lie, like mine, in the past are of little moment; but they have seen much, and what they have seen suggests much for the future.

There lies before your Royal Highness in prospect the occupation, I trust at a distant date, of a throne which, to me at least, appears the most illustrious in the world, from its history and associations, from its legal basis, from the weight of the cares it brings, from the loyal love of the people, and from the unparalleled opportunities it gives, in so many ways and in so many regions, of doing good to the almost countless numbers whom the Almighty has placed beneath the sceptre of England.

I fervently desire and pray, and there cannot be a more animating prayer, that your Royal Highness may ever grow in the principles of conduct, and may he adorned with all the qualities, which correspond with this great and noble vocation.

And, Sir, if sovereignty has been relieved by our modern institutions of some of its burdens, it still, I believe, remains true that there has been no period of the world's history at which successors to the monarchy could more efficaciously contribute to the stability of a great historic system, dependent even more upon love than upon strength, by devotion to their duties and by a bright example to the country. This result we have happily been permitted to see, and other generations will, I trust, witness it anew.

Heartily desiring that in the life of your Royal Highness every private and personal may be joined with every public blessing, I have the honour to remain,

Sir, your Royal High ness's most dutiful and faithful servant,

W. E. GLADSTONE.

Even the House of Lords, which has so often mutilated and delayed great measures on which he set his heart, still has a definite place in his respect, if not in his affection. Indeed, he attaches to the possession of rank and what it brings with it an even exaggerated importance.

In all the petty details of daily life, in his tastes, his habits, his manners, his way of living, his social prejudices, Mr Gladstone is the stiffest of Conservatives. Indeed, he not seldom carries his devotion to the existing order to a ludicrous point, as when he gravely laments the abolition of the nobleman's gown at Oxford, or deprecates the admission of the general public to Constitution Hill.

It is true that Mr Gladstone has sometimes been forced by conviction or fate or political necessity to be a revolutionist on a large scale; to destroy an Established Church; to add two millions of voters to the electorate; to attack the parliamentary union of the Kingdoms. But, after all, these changes were, in their inception, distasteful to their author. He has allowed us to see the steps by which he arrived at the belief that they were necessary, and, with admirable candour, has shown us that he started with quite opposite prepossessions. His mind is singularly receptive, and his whole life has been spent in unlearning the prejudices in which he was educated. His love of freedom has steadily developed, and he has applied its principles more and more courageously to the problems of government. But it makes some difference to the future of a democratic State whether its leading men are eagerly on the look-out for something to revolutionize, or approach a constitutional change by the gradual processes of conviction and conversion. It is this consideration which makes Mr Gladstone's life and continued ascendancy in the Liberal party so important to the country. In spite of all that has come and gone, he is a restraining and conservative force. And those who know him best, as they peer into the future, feel something of that misgiving which filled the air in

Queen Elizabeth's latter days, when, 'all men pointed to the Queen's white hairs and said, "When that snow melteth there will be a flood."'

Mr Gladstone's religiousness, his love of power, his Conservative bias, are aspects of his character which have often been the ground of debate and dispute. There can not be two opinions about his love of beauty. It is a many-sided and far-reaching enthusiasm. Beauty in nature, in art, in literature, appeals to him with irresistible force. For what is merely rare, or curious, or costly, he does not care a jot; but he kindles with contagious enthusiasm over a fine picture, a striking statue, a delicate piece of artistic workmanship. Good music stirs him to his depths. In literature he exacts beauty both of form and of substance. No mere skill in character-painting, or subtlety of analysis, or creative force, will win his praise for a writer who, like George Eliot, is powerful rather than beautiful, or dwells, however skilfully, on the repulsive aspects of life and character.

It is his devotion to spiritual and physical beauty which has made him a life-long, a passionate, almost an adoring, disciple of Homer and Dante. With regard to the former, it is not necessary to follow Mr Gladstone in all the ethnological and religious theories which, in successive works, published in 1858, 1869, 1876, and 1890, he has laid before the world. Whether sound or erroneous, they are founded on an absolute and detailed knowledge of the text—a commonplace but essential equipment for the task of interpretation which even professional scholars too often neglect. Mr Gladstone's published studies in Homer have received high praise from such competent authorities as Professor Jebb and Professor Freeman, though these learned men do not accept all his theories or follow his deductions from the narrative. He has 'done such justice to Homer and his age as Homer has never received out of his own land. He has vindicated the true position of the greatest of poets; he has cleared his tale and its actors from the misrepresentation of ages.'

Speaking to the boys at Eton on March 14, 1891, Mr Gladstone gave this curious fragment of autobiography:

> When I was a boy I cared nothing at all about the Homeric gods. I did not enter into the subject until thirty or forty years afterwards, when, in a conversation with Dr Pusey, who, like me, had been an Eton boy, he told me, having more sense and brains than I had, that he took the deepest interest and had the greatest curiosity about these Homeric gods. They are of the greatest interest, and you cannot really study the text of Homer without gathering fruits; and the more you study him the more you will be astonished at the multitude of lessons and the completeness of the picture which he gives you. There is a perfect encyclopaedia of human character and human experience in the poems of Homer, more complete in every detail than is else where furnished to us of Achaian life.

Mr Gladstone's love of Dante is reinforced by his theological sense. At the most, the theology of Homer belongs to the region of natural religion; but in Dante Mr Gladstone finds a poet after his own heart, in whom passion and pathos and a profound sense of the underlying tragedy of human life are penetrated by the influence of the Christian dogma. His sentiments on this head are well expressed in the following translation of an Italian letter which, on December 20, 1882, he addressed to Professor Giambattista Guilioni, of Rome:

> Illustrious Sir,—Albeit I have lost the practice of the Italian language, yet I must offer you many, many thanks for your kindness in sending me your admirable work, '*Dante Spiegato con Dante.*' You have been good enough to call that supreme poet 'a solemn master' for me. These are not empty words. The reading of Dante is not merely a pleasure, a *tour de force*, or a lesson; it is a vigorous discipline for the heart, the intellect, the whole man. In the school of Dante I have learned a great part of that mental provision (however insignificant it be) which has served me to make this journey of human life up to the term of nearly seventy-three years. And I should like to extend your excellent phrase, and to say that he who labours for Dante, labours to serve Italy, Christianity, the world.—Your very respectful servant,
>
> W. E. GLADSTONE.

Among modern writers his love of Lord Tennyson is essentially due to his love of beauty; and his essay on Tennyson, published in the *Quarterly Review* for October 1859, may be cited as a peculiarly suggestive and delicate piece of critical writing.

In Mr Gladstone's character several seemingly inconsistent qualities are combined; and it is curious to note in a temperament so highly emotional, imaginative, and even theatrical, a strong cross-current of business-like instinct. Those who speculate in matters of race and pedigree might be inclined to suggest that Mr Gladstone owes the ideal elements of his nature to his mother's Celtic ancestors, and the practical elements to those shrewd burghers of Leith and lairds of Lanarkshire from whom, through his father, he descends. But, however this may be, Mr Gladstone's taste for commercial enterprise is as clearly-marked a feature of his character as his rhetorical fervour or his dialectical subtlety.

One of his colleagues said of him not long ago: 'The only two things Gladstone really cares for are the Church and finance.' And though, when we regard Mr Gladstone's present passion for Home Rule, this seems rather paradoxical, still it has a certain element of truth. The Church and finance are the only two departments of public affairs which have interested him keenly and constantly from his earliest days till now, and with regard to which his whole course has been consistent. It was in the realm of finance that his most remarkable achievements were won. He was the first Chancellor of the Exchequer who ever made the Budget romantic. He believes in Free Trade as the gospel of social salvation. He revels in figures; and every detail of price and value, of production and distribution, of money and money's worth, and every form of enquiry and speculation which tends to illustrate these subjects, exercises a resistless fascination over his mind.

The gravity and earnestness of Mr Gladstone's nature are allied with a strong temper. And there are few more serviceable qualities than a strong temper kept sternly under control. Such is the case with Mr Gladstone; and, while it is easy to discern the passionate and impetuous nature as it works within, it is impossible not to admire the vigorous self by which it is turned from harmful into useful channels. He has a grand capacity for generous indignation, and nothing is finer than to see the changing lights and shades on his mobile and expressive face when some

> Tale of injury calls forth
> The indignant spirit of the North.

The hawk-like features become more strongly marked, the onyx-eyes flash and glow, the voice grows more resonant, and the utterance more emphatic. It is droll to observe the discomfiture of a story-teller who has fondly thought to tickle the great man's sense of humour by an anecdote which depends for its point upon some trait of cynicism, baseness, or sharp practice. He finds his tale received in grim silence, and then perceives to his dismay that what was intended to entertain has only disgusted. 'Do you call that amusing? I call it devilish,' was the emphatic comment with which a characteristic story about Lord Beaconsfield was once received by his eminent rival.

In personal dealing Mr Gladstone is no doubt quickly roused; but is placable, reasonable, and always willing to hear excuses or defence. And when the course of life is flowing smoothly, and nothing happens to disturb the stream, he is delightful company. He has a keen faculty for enjoyment, great appreciation of civility and attention, and a nature completely unspoilt by success and prominence and praise.

A most engaging quality of Mr Gladstone's character is his courtesy. It is invariable and universal. A pretty and touching instance of it is contained in the following letter. A young lady of Wigan, who was suffering from consumption, sent to Mr Gladstone on his birthday, which was also her own, a letter containing a bookmark, on which she had embroidered the words: 'The Bible our Guide.' She received in return some gifts suitable to an invalid, together with the following letter in Mr Gladstone's handwriting:

Hawarden Castle, Chester, January 1, 1883.

Dear Madam,—I am greatly touched by your kindness in having worked a bookmark for me, under the circumstances at which you glance in such feeling and simple terms. May the guidance which you are good enough to desire on my behalf avail you fully on every step of that journey in which, if I do not precede, I cannot but shortly follow you.—I remain, dear Madam, faithfully yours,

W. E. GLADSTONE.

Mr Gladstone has the ceremonious manners of the old school, and alike to young and old, men and women, he pays the compliment of assuming that they are on his own intellectual level and furnished with at least as much in formation as will enable them to follow and to understand him. Indeed, his mariner towards his intellectual inferiors is almost ludicrously humble. He consults, defers, enquires; argues his point where he would be fully justified in laying down the law; and eagerly seeks information from the mouths of babes and sucklings. Still, after all, he is frankly human, and it is part of human nature to like acquiescence better than contradiction, and to rate more highly than they deserve the characters and attainments of even tenth-rate people who agree with one. Hence it arises that all Mr Gladstone's geese are swans. He shows what Bishop Wilberforce called 'a want of clear sharp sightedness as to others,' and he is consequently exposed to the arts of scheming mediocrities, on whose interested opinions he is apt to place a fatally implicit reliance.

In order to form the highest and the truest estimate of Mr Gladstone's character it is necessary to see him at home. There are some people who appear to the best advantage on the distant heights, elevated by intellectual eminence above the range of scrutiny, or shrouded from too close observation by the misty glamour of great station and great affairs. Others are seen at their best in the middle distance of official intercourse and in the friendly but not intimate relations of professional and public life. But the noblest natures are those which are seen to the greatest advantage in the close communion of the home, and here Mr Gladstone is pre-eminently attractive. His extraordinary vigour and youthfulness of mind and body, his unbroken health and buoyant spirits, form an atmosphere of infectious vitality. He delights in hospitality, and, to quote a phrase of Sydney Smith's, 'receives his friends with that honest joy which warms more than dinner or wine.' The dignity, the order, the simplicity, and, above all, the fervent and manly piety of his daily life, form a spectacle far more impressive than his most magnificent performances in Parliament or on the platform. He is the idol of those who are most closely associated with him, whether by the ties of blood, of friendship, or of duty and perhaps it is his highest praise to say that he is not unworthy of the devotion which he inspires.

Also available from Nonsuch Publishing

Alexander, Boyd (ed.)	*The Journal of William Beckford in Portugal and Spain*	978 1 84588 010 1
Brontë, Rev. Patrick	*The Letters of the Rev. Patrick Brontë*	978 1 84588 066 8
Broughton, S.D.	*Letters from Portugal, Spain and France*	978 1 84588 030 9
Brunel, Isambard	*The Life of Isambard Kingdom Brunel, Civil Engineer*	978 1 84588 031 6
Coleman, E.C. (ed.)	*The Travels of Sir John Mandeville, 1322–1356*	978 184588 075 0
Corbett, Sir Julian	*The Campaign of Trafalgar*	978 1 84588 059 0
Duff, Charles	*A Handbook on Hanging*	978 1 84588 141 2
Eyre, Lt Vincent	*The Military Operations at Cabul*	978 1 84588 012 5
Fothergill, A. Brian	*Beckford of Fonthill*	978 1 84588 085 9
Fothergill, A. Brian	*Sir William Hamilton: Envoy Extraordinary*	978 1 84588 042 2
Gooch, Sir Daniel	*The Diaries of Sir Daniel Gooch*	978 1 84588 016 3
Greenwood, Lt John	*The Campaign in Afghanistan*	978 1 84588 004 0
Hammond, J.L. and Barbara	*The Village Labourer*	978 1 84588 056 9
Hawkes, Francis L.	*Commodore Perry and the Opening of Japan*	978 1 84588 026 2
Helps, Sir Arthur	*The Life and Labours of Thomas Brassey*	978 1 84588 011 8
Hill, Wg Cdr Roderic	*The Baghdad Air Mail*	978 1 84588 009 5
Hudson, W.H.	*Idle Days in Patagonia*	978 1 84588 024 8
Jefferies, Richard	*Wildlife in a Southern County*	978 1 84588 064 4
Livingstone, David and Charles	*Expedition to the Zambesi and its Tributaries*	978 1 84588 065 1
Matthews, Henry	*Diary of an Invalid*	978 1 84588 017 0
Park, Mungo	*Travels in the Interior of Africa*	978 1 84588 068 2
Scott, Capt. Robert F.	*The Voyage of the Discovery, Vol. One*	978 1 84588 057 6
Ségur, Gen. Count Philippe de	*Memoirs of an Aide de Camp of Napoleon, 1800–1812*	978 1 84588 005 7
Simmonds, P.L.	*Sir John Franklin and the Arctic Regions*	978 1 84588 007 1

For forthcoming titles and sales information see
www.nonsuch-publishing.com